D1359163

CONFLICT RESOLUTION FOR CHRISTIAN COUPLES

PAUL R. SHAFFER

authorHOUSE®

AuthorHouse™
1663 Liberty Drive
Bloomington, IN 47403
www.authorhouse.com
Phone: 1 (800) 839-8640

Published by AuthorHouse   11/17/2015

ISBN: 978-1-4259-6631-7 (sc)
ISBN: 978-1-5049-4706-0 (hc)
ISBN: 978-1-4389-9947-0 (e)

Library of Congress Control Number: 2006909447

Print information available on the last page.

Dedication

I would like to dedicate this book to my father and mother, Paul and Dee Shaffer. They were my early models of Christianity in practice.

So far as I could tell, *every* day of my father's adult life started with reading the Bible. At his funeral, several people credited their coming to Christianity because of him. His first comment to just about any request for advice would predictably be "Who's your source?" because if God is truly your source, then you should have nothing to fear. While he was far from perfect, his desire to live a life pleasing to God was constant.

My mother was a model of grace, striving to understand rather than judge. She had a very hard time seeing anyone in a negative light, and always tried to be the peacemaker. She, more than anyone, got it into my head from an early age that you can accomplish incredible things if you just first believe that you can, and then, with God's help, stay the course.

While my life is not a mirror of theirs, both of my parents were crucial in getting across to me the importance of living a life of significance.

Table of Contents

Dedication v

Acknowledgements ix

Foreword: Theology and Psychology xi

Part I A Christian Foundation

Chapter 1 Christianity 101 3
Chapter 2 Christianity 201 23

Part II Tools for Resolution

Chapter 3 The Conflict Model 49
Chapter 4 When an Issue Exists 75
Chapter 5 Identifying the Issue 95
Chapter 6 Validating the Issue 111
Chapter 7 Processing the Issue 131
Chapter 8 Resolving the Issue 157

Part III Strategies for Change

Chapter 9 A Model for Change 179
Chapter 10 Healthy Routines 191

Part IV Unique Situations

Chapter 11 Affairs and Conflict 215
Chapter 12 Separation and Conflict 255

Afterword: Balance 283

Appendix Tools & Exercises 287

Acknowledgements

I would like to thank some of my Christian friends who have meant a lot to me over the years. My friends from college: Lori Sheridan-Black, Chuck Day, Glenda Tolefson, Christia Prather-Caudle, Lani & Randy Juengel, and Kent & Carol Sivadge. And my North Carolina friends (past & present): Wanda Belote, Harriett Feimster-Cathcart, Debbie Daurity-Medves, Eileen Sercu, Lou & Marisa Sellman, Jodye McGray, and Laura Martone.

Of special note, thanks to Kim Spies and Jeff Seiler for their help in editing this book!

Foreword:
Theology and Psychology

I work with both secular and Christian couples in my practice, and, while there is always a spiritual component to the work that I do regardless of the group, there are sometimes places I can go more easily with Christians because of the shared belief system. But if you ask me "Is it easier working with clients who endorse the same faith as you?" the answer is more of an "It depends". Just because someone carries the label of "Christian" does not ensure that the same values or lifestyle exist. And, often, working with some Christians, if there is too much rigidity in their thinking, the work is harder, not easier, because you must justify what you're doing every step of the way.

While some still consider Christian theology (the study of God, and man's relationship with God) and psychology (the study of the human mind and behavior) to be strange bedfellows, this doesn't have to be the case. Some of this fear may stem from Biblical references warning Christians to not rely on man's wisdom (Proverbs 3:5 and Colossians 2:8, for example). Yet, if this is adhered to strictly, the only "safe" book to read is the Bible, which eliminates many other excellent references that can effectively round out one's faith. The best rule is what applies for most situations in life, "Be careful of the extremes," both extreme psychology *and* extreme theology.

There *are* different fly-by-night counseling approaches that catch the public's attention, often due to their degrees of the bizarre, only to fade in time as is typical of passing fads. However, some churches respond by "throwing the baby out with the bathwater". It may be falsely concluded that *all* psychology or outside counseling is evil or, at best, misguided, which is both an overly broad and inappropriate generalization.

At the same time, there are also extreme theologies - those that are somewhat cultic in nature and attempt to control and isolate their followers by keeping them segregated from the rest of the population, even to the degree of not allowing medical intervention for the sick. Or those theologies that promote viewing anyone outside their specific faith as "the enemy". It would be just as wrong for the general public to make the broad generalization that, therefore, all theologies are unhealthy attempts at social control, or are elitist in nature, and should be avoided.

If your faith is a mature one, then you have a working knowledge of what the Bible says and reading from other sources should not easily "corrupt" your belief system. With spiritual maturity, you are able to use discernment in examining other sources of information, knowing, because of your familiarity with Scripture, what lines up with it, and what does not. As Paul himself said, "**I believe *everything that agrees with the Law* and that is written in the Prophets...**" (Acts 24: 14)

For the person new to the faith, or with an undeveloped faith, there is reason to be much more cautious since knowledge of what is Biblical and what is not can be lacking.

Many forms of psychology, while secular, still contained truths that made them quite successful in seeing positive change in clients. During the last 20 years, Christian pastors and counseling professionals (such as Minirth & Meier, Cloud & Townsend, LaHaye and others) took those approaches and integrated them with Christian terminology, being able to then use them with Christian populations. Does that mean that, because the initial concepts came from a secular source, the entire approach should be discarded as corrupted or "humanistic"? I don't think so.

Real truths are universal. They hold true for both the Christian and the non-Christian. The *natural* law of gravity affects both Christians and non-Christians whether you believe in it or not. If I step off a cliff, unless a miracle occurs, I'm going to fall and hurt myself. The Bible does not discuss the law of gravity, yet it doesn't make it any less real.

The *supernatural* law of faith, while central to living as a Christian, works for both the Christian *and* the non-Christian. The "law of attraction" that is being promoted in secular society today is based on the supernatural law of faith. If I have faith in my ability to accomplish a task, I'm much more likely to be able to achieve it versus someone who is riddled with fear and self-doubt.

The difference in terms of these laws between the Christian and the non-Christian is that the Christian has direct access to the divinity which governs these laws, allowing for a more direct path to miraculous intervention.

* * *

In my work, I attempt to use Christianity as a filter, striving to use approaches that coincide with a Biblical foundation. From my point of view, psychology can be an excellent complement to a sound theology.

I very much see the Bible according to "**All scripture is inspired by God and useful for teaching the truth; rebuking errors, correcting falsehoods and giving instruction for right living**" (II Timothy 3:16). It is an excellent reference for teaching healthy living (physically, mentally, emotionally and spiritually), and one of the best avenues for developing an active relationship with God.

Psychology, used with discretion, often acts as a necessary *supplement* for the Christian lifestyle, providing specific strategies and methods for living it. The Bible tells me that I should forgive others, but most people still have difficulty understanding on their own *the process* of forgiveness.

The Bible says that "a kind word turns away wrath", which is true, but much of anger management is a *skill*, not something you acquire just because you know you're supposed to do it. While the Bible gives us examples and models, we often still need actual *methods* laid out for us in order to duplicate the desired behavior - something that counseling techniques provide.

I hope that you're able to approach the concepts and strategies in this book with an open mind and either an eagerness to learn, or, at the least, have what you already know affirmed. As with any book, take what is helpful, and leave the rest behind. I hope that you'll approach it as you would an honest friendship: expecting that there could be things that require you to stretch a bit in your thinking, exercising patience at the times when the pace doesn't match your own, and avoiding making assumptions about where I'm coming from before you've heard me out.

*   *   *

In writing a book, the writer must decide up front how to handle possessive and personal pronouns. For the purposes of this book, I'm choosing to use the masculine pronoun (he/his/him), not with the purpose of pointing the finger at men, or the likelihood that the majority of people reading this book will be women, but for consistency's sake. No offense to men OR women intended.

Part I

A Christian Foundation

Chapter 1
Christianity 101

"The wisdom of the prudent is to give thought to their ways, but the folly of fools is deception." (Proverbs 14: 8)

Conflict is inevitable in any relationship, whether you're a Christian or not. Yet many people enter into relationships with the expectations that, if it's a *good* relationship, if it has God's blessing, there should be *no* conflict. So when conflict inevitably *does* occur, people often end up incorrectly concluding that the relationship was a mistake.

People will deny, avoid, repress or ignore conflict in hopes that it will go away. But *a healthy relationship is often determined by how smoothly conflict can be negotiated, not ignored.* It is a skill that, even if not modeled by your caregivers while you were growing up, is learnable. It all comes down to:

- Having a good foundation from which to work
- Having a good selection of tools to handle whatever problems come along
- Knowing which tools to use and when
- Following through in using them consistently

When I use the word "foundation" I'm referring to the attitudes, expectations, understandings and beliefs that you bring to the relationship - not just those pertaining to romantic relationships, or the roles of husband and wife, but also how well you understand yourself.

- If your *attitude* about a relationship is based solely on the amount of energy your partner is expending for you...

- If you're entering a relationship *expecting* that God's going to do all the work to make necessary change occur...

- If your *understanding* of relationships is limited because you grew up in a family that didn't model healthy conflict...

- If your *belief* about relationships is that it's all about unconditional love, and accountability is just another form of judgment...

...there are going to be problems.

Understand that the foundation is the core of the relationship. *If the core is unhealthy, then everything else that happens within that relationship is perceived through that unhealthy filter.* Yes, even if you have a healthy foundation, there will still be problems, but the healthier the foundation, the more easily those problems can be resolved, and the less work there is overall.

*   *   *

One of the difficulties in starting counseling with a new couple is that you can't just assume that everyone is already speaking the same "language". So, much of the early part of starting to work on communication and conflict resolution is educational - bringing everyone up to speed on the core concepts that are necessary to know if better skills are going to be developed.

In these first two chapters I want to spend some time reviewing some of the basics of the Christian faith (as it pertains to relationships) before we add on the basics to conflict resolution. It's not wise to just assume that everyone already knows them.

The more grounded our Christian foundation (its core values guiding how we live each day), the more in touch we stay with the Biblical guidelines for our behavior in our relationships. If our behavior has deteriorated, it's typically because we have started to stray from remembering what it means to be "Christ-like".

First things first, *religion is not the same as spirituality*. As I am defining it, to be *religious* is a measure of how frequently you practice a certain set of traditions or rituals attached to your particular belief system. Going to church regularly and being actively involved in church activities may qualify you as being "religious" but it doesn't automatically mean that you are also "spiritual". Being "spiritual" has more to do with the *depth* of your relationship with God, and how much your Christianity is integrated into your overall lifestyle.

As with romantic relationships, you can fill the *role* of partner, doing what is expected of you, but still have little emotional connection to whom you're in relationship with. Just because you complete the duties and routines that are part of your relational obligations, does not assure any depth exists to the relationship.

Many Christians, when put to the test, fail to remember to actually turn to their personal faith to help deal with whatever their struggles may be. Sometimes this is because:

- while they publicly endorse those beliefs, they have never actually lived their lives *based* on those beliefs. It is a *nonexistent* faith.

- sometimes people make such a strong distinction between the *physical* and the *spiritual* that it never occurs to them to apply their spiritual beliefs to the physical world. Someone else has to make the connection for them before they see it (which is what many depend on church for).

- some people fear the idea of putting their faith to the test because, underneath, they either doubt the strength of their own faith, or doubt if God will really come through for them. But, in the meantime, it's a nice security blanket that helps them through. This is an *immature* faith.

5

Everyone, at some point or another, if they are to develop a *mature* faith, has to go through a time of searching and questioning what they believe versus what others would have them believe, arriving at what is actually their *own* faith, not a borrowed one.

This is not an overnight process but involves time, trials, testing and experience. If we live our lives so safely that we never allow for risk, never put ourselves in a position where we have to depend on God for a need, we fail to allow ourselves the opportunity to grow in faith.

The core "tools" of a mature Christian faith consist of:

- Biblical knowledge
- Prayer
- Fellowship
- Ministry

Biblical Knowledge

"Your word I have hidden in my heart, that I might not sin against You." (Psalm 119: 11)

As there are "tools" in the mental health field for dealing with conflict, there are also spiritual tools we have in our possession. Those tools, aside from helping us deal with other people, are also vital in helping us establish an active relationship with God.

If you were to try to develop a deep friendship with someone, how would you go about it? Well, you'd probably have to spend time with them. You'd need to come to understand how they act, think and feel. Through experience in being around them, you'd come to see how their views actually play out in the everyday world. Crisis reveals character, so you'd also need to see what they were like in hard times as well as good. A deep relationship requires intention and commitment. The same is true of a relationship with God.

One of the most immediate tools necessary for the Christian walk is the Bible. For it to be effective, we need to spend time reading, learning and applying what it has to say. While many of us choose to substitute reading by going to church, if you want a personal relationship with God, you need to be reading those words yourself. It would be like being married to somebody who has all of these profound things to bring to a relationship but you keep going to your next door neighbor to find out more about your partner's special qualities. I would think that, if it were your partner, you'd automatically be eager to go to the source to experience that relationship directly.

The significance of the tearing of the veil in the temple when Jesus was crucified was that Christ's sacrifice restored our direct relationship with God. We no longer needed the priests to be our intermediaries. Jesus is now our intermediary. But, for many of us, we live like that veil is still in place, and depend on other people to interpret God to us.

True, you probably don't have a seminary degree and so it helps to have someone who can put things in context for you, such as a pastor. But it doesn't change the fact that it's still *your* relationship with God, and nobody can have that relationship for you.

Biblical knowledge provides for four things: 1) understanding God's character, 2) guidelines for our behavior, 3) emotional support for when we're experiencing trials, and 4) promises which grant us some degree of control over our life circumstances.

Understanding the Rules

Often we respond to the "do's" and "don'ts" of Christianity as we did to the rules of our parents: with compliance, passive-resistance, opposition or outright rebellion.

Most people are familiar, to a degree, with the Ten Commandments of the Old Testament. They can probably recite at least three or four. For many, the concept attached to the commandments is that, if we violate a commandment, we stand in God's judgment.

In the New Testament, Jesus narrowed the focus to six Commandments.

"...But if you want to enter into life, keep the commandments."

He (the rich man) **said to Him, "Which ones?"**

Jesus said, "'You shall not murder,' 'You shall not commit adultery,' 'You shall not steal,' 'You shall not bear false witness,' 'Honor your father and mother,' and 'You shall love your neighbor as yourself.'" (Matthew 19: 17-19)

Notice that Jesus' focus wasn't about punishment for violating the commandments, it was about "if you want to enter into life". The commandments *aren't* there to warn us that God is going to zap us with a lightning bolt if we disobey them. *The commandments exist as guidelines for living a healthy life.*

In the same way that a parent tries to warn his children that certain actions are going to harm them because of the built-in consequences, God put the commandments in place as warning markers for His children. Think of it as for each choice you make you open a door into your life that allows things to enter. If the choice was a good one, then that open door will provide new and promising opportunities. If the choice is a poor one, we may experience some things that are going to haunt us or cost us in different ways. *Good choices widen our options, while poor choices narrow them.*

The more we understand the reasons for the commandments, the harm that violating them can cause us, and the life we can gain by respecting them, the more likely we are to truly embrace them rather than just view them as another list of rules.

Guidelines for Our Behavior

When it comes to your romantic relationship, Biblical knowledge provides guidelines for your behavior within that relationship. So, how often do you actually turn to it for relationship guidance?

Some of what the Bible has to say is specific to husband and wife, such as "...**each one of you also must love his wife as he loves himself, and the wife must respect her husband.**" (Ephesians 5:33). And some of it is about relationships in general but can still be applied to you and your partner, such as **"An honest answer is like a kiss on the lips."** (Proverbs 24:26).

If reading the Bible is going to be meaningful for you, you have to move beyond being a passive reader. Learning by *association* is a skill that requires a higher degree of focus and thought, because you're doing more than just taking information in, you're intentionally looking to see how that information applies to both your own life and your understanding of God. Typically this is what a pastor does, making those connections for us, but ideally it's learning how to do this for ourselves.

Prayer

"And when you pray, do not be like the hypocrites, for they love to pray standing in the synagogues and on the street corners to be seen by men. I tell you the truth; they have received their reward in full. But when you pray, go into your room, close the door and pray to your Father, who is unseen. Then your Father, who sees what is done in secret, will reward you. And when you pray, do not keep on babbling like pagans, for they think they will be heard because of their many words." (Matthew 6: 5-7)

If the Bible provides our avenue to knowledge of God's personality, containing His words of guidance and directions on how to live a Christ-like lifestyle, the spoken *prayer* is what provides for our direct communication with Him. Prayer is our avenue for communicating our innermost thoughts, fears, concerns and praises, as well as where we express our needs and requests for intercession.

Many Christians can be awkward with prayer because of their personal image of who God is. If we view God as this impersonal deity who sits in judgment on a throne somewhere, the idea of striking up a conversation can be rather intimidating. However, *if we view God as our spiritual Father who loves us and truly has our best interests at heart, approaching Him in prayer can be a more natural endeavor.*

If our relationship with our earthly father, or authority in general, was a difficult one, sometimes this also inhibits how we see, and trust, God.

- If we had a disciplinarian for a parent, we may tend to live in fear of God's punishment.

- If we had an inconsistent parent, then our issues with God may be around trust. If we don't trust authority, sometimes it's difficult to extend that trust to godly authority.

- If we had a parent who used guilt as a weapon, we may struggle with feeling condemned versus convicted.

- If we experienced only conditional love, we may see God as loving only so long as we are living perfect Christian lives.

There are any number of ways that a prayerful relationship can be sabotaged, but the bottom line is, we can't avoid direct communication with God if we're wanting to develop a relationship with Him. We can't allow the negative lessons we've learned from earthly fathers and authority figures, to keep us from experiencing God's grace, His forgiveness and peace.

The New Testament states that there are any number of reasons to seek out God in prayer, a few being:

- To be healed and see others healed (James 5:15)
- To be forgiven (Luke 18:14)
- To make our needs known (Philippians 4:6)
- To change the hearts of our enemies (Matthew 5:44)
- To cope with temptation (Matthew 16:42)
- To seek protection (John 17:11)
- To increase in faith and relationship with God (Ephesians 1:18)
- For the good of others (II Thessalonians 1:11)
- To escape trouble (James 5:13)

The Serenity Prayer

When we pray we need to turn over the things that are beyond our control to God, but we also need to assume responsibility for what remains our part. On more than one occasion I've heard fellow Christians talk about how they were waiting on God to fix their relationship, rather than focusing on what they themselves could do.

One of the key principles for balanced mental *and* spiritual health, is found in *the Serenity Prayer* by Reinhold Niebuhr, used widely throughout 12-step support groups. It summarizes the path to finding that state of balance we all desire.

"God grant me the serenity to accept the things I cannot change; courage to change the things I can; and wisdom to know the difference. Living one day at a time; Enjoying one moment at a time; Accepting hardships as the pathway to peace; Taking, as He did, this sinful world as it is, not as I would have it; Trusting that He will make all things right if I surrender to His Will; That I may be reasonably happy in this life and supremely happy with Him Forever in the next."

Too often, we will attempt to put things in God's hands that are really ours to deal with. We may pray for patience, or discipline, or virtue, but these are all things that we have to work at ourselves as well if they are going to have any meaning. It is our character that we are building. It wouldn't be true character if it was just handed to us by God. *God blesses our efforts in attempting to walk the walk*, but He's not going to take that walk for us.

The Lord's Prayer

"This, then, is how you should pray:
'Our Father in heaven, hallowed be your name, your kingdom come, your will be done on earth as it is in heaven. Give us today our daily bread. Forgive us our debts, as we also have forgiven our debtors. And lead us not into temptation, but deliver us from the evil one.'"
(Matthew 6: 9-13)

Jesus mapped out this model for us to use when we pray. As your personal walk grows, you're not restricted to that prayer, but it can still serve as a template from which you're guided. The Lord's Prayer consists of five primary aspects:

- Praise

- Acknowledgement of His will
- Bringing our needs to Him
- Repentance from our wrongs
- Requesting his guidance and protection

These aspects are what God is wanting from us in our communication with Him, what He values as important.

These aspects are also some of the most central elements required in the communication we have with our partners.

- We need to be able to praise and support each other.
- We need to be respectful of each other's rights in the relationship.
- We need to be able to bring our needs to each other.
- We need to exercise humility by being able to admit our mistakes and wrongs to each other.
- We need to be able to approach each other for guidance and counsel

And, just as with God, we need to be engaged in regular communication with each other, sharing from the heart.

Fellowship

"For where two or three come together in my name, there am I with them." (Matthew 18:20)

Many people go through their lives without ever experiencing *true community*. For those that have, they understand the incredible "connectedness" that can occur from experiencing being a part of a group on this level. *True* community goes beyond mere socializing. It involves a degree of acceptance and commonality that is incredibly intimate, and is perhaps best described as a deep sense of *belonging*.

Many war veterans experienced this during combat with their units. People who have lived through catastrophes together are often bonded in this way. The early Christians, being tortured for their faith, experienced this. But often, even though we congregate in churches on a regular basis, we still fail to experience and cultivate true community in the present day.

Scott Peck wrote "The Different Drum" which explored the process of developing community. He identified four stages:

- Pseudo-community
- Chaos
- Emptying
- True Community

In *pseudo-community*, we go through the socially-appropriate rituals. We smile. We say all the "right" things. We give the *impression* of connectedness, but it is superficial and never really goes below the surface in any meaningful way.

During the *chaos* stage, we begin to be aware of our differences. We begin to discuss how we *really* feel, think or believe, and there is often the experience of conflict with opposing views. During this time, there is often the attempt for opposing sides to try to *convert* the opposition to their way of thinking or doing. Judgment and rejection may also be part of what occurs.

The third stage is *emptying*. If we are able to move past chaos, sometimes it's because we are *consciously choosing to respect each other's differences.* We have moved past the instinct to convert, and are working at accepting and letting go. Typically this is possible *only if there is some greater purpose still held in common*, such as, whatever the individual doctrines, the different sides are still trying to effectively serve God.

True community is obtained when we've successfully emptied ourselves of the differences that drove us apart, focusing on the greater commonality that brings us together.

It's easy to see how this applies not just to a community, but to the couple. Our individual differences move us apart. They tend to create an environment ripe for rejection or judgment. Only by learning how to move past those differences, focusing on the greater purpose of maintaining a loving, godly relationship, do we experience the closeness and acceptance we desire.

Many couples will move out of the chaos stage by retreating back to pseudo-community. The differences will come out and things will get heated, so, in order to restore peace, they go back to not addressing issues, pretending like everything's okay again when it's not. This isn't "emptying". It's denial or avoidance.

Part of "emptying" in a committed relationship has to do with whether what we are trying to empty ourselves of is a *need* or a *preference*. We *do* need to move past our different preferences and not hang on to petty things (just as opposing doctrines often get stuck in debating points that are irrelevant to the big picture). But we still need to apply *accountability* for actual relationship needs. To "empty" ourselves of a legitimate need is trying to pretend we don't need to eat when we're hungry. Needs, by definition, need to be met. If we don't meet them in healthy ways, we will often, unintentionally or unconsciously, try to meet them taking unhealthy paths. So, for needs, a second path to true community, rather than emptying, is through *conflict resolution* which attempts to *structure* the chaos.

We *accept* the differences related to preferences. We *work through* the differences related to needs.

As a couple trying to hang on to true community (true relationship), the greater commonality that keeps the relationship focused and united can be several things. It can simply be about living a life together that is pleasing to God. It can be focused on making a difference in life developing our particular God-given talents. It can be about supporting each other's life dreams and vocational goals. It can be about continuing to grow together as a couple: learning, keeping the routines healthy, seeking out new experiences together, and embracing life as a progression.

The most common shared visions that couples gravitate to in a marriage are either 1) raising a family, or 2) working towards retirement. But the problem with using these as the vision is that *neither* attaches a priority on the relationship. The family focus is on raising the kids. The retirement focus is on the jobs and the income. Too often, what sets off a "mid-life crisis" (beyond mid-life) is we've hit the "empty nest" stage now that the kids have moved out, or now that we've retired we don't know what to do with each other after all of this time. For couples that have a relationship vision that takes into account the progression and health of the two (how we keep each other fit and continue to grow), the empty nest and retirement transition points are smoothly managed because the vision didn't stop there.

When both members of the couple are actively involved in supporting that common vision, just like an athlete dedicated to maintaining his physical health, doing anything that is destructive or counter to that healthy focus tends to stand out like a sore thumb. It becomes much easier to spot it when the relationship starts to drift because it's so visibly inconsistent with the strong positive current that has been created. Everything is on a more conscious level, and approaching necessary change is openly practiced without condemnation attached. The lifestyle remains focused on the health of "us", rather than over-absorbed with self, or the wrong others.

The Male Dilemma

Men, especially, tend to be loners, ignoring relationships of depth with those other than their partner until they find themselves in crisis and with no one to turn to. Men are supposed to be strong and self-reliant (that's how they're raised to think) but they have to be careful that they don't interpret that as above needing others.

Even God is relational. He created us in order to be in relationship with Him.

We can't afford to think we can be islands to ourselves - that all we need is God, a good job, and our partner. Yet this happens over and over again. *Even Jesus had his twelve disciples, and, yes, he did look to them for support, not just to teach.*

We need to be open enough to be accountable to our Christian peers. By soloing it we run the danger of getting off-track, without anyone to correct us if we're headed for the rocks. It's a dangerous place to be, thinking we're above needing help with anything, or that our view of everything is naturally the right one and we don't need anybody else's counsel.

It's often more difficult for men to start friendships because the social "rules" between men are more about respecting each other's space than getting into each other's space. Exploring personal territory is not quickly ventured and it takes longer to earn trust before a man usually opens up to another man. At the same time, even though the process is a slower one than with women, it doesn't change the fact that it's still a necessary thing (to have at least one or two close friends that serve as support, confidante and sometimes mentor). It's too much to expect all of that from just your partner.

We need to use discernment in choosing our close friends - seeking wise, insightful, and spiritually-grounded individuals. It's a great help to have friends with healthy marriages who inspire our own. Ideally, knowing at least one couple that has gone further down the road than we have, who can help show us the way back if we start to wander off the path.

Avoiding Intimacy

One of the problems typically seen in the Christian community is how we have difficulty approaching honesty with each other. Even though we are supposed to be actively practicing grace, we often don't open up on a truly personal level with each other for fear of being judged. My own experience with fellow Christians is that they can often be harsher judges, more critical and less forgiving, than much of secular society.

Because right and wrong, the presence of sin, are such central concerns for the Christian, it makes sense that one would be more aware or watchful of it in others. Yet we need to realize that a big part of why people were drawn to Jesus was because of his openness to receive them as they were. He did not avoid accountability, but *his first priority was to develop a relationship with the people first.*

So, too, we need to create a Christian atmosphere both in the church and outside of the church where honesty and need can be openly expressed, not instantly judged.

Over the years I've done several church "life-groups".[1] I remember one in particular where the group quickly developed into two specific sub-groups of people: those who were coming just to socialize, and those who were coming to share. The "socializing" group was uncomfortable with the "sharers" because the "socializers" weren't coming for, what they saw as, "therapy." While the "sharers" were coming for support from their fellow Christians, but being dismissed by the "socializers" as that not being the place. In my mind, the life-group's focus was to provide *both* a time of socializing as well as a deeper time for learning and support. For those looking for just the "lite" experience, without wanting to touch on anything serious, *they* should have been looking elsewhere.

My issue is with those Christians who just want to superficially remain on that pseudo-community level, and never be bothered with others aside from interacting only when they want to have "fun". We are not called to this faith in order to remain self-absorbed and beyond connection with the world around us.

Ministry

"There are different spiritual gifts but the same Spirit; and there are different ministries and the same Lord; and there are different activities but the same God who produces all of them in everyone." (I Corinthians 12: 4-6)

Many who think of the term "ministry" immediately think of the act of witnessing, or the evangelical call to take God's Word into the world. So if you haven't been called to be a pastor or lean towards being an introvert who values privacy and not intruding on other's lives, the idea of ministry can be something you leave for everyone else. But let me challenge that thinking just a bit.

---

[1] A "life-group" is a small church-driven group that meets for study, support and fellowship outside of the church.

One sign of emotional maturity is an awareness, respect and regard for the feelings, rights and needs of others. If we've matured, we've expanded our view beyond just ourselves to consider how our lives negatively or positively impact the people closest to us (and even those not so close that we come in contact with every day).

As we age, we become more concerned with what, if any, difference our life has made for having lived. We start to consider the significance of our existence, what we are leaving behind to say that we were here.

As Christians, one of our most direct connections to God is through our creative talents, whatever they may be, just as one of the primary aspects of God is "God the Creator". One of the ways we were created in His image is evidenced in how man himself constantly strives to create: through technology, the arts, industry, and relationships.

Often, *when someone has developed his personal creative talents, there comes with it the greatest sense of peace and satisfaction because the resulting feeling is that he is living out his purpose.* He is doing what he was put here to do.

This is symbolized in the Parable of the Talents in Matthew 25: 14-30, where the master gave his servants each a talent (in this case meaning money) and then went away for a while. When he returned he asked each of them what they had done with the money. He was pleased with those who had invested and increased what he had given them. He was upset with those who had done nothing with it (buried it in the ground).

Our skills and talents are part of what define us, and give us a better sense of direction and purpose in our lives. When we waste the skills and talents that we possess, we typically end up feeling lost and adrift, without a clear sense of personal identity.

Healthy self-love is shown in developing these abilities in ourselves, because they are a direct connection to our future, not just an immediate gratification. Healthy love of other is shown in inspiring and supporting our partners and loved ones in developing *their* own gifts.

When it comes to ministry, often this means taking a look at these personal talents, skills and gifts and how we're using them to benefit others, more-so than just ourselves.

Often, when we think of tithing (giving 10 percent of our income back to God), we think only in terms of money, when in fact tithing can be *anything* that we have to give whether it's money, material possessions, our talents and skills, our knowledge, or even just our time.

*   *   *

Ministry is also an outcome of past hardships. It is not uncommon to see someone who has gone through a particular trial in his life (medical issue, divorce, addiction, significant loss) who then turns around and begins to use that experience to minister to others who are still going through such things. The historical negative becomes transformed into a present positive.

—————

Ideally, before a couple passes judgment on each other for the conflict going on in the relationship, they need to first look at how healthy the spiritual foundation is, and work at getting their own house in order. That doesn't mean forcing your partner to comply with your version of Christianity. It means looking at the condition of your own spiritual life (devotions, prayer, fellowship, ministry) and doing what's needed to restore balance.

Summarizing this chapter, the core of the Christian walk is centered on 1) Biblical knowledge (what God has to say to us), 2) prayer (what we have to say to God), 3) fellowship (what God's people have to share with each other), and 4) ministry (what we have to give back to the world). Isn't it interesting that that's all about relationship?

Discussion Questions:

1. **When it comes to the guidelines for our behavior, in thinking over your current problems in your relationship, what does the Bible have to say about what you should do?** If you don't

know, what's keeping you from finding out? If what the Bible says you should do is different than what you are actually doing, and you are committed to being a Christian, how do you justify that discrepancy? What do you need to do to bring your actions in line with the guidelines?

2. **Are devotions a shared activity you have with your partner?** If not, why not? If you're both of the same faith, then this is an opportunity for growing together on a spiritual level.

3. **How is your prayer life?** Do you feel like your prayers are routine to the degree that it is a one-way monologue that rarely changes? Does it involve listening as well as speaking? How do you think you can improve on it?

4. **Do you pray together?** Again, this is a very intimate thing, so being able to share your relationship with God with your partner can be very helpful in working towards intimacy in the relationship.

5. **Have you ever experienced being part of a "true community"?** Have you ever been part of a peer group that knew you, faults and all, and still accepted you? Are you still a part of such a group in the present? If not, are you taking any intentional steps to be a part of one again?

6. **Of the four stages of community, what stage would you say your relationship is in most of the time?** Does it move back and forth between approaching chaos and then retreating back to a pseudo-relationship? What keeps it from arriving or remaining at true community? Is there a long-term common vision for the relationship other than raising a family or reaching retirement? Does that common vision help keep the relationship, especially the emotional/spiritual connection, fit?

7. **Do you feel you are above the need for spiritual peers?** Do you understand how going without this support and this accountability can be a dangerous thing? If lacking, what

realistic steps can you take in your current situation to start developing healthy peer relationships?

8. **Are you involved in any type of "ministry", any way that you give back to your family, friends, Christian community, or the rest of the world?** If not, what's held you back? Do you know what your personal skills and talents are?[2] How have you, or would you, go about developing them? Have you every filled out a "spiritual gifts" inventory?[3] Have you ever helped someone get through a hardship that was something you yourself had gone through in the past? Have you ever thought of applying that experience to a ministry?

---

[2] Skills and interest testing/inventories are available online and through most local universities.

[3] Again, available online.

Chapter 2
Christianity 201

**"By this all men will know that you are my disciples,
if you love one another."** (John 13:35)

The power of a person's Christian witness to the rest of the world should
be a visible thing. It's just as much about what you *model* as what you say.
And as far as what you say, your own particular story is the only thing
you have that's uniquely yours to share.

A non-Christian should be able to look at a Christian's life and see
something about it that is *desirably* different. I know many Christians
who aggressively witness to others, but the way they go about it does
not make anything about the Christian life actually desirable. So, too,
many will attempt to verbally promote a Christian life to others, but
their own personal life remains a complete train wreck. Hypocrisy
becomes a concern.

Many non-Christians live very moral lives. Just because Christians
embrace morality as well does not make us stand out. Hopefully, what
makes us an effective witness is being able to model something that the
rest of the world struggles to find (a deeper sense of meaning, peace,
joy, and virtuous love), rather than coming to God solely through fear
of judgment and eternal damnation.

If my life as a Christian is all about following a strict code of Biblical rules, obsessing about the right and wrong of everything because I'm in constant fear of God's disapproval, or judging everyone else for how closely I feel they come to living up to my list of "shoulds", the likelihood is that I've just found a new way to lose my joy and peace. I've created a new way to be in bondage even though I'm now supposed to be free. Why would a non-Christian want to share in that?

As Jesus said, "**Come to me, all you who labor and are heavy laden, and I will give you rest. Take my yoke upon you and learn from me, for I am gentle and lowly in heart, and you will find rest for your souls. For my yoke is easy and my burden is light.**" (Matthew 11:28-30).

In other words, *if we haven't found freedom in Christianity, then we haven't been living it the way that Jesus taught it.*

Law Versus Relationship

"So the law was put in charge to lead us to Christ that we might be justified by faith. Now that faith has come, we are no longer under the supervision of the law." (Galatians 3:24,25)

Man has a dual nature: order and chaos. To create and to destroy. While the creative side strives to improve and progress, the downside of its positive need for order is when man begins to *over-structure* and *over-control*, becoming a part of the problem rather than the solution.

The Jewish law, aside from the books of Moses (the first five books of the Old Testament), is summed up in the Torah. The Torah was what the Pharisees of Jesus' day were bent on enforcing throughout the Jewish community. To violate their religious laws often meant criminal charges and serious physical punishment. The Jewish law became one of micromanagement, where more and more detail was added onto every facet of living, to the point where it was difficult to do *anything* without having a "right" or "wrong" attached to it.

In the modern age, for Christians the Bible is still the spiritual law, and there still remains the trap for us that the Pharisees fell into. If we become *legalists*, our primary focus is on living *the letter* of the law. But legalists adhere to such a strict translation of the Bible that they lose the greater meaning behind it - the *spirit*, or the *heart*, of the law.

Aside from the fact that it is impossible to be justified in God's eyes by what we do, God isn't concerned about the letter of the law, but our desire to know Him (our hearts).

The added layer to this is that *the more we are focused on a relationship with Him, the more we automatically live the heart of the law because His nature is being reflected in us.* It's a matter of focus that makes the difference between bondage and freedom.

When it comes to romantic relationships, we similarly have a choice as to what we focus on: the role or the connection. When we become more focused on filling the relationship role (the obligations, the "to do's") we risk turning it all into work, and ultimately losing the connection. When we focus on maintaining the connection (the intimacy, the courtship) it makes the work ultimately so much easier to do.

*   *   *

More than our relationship with God and our relationship with our partner, for the Christian, it's about how we *integrate* the two relationships - two people with Christ/God at the center. Because the couple are both striving to live a Christian life together, that common vision keeps the relationship focused and mutually accountable to the values of their shared faith.

The Problem of Sin

"For all have sinned and fall short of the glory of God." (Romans 3:23)

For Christians, the stigma of "right" and "wrong" is usually attached to the even more weighty word "sin". If you have done somebody wrong, you have sinned against him. And, usually, to be *accused* of a sin has an aspect of judgment attached. There is automatically a comparison drawn between the sin and your character for committing the sin.

In a healthy relationship, the assumption is that both parties are interested in and dedicated to the health of that relationship. Yet, since both individuals in the relationship are human, things aren't going to be perfect. It's how we deal with these imperfections, and the sins that occur, that often determines whether the relationship will move in a positive or negative direction.

So if somebody asked you what a "sin" is, how would you define it?

The Bible defines sin in James 4:17 as "...**to him that *knoweth* to do good, and doeth it not, to him it is sin.**" In other words, *conscious* awareness of right and wrong, and *intentional* choice of refraining from doing what's right. For some people, that definition in itself is new information. Sin isn't making *mistakes* with our words or actions, it's intentional, conscious acts of neglect (sins of *omission*) and physical, emotional, mental, or spiritual harm (sins of *commission*).[4]

Of course, that leaves us to decide whether or not our partner's actions were intentionally done to hurt us. When the benefit of the doubt no longer is being given in a relationship, the automatic assumption is that our partner is doing and saying things with a conscious desire to be hurtful. Yet, we're looking at our partner as if they knew exactly how we would react to an action or statement when quite often they either didn't or weren't taking it into consideration. *We're sometimes giving our partners too much credit to know in every moment how we think and feel, and we have too much confidence in our own ability to know what they are thinking and feeling.* Most people don't intentionally set out to be hurtful in a relationship (unless a fight has already started) because most people do not enjoy creating conflict.

The word "sin", in its original context, was actually a term that was used in archery when an arrow missed its target. It meant *"to miss the mark"*. Somehow, saying, "You've missed the mark" does not have the incredibly negative connotation that goes along with "You've sinned," or

---

4 *Sins of omission* are where we see an opportunity to do good yet we choose to do nothing, or when honest information is intentionally withheld, making what we're saying only a partial truth. *Sins of commission* are where we see the choice between right and wrong and we choose wrong.

"You're a sinnner". A mistake, even an intentional one, can be repaired because you just try again (pick up another arrow).

This can be tricky territory since there are at least two different paths to addressing fault and they are approached from different directions.

For some, looking at our sins as "missing the mark", *without* the emotional baggage, makes it easier to accept responsibility for those errors, to learn from them, and make the necessary changes so as not to repeat them. That isn't saying that the wrong goes ignored. It's simply approached without the judgment attached.

However, others aren't motivated to repent until it has gotten to the place where a judgment has rightfully been earned, such as when a *pattern* of negative behavior exists. The weight of that judgment, the conviction of it, finally motivates them to change.[5]

Grace and Accountability

"If someone is caught in a sin, you who are spiritual should restore him gently." (Galatians 6:1)

An essential part of understanding the Christian life is grasping that *you are saved by grace, not works* (Ephesians 2:8, 9). In other words, you don't *earn* your way into heaven. Salvation is a gift.

But, once a Christian, there *is* the expectation that you will *act* like a Christian - a follower of Christ. If the majority of your life is not in accordance with Christ's ways, it would certainly lead one to doubt the sincerity of your commitment to Him.

How well we deal with accepting responsibility for our mistakes and faults, being honest with ourselves and our partners, often comes down to knowing how, and when, to apply grace. Grace, in part, is the act

---

[5] There are individuals who, due to emotional immaturity, insecurity, or having become over-sensitized to criticism in the relationship, cannot accept criticism in *any* form. Any feedback is automatically seen as a negative judgment or rejection. In order to move forward, they have to understand that there is such a thing as *positive* criticism, and value it as healthy if the relationship is going to improve.

of approaching yourself, or another, with an attitude of acceptance - accepting both the good *and* the bad.

God has accepted us *despite* our sin. Throughout the Bible, God worked through imperfect people. Aside from Jesus, *all* of the main players in the Bible who were favored by God were also flawed in different ways.

For the couple, part of grace is actively seeking, finding, and recognizing the good in each other - trying to see each other through God's eyes. It separates the destructive *behavior* that occurs (the negative choices) from the *character* of the person engaging in that behavior, recognizing that just because someone does something foolish in a hasty moment, it doesn't make them a fool.

This attitude of acceptance allows us to hear and share advice or concerns with our partners, because it is removed from judgment or reaction. Knowing that we are accepted, and modeling acceptance, we no longer need to be constantly fearful of rejection. We have given up wearing masks with each other.

That doesn't mean we stop editing what we say, or thinking through what would be upsetting to each other. We still need to be mindful of what is hurtful. Being respectful of each other is always taking each other's feelings and limitations into account.

The need for grace is obvious. Since every couple consists of two imperfect people, there needs to be room to allow for mistakes. Without grace, there is only criticism, rejection and judgment - no room for error.

As I mentioned with emptying, there are things in a relationship that often ultimately need to just be accepted and respected. With grace, we are no longer continuously attempting to convert our partners to our way of doing things. We can respectfully "agree to disagree".

Yet, grace, by itself, is still a relationship out of balance. *Unmet relationship needs* still need to be addressed. There are things that are destructive to the relationship that, left ignored, will harm or ultimately ruin the relationship. To rely solely on grace, hoping that things will just change on their own, or thinking that we're somehow supposed to accept the unacceptable, becomes an issue of neglect.

In both our relationship with God and our relationship with our partners, *grace must be balanced with loving accountability.* While we accept each other for who we are, we are still held responsible for our *choices*, and the things that need to change, in order for the relationship to work. (I'll go into this in more detail in the "Tools" chapters.) While God forgives us of our sins, there are still *consequences* for our choices.

Trying to maintain this balance is trying to keep in perspective what is really a big issue that requires accountability versus a smaller issue that, while maybe worth mentioning, may end up being something we need to let go of and accept, if it looks like it's not going to change.

* * *

For many Christians, it's easy to fall into one of the two extremes: grace without accountability, or accountability without grace. If I make everything that is negatively done against me "okay" by not saying anything, I am enabling bad behaviors in others. On the other end, if I'm constantly criticizing others for their less-than-Christian behavior, I run the risk of developing a negative focus, losing my Christian witness, and being judged in turn.

Spiritual Warfare

"Put on the full armor of God so that you can take your stand against the devil's schemes. For our struggle is not against flesh and blood, but against the rulers, against the authorities, against the powers of this dark world and against the spiritual forces of evil in the heavenly realms. Therefore put on the full armor of God, so that when the day of evil comes, you may be able to stand your ground, and after you have done everything, to stand."
(Ephesians 6:11-13)

While Christians accept the existence of a *personal* God (a god who is interested in a personal relationship with the individual), it's surprising to meet Christians who don't believe in a personal "evil" as well. The idea of a real Satan and his demonic forces perhaps seems too Hollywood or too uncomfortable for some to entertain. But the Bible doesn't really allow for the acceptance of Christ for who he said he was without also recognizing the existence of his enemy.

At the start of his ministry, Jesus endured the temptation in the wilderness, being directly confronted by Satan several times. There are numerous incidences throughout the New Testament where Jesus or his disciples exorcised demonic influences. Satan is credited as being the reason for man's fall from grace, removing God's creation (man) from His favor. Jesus' purpose in coming was to *restore* our relationship with God. **"The reason the Son of God appeared was to destroy the devil's work."** (I John 3:8)

Satan is described in the Bible as "the father of lies", assailing mankind through temptation, deception, distraction and distortion of truth. His is a very *subtle* corruption of what is good, a slow seduction that distances us from God, **"for Satan himself masquerades as an angel of light. It is not surprising, then, if his servants masquerade as servants of righteousness."** (II Corinthians 11:14)

This distortion starts with the visual we typically attach to Satan. Movies and books depict him as a horned and hoofed monster. Yet the angels of the Bible were described as beautiful, and Satan was said to have been one of them before his fall from heaven.

When we talk about the demonic, or spiritual warfare, it's easy to become paranoid and overwhelmed with fear of the unknown. We think "better not to think about it" than to let our minds run wild, jumping at shadows. And, certainly, evil has been done in reaction to our fear of the supernatural - witch hunts, labeling the unknown as black magic, doctors put to death because their medicine was thought to be sorcery, schizophrenia once thought to be demonic possession, etc.

As Christians, much of our role is leaving what's beyond our control regarding the supernatural in God's hands. But the Bible also tells us that, whether we like it or not, we're also a part of the fight.[6]

In a war, from a strategic point of view, if you know your enemy, then you know his methods of attack and can be better defended. We need to understand how Satan works in the real world in order to know when we're being played.

Deception

Orson Scott Card, a well-known Mormon writer, is one of my favorite authors of fiction. Card has an incredible understanding of people, especially children. He also has very wonderful insights into God's nature and the subtle workings of evil. He is most well known for his science fiction book "Ender's Game" which was made into a movie, but my favorite of his books is the series called "The Tales of Alvin Maker". The stories follow a gifted boy named Alvin from childhood to adulthood, exploring the moral development of his character as he discovers and attempts to live out God's purpose for his life.

Satan is a very present character in this series. Card's name for Satan in these books is *"the Unmaker"*, which is very appropriate since, as it is God's nature to create, Satan's purpose is to *undo* God's creation.

A committed, loving relationship is something that you *create*. Hopefully, as Christians, you've sought God's blessing on your relationship. Unfortunately, that also makes it a target for the Unmaker. And, subtle as he is, we never tend to consider that what's unmaking our relationship is anything other than ourselves or our partner.

---

6   Scott Peck's book "People of the Lie" started off as a study of human evil. During the writing of it he converted to Christianity because of his personal experience witnessing a demonic possession (and exorcism) in a treatment facility specifically designed to address such cases with a patient of his own that he had referred there. Here was a psychiatrist, familiar with schizophrenia, who could not explain what he saw within the definition of that disorder or any other. Of significance, the possessed all responded to the authority of Jesus' name.

To put our relationship's conflict into perspective on the spiritual level sometimes allows a couple to stop looking at each other as the enemy, and to become a united front against allowing "the Unmaker" to continue to manipulate their lives. This is most visible in cases where things have become emotionally reactive and the couple is now acting totally out of character. Their anger continues to keep things fueled and they're no longer in control of themselves - like puppets on strings. It's almost like you can hear evil laughter in the background as they're going at it, seeing these committed Christians treating each other in such destructive, disrespectful ways, and watching another creation unravel.

C.S. Lewis' book "the Screwtape Letters" is another excellent example of how our own thoughts, even those that start out with excellent intentions, can become corrupted, distorted, and lead to our eventual downfall.

The initial *deception* starts with us thinking that we're above such things. *We* wouldn't cheat on our partners. *We* would never say such a thing. *We* could never be so misled. *We* would never treat our partners like that. And by putting ourselves above it, we aren't watchful when it starts to happen, because we're convinced it couldn't happen to us.

Temptation

Temptation is the most obvious form of spiritual warfare, whether it's through sex, drugs, money, food, or material things. Since we're all human, to experience temptation is natural. The point where it becomes a sin is the point at which we begin to dwell on it - when we let it take root.

The myth of temptation is, "How can it be wrong, if it feels so good?" We tell ourselves we'll stop going there, waiting for it to no longer feel good, but the power of its temptation is that it *does* feel good and often *continues* to feel good. Our lives may start to fall apart because of the priority the temptation takes in our life, yet we keep hanging onto it because now it's the only thing left that gives us some relief. Like the sirens in mythology that lure the sailors to steer the ship onto the rocks.

Distortion

Our underlying needs are always legitimate. The problems are almost always in how we go about trying to get those needs met.

Affairs will frequently start out as benign relationships. The primary, legitimate need that fuels them is typically that of support or fun - a friendship. But as intimacy deepens, it will sometimes become corrupted into selfish desire.

Unhealthy love is a *corrupted* form of healthy love. When we show love to ourselves, we can feel like it's healthy because it makes us feel good for that moment, yet it can be completely selfish and unhealthy if it's going to cost us tomorrow, or chronically puts our need above everyone else's. So what feels like "taking care of me" can actually be neglecting what's really best for me.

Satan takes healthy things and corrupts them just enough that they are no longer serving a healthy purpose for us. But *we remain attached to them because of the healthy need they are still attempting to satisfy.*

Distraction

In this day and age, the subtler form of spiritual warfare (but probably the most effective in leading Christians astray) is positive or negative *distraction.*

In terms of the positive, we have so many choices in this culture, so many options with what we see on TV, with our I-phones and I-pads, with how we spend our free time. Yet, the majority of it simply keeps us occupied, accomplishing little other than to either rescue of us from boredom or help us get our minds off of our stress.

In terms of the negative, much of mental illness revolves around distraction. Addictions keep us over-focused on the object of our addiction. Depression and anxiety keep us ensnared in torturing ourselves with anxious or depressed thoughts. Obsessive-compulsives lose themselves in generating new nonsensical rituals or going down endless mental rabbit trails. Ultimately, what each does is to distract us from living our lives more effectively. We get lost in these paths that remove our focus from the simplicity of being able to rest in the moment, to just "**Be still and know that I am God.**" (Psalms 46:10).

At times, I tend to visualize life as this big novelty shop that each of us has to pass through. Every item in the shop represents something more than just an object: an experience, an opportunity, an idea, an activity, a ministry, a skill, or even a relationship. Some of the items that we find in that shop are a unique fit for us and will add something wonderful to our lives and our identity. But some of the other items are traps that can prey on our particular weaknesses, mesmerizing us, keeping us stuck from making any meaningful progress forward. For those who become mesmerized, they've just been effectively removed from the part that they were supposed to play in "the war", and it didn't even require anything other than a distraction.

That's why it's so important that we are making *conscious* choices of how we spend our days (considering the bigger-picture positives and negatives of the "items" we daily choose to focus on) if ours is to be a life of meaning versus a life misled by distraction.

*   *   *

Let me balance what I'm saying about spiritual warfare. I'm *not* saying that every relationship's problems are due to Satan manipulating us. Sometimes we do a great job of ruining things all by ourselves. What I *am* suggesting is if we don't take into account Satan's willingness to use our weaknesses against us in order to undo our relationships, if we don't stay spiritually guarded against his subtle corruption of what is good, then we remain vulnerable and at risk of being used and manipulated by him.

Spiritual Consequences and Boundaries

"**We have renounced secret and shameful ways; we do not use deception, nor do we distort the word of God. On the contrary, by setting forth the truth plainly we commend ourselves to every man's conscience in the sight of God.**"
(II Corinthians 4:2)

A man named Kohlberg came up with the theory of moral development many years ago. In it, he described three different levels of moral reasoning that reflect an individuals' developing maturity.

A person who is operating at the lowest level of Kohlberg's scale follows moral rules out of fear of punishment. If the rules were not in place, or there was little likelihood of being caught, that individual would probably not be a respecter of those laws.

The second level is where individuals follow rules in order to gain social approval, or out of a sense of duty ("It's the right thing to do"), or obligation to society.

The third level is respecting moral laws because of a sincere interest in the welfare of others. The focus is no longer on self or image and there is a deeper understanding of the reasons behind the rules.

Kohlberg felt that the majority of society never make it to the third level.

Despite being Christians, many of us still choose our behaviors based on the presence or absence of *visible* consequences. Even though we say that we recognize that there is a spiritual world, we don't seem to give weight to spiritual consequences (aside from the possibility of God's punishment). So all of those unhealthy things that we continue to do in private, where others can't see, are doable because we think it's not hurting anyone. We fail to take into account the impact our choices have on the condition of our soul - affecting our self-respect, our integrity and our closeness to God. *Those choices over time reshape the lines of our identity and how we are willing to compromise our personal standards.*

For example, one subtle but progressive consequence for the use of pornography is that it makes it more difficult to be aroused by only your partner. Because your partner can't compete with the fantasy image, you become more dependent on using those images to sustain your desire. Even though you may never accept the label, or judgment, of being a "pornographer", you're still suffering the natural consequences of being one.

If our behavior was ever brought to light and we were publicly exposed, we'd be humiliated and maybe find the motivation to actually change. But it's unfortunate that it has to get to that point before we exercise accountability with ourselves.

Many don't take the time to consider where their present behavior is taking them. Sometimes they do see, but they gamble that they can stop any time, and they won't let it go that far - until they're already there.

Why don't we care enough about ourselves to put more of a priority on our private character? Kohlberg would say that it's because, morally, we are still operating on a very immature level, only staying within the lines when we are at risk of getting caught.

*   *   *

So what about when our inappropriate behavior in private isn't really private because we are doing it in front of our partner, and maybe even our kids? For example, abusing substances, throwing tantrums, making threats, passing character judgments, no longer treating the relationship as a priority, or no longer being respectful. We wouldn't do that if company was present, or if we were in public, but somehow, when it's just us and our partner (the person we're supposed to love the most) it's become okay. What happened?

When it comes to healthy, personal boundaries in a relationship (those relational lines that allow us to continue to see our partner as separate and "other"), the struggle is always with how we continue to maintain them over time. There are several factors that contribute to boundaries deteriorating:

- too much familiarity
- stress
- distraction
- too much routine

The boundaries begin to fade or fragment, and now the behavior that we normally held in check starts to trickle out on our partner, because in that moment we are no longer really seeing them as separate. They have become an extension of us - something to react to, not someone to respect.

If we struggle with anxiety, now our worry and fears include them. If we have unresolved anger, our upset erupts openly. If we have a critical inner voice, now our partner is part of what and who we judge.

In those situations, our filters (how we edit) have been dropped. So now the things that we used to manage start managing us. And behavior that we wouldn't ever display in public now starts to be modeled in front of, or directed at, our partner. (And because our kids are also in our inner circle, sometimes it includes them as well.)

For couples that have become reactive, they are so overly focused on trying to control each other's behavior that they ignore accountability for their own inappropriate behavior. They complain about how hurtful the other is even as they are creating some new wounds themselves.

With all of this, there has to be a point of self-awareness, waking up, where someone finally looks at himself and says, "What am I doing? How is this even close to acting like a Christian?"

Sometimes it's not our own voices, but our partners' voices that we need to listen to when they are trying to make us self-aware of our less-than-healthy behavior. That *is* part of why we need these relationships, to help balance us when we are falling out of balance.

Restoring boundaries has to do with:

- intentionally practicing respectful communication
- better managing our personal stress
- continuing to attach a priority to the relationship connection
- not letting the routines become too routine[7]

As Christians, we have the added benefit of the presence of the Holy Spirit. While we would choose to focus on things other than our own

---

[7]   Which we'll talk about in Chapter 10.

accountability, if we are continuing to work at maintaining a relationship with God, the Holy Spirit continues to deal with us about our choices far longer than we would choose to think about them. If we are no longer hearing that voice, it's likely that we are either actively ignoring it, have already distanced ourselves from God, or our own emotions (or neediness) are drowning it out.

Toxic faith

While faith and spirituality can be a very good thing, helping to keep us grounded, centered and at peace, throughout this book you will hear me say, "The problem is with the extremes".

A faith can be overly flexible to the point that everything becomes relative and it stands for nothing. Yet a faith can also become so rigid that it becomes closed to new information, so narrow in its thinking that it ceases to grow, only feeding off of the things that support its specific doctrine.

The term "toxic faith" has been around for several years now, recognizing the fact that sometimes it is our own particular set of spiritual beliefs that is causing problems for us. While this can be due to rigidity, it can also be due to embracing a particular belief, or set of beliefs, that is either destructive in itself or destructive in how we interpret or apply it.

1. A toxic faith can over-focus on judgment.

There are those individuals who have taken on their interpretation of God's role by going around pointing out the sins of their fellow "brothers and sisters", making open judgments, and completely disregarding **"judge not lest ye yourselves be judged."** While the New Testament *does* promote Christians being accountable to each other, we still have to consider the line between accountability and judgment.

Often, as a couple, one's own religious convictions can result in a constant judgment of the partner. Because of that continued condemnation, the partner isn't inspired to change but is pushed away by the attempts at lecturing, punishing, and converting. If the initial focus had been on *modeling* a healthy Christian life, ideally, the positive example set would have served as a better witness than any attempts to persuade or convert.[8]

For black-and-white Christians, everything comes down to "right and wrong", "good or evil", which means everything requires a judgment to discern between the two. This is a very easy trap for Christians to fall into since the Bible will often talk in similar terms. But the truth is that *there are many things* (money, material things, alcohol, music, food, dancing, etc.) *that are neither good nor bad. It's what you do with them that decides the difference.*

I'm not saying that everything is relative. There are still absolutes. It's just that there's a lot of things in between that don't fall into either category.

With couples who oversimplify, the thinking is often, "If I think I'm right, then you must be wrong." But in reality *each* person typically has some valid points in a disagreement. There are at least some *partial* truths to both sides.

When a "right/wrong" mentality becomes the habitual way of thinking, it gets carried into the everyday things such as how you fold the laundry, or keep the house clean, or what you choose to do with your free time. Yet, these are *lifestyle preferences* more-so than values. For the person who has an overly long list of "shoulds" ("This is the way it *should* be done.", "This is what you *should* be thinking.", "This is what you *should* be doing."), their parental mindset robs them of ever being able to just relax and be at peace. Left unchecked, they can become very critical, unhappy people.

2.   A toxic faith can *isolate* God rather than *include* God.

When people do priority lists (God, family, spouse, job, hobbies, etc.), debating what should fall into the top 3, the initial error is in listing God

---

[8]   Part of this obviously depends on the destructiveness of the partner's behavior. Tolerance isn't possible when substance abuse, affairs, or physical or emotional abuse are the issues. In those situations, tolerance becomes enabling (making it okay).

as a separate priority, because God is the one "category" that needs to be *incorporated* into all of the others, not set apart.

With attaching a healthy priority to our partner, including God becomes how we are now trying to be a *godly* partner. As a parent, it's how we try to be a *godly* parent. By taking care of our bodies (through diet and exercise), we are respecting God's instruction to take care of these "temples" He has given us. By maintaining a social life with fellow Christians for our support system, we are respecting the Biblical instruction to not forsake gathering together. *All healthy priorities overlap with God as our priority so long as we continue to consciously, intentionally bring Him into each of them.*

In the addictions realm, it's not unusual for someone to replace one addiction with another. Sometimes, religion becomes the new addiction. On the surface, religion is certainly a more positive addiction of choice. The focus is now on regularly going to church, volunteering, maybe even teaching a class, participating in outreach programs, etc. But, sometimes, if you go into the home and talk to the spouse or the kids, you will find that the relationships themselves haven't changed. They're still being neglected because God was being treated as an isolated priority, not an integrated one.

3. A toxic faith can be overly rigid, cutting itself off from anything that could potentially challenge its truth.

Sometimes these are the people who can be quite vocal in telling others about their faith, yet, if you offer either a different perspective or question theirs, you are automatically met with a judgment, a dismissive response to what you have to say, or a defensive reply that allows for no further discussion. This might be due to being close-minded, overly sure of themselves, or stubborn. But sometimes that seemingly strong conviction is actually something quite fragile.

For the latter, hanging on to their particular pieces of theology is where all of their security comes from. To consider any contrary (or sometimes even complementary) information, is too much of a potential threat to their oversimplified foundation. Their need to be right has an almost urgent feel to it. The fear of being wrong, and the internal discomfort that that creates, doesn't allow for any true discussion.

Insecure people often *overcompensate* by projecting an attitude of competence and confidence to cover up their inner fears. Those fears are usually about some form of inadequacy, somehow being exposed as incompetent or unlovable (which would lead to feeling rejected, judged or abandoned). As a result, they tend to reject before they can be rejected, judge before they can be judged, abandon before they can be abandoned.

For insecure *black-and-white* people there are only two options in relationships: acceptance or rejection. They are quite comfortable with the strokes or compliments others may provide, but *any* form of criticism (even healthy, necessary criticism) is automatically experienced as rejection or judgment. This creates a dilemma for their relationships because the only way for a relationship to truly progress and grow is to be open to feedback and suggestions, which they're not.

There's frequently an inner paradox that goes on with them in that, while they are oversensitive to criticism, they typically have an overly active inner critical voice of their own that continuously draws a sense of their self-worth from making comparisons with others. As a result, being in the presence of highly competent people, while they may enjoy being treated as a peer by such, can also make them feel inferior. So they eventually have to resort to finding qualities about those people that they can judge. Being in the company of people less competent than they makes them feel better about themselves, safer.

Black-and-white thinkers have to train themselves to start looking past the oversimplified extremes in order to discover middle ground. With accountability, that middle ground means being open to healthy criticism. With relationships, that middle ground means being able to explore healthy compromise. In all other things, that middle ground is called moderation and balance - something extremists easily overlook. Extremists lean towards excess or abstinence.

*   *   *

41

Cults isolate their members from the outside world. They don't want any other influences interfering with the doctrines that they're promoting.

On a broader scale, we do this to ourselves when we overly depend on getting all of our Christian instruction through just one source (be it a particular pastor, speaker, author, TV or radio show). By doing this, we are automatically putting ourselves in a precarious position by relying on that particular individual's interpretation as being an unbiased and accurate one.

"Not many of you should presume to be teachers, my brothers, because you know that we who teach will be judged more strictly. We all stumble in many ways. If anyone is never at fault in what he says, he is a perfect man, able to keep his whole body in check." (James 3:1)

Even if you have a source whose theology is consistently sound, by overly depending on someone else's teaching without ever questioning it, or taking time to develop your own knowledge (through reading, discussion, Christian peers, prayer and application), you are still relying on a *borrowed* faith.

4.   A toxic faith can over-spiritualize.

People who over-spiritualize read too much meaning into mundane events. Just as Satan isn't responsible for every bad thing that happens, so, too, every occurrence in our lives is not because God is behind it, trying to tell us something. When things go wrong, too often people will assume that somehow they have displeased God and now they're being punished, forgetting that this is a fallen world, after all. For the Christian, it's knowing that, **"in all things God works *for the good* of those who love Him, who have been called according to His purpose."** (Romans 8:28)

It's a very good thing to continue to try to search for what God may have to teach us, or what His will is for our lives, but the concern is when personalization has gone to such an extreme that we're running ourselves ragged reading too much meaning into things, to the point that, once again, we've found another way to lose our peace.

Even when things go wrong *because* of something we've done, sometimes the outcomes are just due to *natural* consequences. For example, what are the physical consequences for unresolved anger? Ulcers, arthritis, musculoskeletal problems, and other physical ailments. God isn't dropping that on us. We're doing it to ourselves!

And, sometimes, the stress that creates those physical problems comes from unsound theology. We're convinced God hasn't forgiven us. We don't feel worthy enough to be forgiven. We're trying to earn our salvation. We're waiting for God to deal out justice to those we feel need to be punished. We're not able to trust God with something important to us.

When we have a *lack* of information, we tend to fill that void with our own issues, our own fears, or even our own wish fulfillment ("I really think this is God's way of saying I should go ahead and get that car!").

* * *

For relationships, it's always a dangerous position for one partner to appoint himself as the only one who hears from God. First off, how do you argue with that? It creates an imbalance for the relationship - a way that one partner can always dominate the decisions, or always be right.

It's wiser to stay with "I *feel* like God is saying...", rather than "God told me...", since the first allows that we could be wrong, which is a real possibility. It acknowledges our humanity, that we are not beyond making mistakes. We need to remember that some of this world's greatest tragedies involved people who were completely convinced they were either chosen by, or spoke with God. Even if true, being chosen by God for something does not put us above error. Moses, chosen by God, successfully led his people out of Egypt, but his impulsive error with striking the rock kept him out of the Promised Land.

God *does* attempt to communicate with us in various ways, but you need to use discretion and wisdom in interpreting the signs. If we need to be making a big decision, while still praying for guidance, it's a good policy to consult with others whose spiritual judgment and common sense you value before drawing a firm conclusion as to what the "right" path to take might be. "**Plans fail for lack of counsel, but with many advisers they succeed.**" (Proverbs 15:22)

We need to recognize that there are many decisions in life that we may treat like moral dilemmas, but they really have no one God-ordained choice (what car we buy, what house we choose, what gym we go to). In those situations, making a good choice, even if it's not the "perfect" choice, is still good enough. We shouldn't be over-stressing that God has abandoned us, or we missed hearing His will, if our choice doesn't turn out as well as we would have liked. What's more important in those circumstances is *being committed to making the most out of whatever choice we made.*

In summary, Christianity should be something that sets us free, not creates greater bondage. Accepting that we are human (that we are capable of wrong), rather than having to always "have it together" (deflecting or rejecting any criticism), can be freeing in itself. To admit that we make mistakes sets a much more realistic expectation for ourselves and our relationships. What's more important is that we're willing to take responsibility for correcting whatever those mistakes may be.

Ultimately, the daily criteria for the choices that we make in our relationships should come from our familiarity with the personality of Jesus, our best example of godly behavior; God in human form. If we *know* his character, consistently shown in the gospels, it shouldn't be difficult to answer "What would be the 'Christian' thing to do?"

Discussion Questions:

1. **Is your relationship with God based on trying to achieve his approval through deeds, or is the focus on drawing closer to Him?** Do you feel freer as a Christian, or more stressed with everything you're supposed to be doing as a Christian? If more stressed, what would you need to do different than what you are in order to restore healthy freedom?

2. **Is your relationship with your partner primarily about performing *tasks* in order to avoid their disapproval?** If so, what would the two of you need to do to move the relationship back to a position of freedom and choice, where the relationship, and not the lists, is the focus?

3. **When you think of sin in the original archery context, "to miss the mark", does that change the weight you otherwise might attach to a Biblical sin?** Does the guilt or shame attached to admitting a sin make it easier or harder for you to own it?

4. **Do you believe in the existence of a personal Evil called Satan?** If so, do you believe that one of his purposes is to undo God's creations? Does that include your own relationship? Does thinking about the reality of spiritual warfare put a different perspective on the difficulties that arise between you and your partner?

5. **When you're by yourself, what level of moral development do you live by?** If there is an inconsistency between your public self and private self, how do you rationalize it? Has your partner lost respect for you because of that inconsistency, or vice versa? How well does your partner know your private self or do you have to maintain a different face? If you have to present a certain image to your partner, how does that interfere with feeling accepted for who you are?

6. **Have you ever seen someone practicing toxic faith?** What was your experience when you were around them? Do you, or does your partner, view how the other practices their faith as being problematic for the relationship? If so, if respect was restored for each other's opinions/insights, how much would that help the relationship?

7. **Do you automatically perceive new information that is different from your own beliefs as a threat to your faith, or as new information to be considered, measured out, and possibly used to further refine your faith?** How do you measure your own flexibility - knowing if or when you're being too rigid?

8. **How do you decide the difference between what God wants you to do versus what might just be your own magical thinking?** How much do you allow your partner's perspective to balance your own when it comes to interpreting God?

Part II

Tools for Resolution

Chapter 3
The Conflict Model

"A gentle answer turns away wrath, but a harsh word stirs up anger."
(Proverbs 15:1)

When it comes to anger, there are natural dilemmas that exist when dealing with how you do or don't express it. If you squash your anger, pretend or act like it doesn't exist, you may have saved the day today, but it's going to eat away at you inside and either explode somewhere down the road or find other ways to get out. If you "let it fly", you risk saying things that you're probably going to regret, and maybe don't even mean, but, once said, can't be undone.

Many people who have issues with anger do so because they feel, or the partner feels, that it's *not* okay to be angry. Because there is no "allowed" outlet provided for their upset, things build to a point where they finally explode. But one of the central concepts of conflict resolution is that *it's okay to express your anger as long as you do it appropriately* - ideally, in a way that creates understanding, not further damage.

Controlling our temper is difficult because it goes *against* our natural instinct when we feel attacked or hurt. While our emotions are telling us to defend ourselves by retaliating, or to run away, we're consciously choosing to ignore them, to stay put, to think things through and to work it out.

Learning how to manage our anger effectively is a skill, and, being a skill, it is learned. You aren't born with it. Sometimes we see it modeled for us by our parents, but other times we have to figure it out for ourselves. It's learning how to control our nature until the control part itself becomes more natural for us.

Anger stems from hurt feelings which, in turn, stem from unmet or injured needs. As I said last chapter, needs, by nature of their definition, are always legitimate. They *have* to be met. *The problem is always in how we go about trying to meet them.*

In a romantic relationship, you need both emotional intimacy and security. So if you've got an issue with your partner, intimacy demands that you share that with him at some point or you will be moving towards *false* intimacy. Emotional *security*, in part, comes from knowing that you're safe in sharing your pain with your partner, that he can handle it respectfully and lovingly, even when it's directed at him.

Conflict resolution attempts to meet those underlying needs, but in a way that doesn't further complicate the issue.

*   *   *

There is a natural progression as to how anger escalates over time, and what it becomes if it goes unchecked.

Frustration often comes from circumstances where somebody said or did something you perceived as negative, that you can't easily change, or is beyond your control.

Anger usually comes into play when frustration has gone unresolved over time, or if you feel you've been intentionally wronged.

Resentment usually sets in when your anger has no outlet or no resolution.

Bitterness results when chronic resentment has hardened your heart. Only a conscious act of true forgiveness can begin to reverse the process.

*   *   *

Because the extremes are the easiest options to see, people often either stop too short or go too far in trying to resolve conflict. Our instincts also operate in extremes. When there is the presence of a threat our instincts are very basic: fight or flight. Attack or withdraw.

Many are great at starting arguments, but never get far enough into the conversation to accomplish anything. They complain and retreat. If you're tempted to withdraw from an argument before you've been successful at explaining yourself, or have yet to reach a resolution on the issue, you probably need to face the discomfort of conflict and hang in there longer.

However, if either you, or your partner, are starting to lose your temper, and attempts to get the conversation back on track have failed, it might be better to shut things down and re-approach later on. (*Re-approaching* being the most important part, since many simply abandon the issue and it never gets resolved.)

If I've already said what I needed to say, have reached a workable solution, but now I'm tempted to go back and underline my points, I probably need to stop where I am. Some can actually reach a solution, then take it too far and undo everything they've accomplished.

Words of Power

The Bible is full of evidence that there is power in the spoken word. God *spoke* Creation into existence. The Bible didn't say He thought it into existence. Each aspect of Creation was verbally *commanded* into being.

"And God *said*, 'Let there be light', and there was light." (Genesis 1:3)

So, too, Jesus performed miracles by the command of his words.

"When evening had come, they brought to Him many who were demon-possessed. And *He cast out the spirits with a word*, and healed all who were sick," (Matthew 8:16)

Not only do God and Christ's words have power, but the Bible also attaches a good deal of weight to our *own* words.

"The tongue has the power of life and death…" (Proverbs 18:21)

Words can be used for good or evil, to hurt or to heal, but the weight that they possess is the emotional weight that we attach to them. The same word for one person can leave him completely unmoved, while, for the next person, it can set off all sorts of associated memories or feelings. Words are incredibly powerful and we need to learn when, and how, to use them.

Most of us are very skilled at knowing how to use words as weapons. We have been entrusted with the knowledge of each other's most private fears, failures, embarrassments and guilt. We have listened to our partners share these with us in confidence and felt closer to them for trusting us. Yet, when things "hit the fan" and tempers start to flair, how do we repay this most loved one for their past trust? Well, we prove our own untrustworthiness by using those most private things against them, violating the intimacy that was gained. And then, days after the smoke has settled, we have the nerve to express our frustration when we find they are hesitant to share with us again. We desire intimacy but so often abuse it once we've gained it.

By the time we are adults, we are typically very protective creatures who trust only in the smallest of degrees. We guard our secrets closely and to risk trusting another with them takes courage. For those who have already been hurt or betrayed in the past, it takes *incredible* courage.

Trust is the foundation of any relationship. If you don't have trust, then you don't have anything to build on. We *create* trust through the loving consistency in our words and actions. Thinking in these terms, it's easy to see how a lover can become an enemy - how love can shift to hate, if the trust is violated. If I am rejected by a stranger it means nothing because they meant little to me, and they really do not know who I am. If I am rejected or betrayed by my partner, it is the essence of who I am that is being judged, violated or discarded by the very person I trusted the most.

People are often quite fragile when it comes to the opinions of others. Sometimes you can make or break someone else's day by a simple compliment or criticism. You can enforce your child's self-confidence or contribute to his fears based on what you verbally choose to recognize about him or his world.

Even in your own life, outside of any relationship, *the words you tell yourself shape the quality of your existence.* You can impact the likelihood of having a great day or a bad one based on what words you tell yourself at its start. If you say to yourself, "Today's going to be a great day", then you've already chosen, at least to a degree, that today's going to be something to look forward to. If you get up and the first thing out of your mouth is "Oh, no, what's going to go wrong today?" you're already focused on finding the things that will confirm your fear of the day going badly.

Words can be so incredibly powerful and yet we often treat them with no regard. We gossip. We wound. We ramble on. But when we start to take back conscious control of what comes out of our mouths, and what words we tell ourselves in our thoughts, we begin to harness an amazing tool for moving our relationships, and our life, in positive directions.

Adult – Parent - Child

Eric Berne had a theoretical approach to relationships back in the 70's and 80's called *transactional analysis* that is really helpful in gaining perspective with what happens when we argue. Berne said that there are three different types of communication "roles" that we assume: the *Adult*, the *Parent* and the *Child*.

Of those three roles, the Adult is the most balanced and mature. When it comes to conflict, the ideal combination we want in the relationship is Adult-Adult.

Naturally, as adults, we expect to be treated as another Adult (with respect, equality, and fairness) but often we are not actually *acting* like an adult when we get upset.

In chaotic relationships, where both adults are emotionally immature, conflict deteriorates into Child-Child. Because not even a parent is present, there's no telling how dangerous the interaction might become.

Since couples tend to naturally attempt to balance each other, one way we balance a partner who is acting like a Child is to take on the role of Parent to that Child. It's not even a conscious choice.

Understand that just because a relationship is *balanced* does not mean that it is *healthy*. I can be married to a very hot-headed woman and, because I'm passive, things balance out. I absorb her temper blasts like a sponge so, ultimately, there's peace, even though I've become a doormat in the process. But that doesn't mean that I'm happy or that the relationship works.

The Parent-Child pattern is one of the most typical for adult couples. Whoever is acting as the Child will often do the very things that force the partner into being the Parent even though *neither* wants to have that role.

The reactive Child tantrums, insults, and attempts to manipulate.

The reactive Parent punishes, judges or attempts to control.

Since we've all been children, we are familiar with childhood strategies to get our way. And since we've all had caregivers in one form or fashion, we are familiar with parental strategies to gain our compliance. Not as many of us have had Adult behavior modeled for us.

The Adult isn't interested in control strategies, and sees them as the distraction that they are from getting to the real issue. So the Adult sidesteps the temper tantrum or judgment directed his way and remains focused on getting to the underlying unmet or injured need. *The only person the Adult is concerned about maintaining control over is himself.*

The Adult attempts to restore the Child to a peer level by modeling mature behavior, not demanding it.

The Adult talking to the Parent stays focused on finding a mutual compromise that addresses the needs of both.

The Parent and Child are easily pulled into a conflict, and quickly lose perspective. The Adult takes an emotional step *back* from the conflict (though not out of the conversation) in order to keep perspective. He can discuss and confront, but he doesn't get sucked into it. His agenda is to get to the heart of the issue (and possible solutions), not get distracted or pulled into a reactive cycle.

The inappropriate Child or Parent behavior may still need to be addressed (since Adults *do* hold each other accountable), but usually *after* the current issue has been resolved. Otherwise, attempting to manage the other's reactive behavior is successfully diverting the Adult from the current issue.

While there is a *tendency* for each of us to gravitate to a particular role, often in a relationship, and even within a conversation, the roles may switch back and forth, acting as the Child one moment, and the Parent the next.

Outside of conflict, we are not always striving to be the Adult. Sometimes it's okay to be the *positive* aspect of a Child, enjoying life and just being in the moment without having to consider responsibility. And sometimes it's okay to be the *positive* aspect of a Parent when that parent is a supportive one, attempting to educate, not control.

The concern would be when any one pattern became too rigid and did not shift to meet the needs of what was most appropriate in the current situation, or when the role of Adult was consistently absent during conflicts.

The Model

The key to the dilemma of what you do when you've been hurt is in knowing *how* to express it. Much of the information we attempt to share in negative ways is still useful, it's just that we aren't delivering it in a way that's going to accomplish anything other than to escalate the situation.

What's going on with you when you're upset is more than just being angry. There are reasons *why* you're angry that need to be discussed.

You need to remember that your partner's personality and perceptions are different than your own. Even though you're both humans, you talk, think and feel things differently. You may have a lot in common, but you're not identical. You can't afford to assume that you're automatically understood, and you need to model what you want in return. If you want respect, then show respect. If you want love, then show love. But try to do it in a way that's meaningful to your partner. Even in the midst of conflict.

Why would you expect a verbal attack to draw you closer again, or withholding to create better understanding? A verbal attack pushes you further away from your partner. Withholding creates a gulf between the two of you. If what you really desire, past the anger, is restored closeness, then you need to forget the attack, or the withdrawal, and work towards a better way of being understood or seeking a resolution.

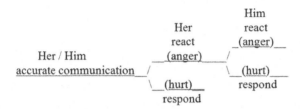

Above is a two-way model for resolving conflict where anger (or any strong emotion for that matter) is playing a part. It's a two-way model in that either party can intervene at any point to change the direction of the conversation - to escalate or deescalate the situation. It can be used for dealing with either misunderstandings or when an actual issue is present.

Let's take it one piece at a time, since the diagram will make no sense until we start playing it out.

The straight line, labeled "accurate communication", is Hank and Harriett having a conversation. At this point, for the most part, Harriett's interpreting what Hank's saying accurately. They are hearing and understanding each other and generally getting along. (Realize that communication, with its nuances, tone and semantics, is never 100% accurate. It is more like a bumpy line than a straight one.)

Conversation, when it's done respectfully, is like a game of tennis. One person is talking at a time. When he's said his piece, then the ball is over in her court to add to what he said or move the conversation in a different direction. So, too, the conflict model is taking turns back and forth, moving things through to a resolution. Obviously, one of the difficulties for many arguments is that no one's taking turns. It becomes a struggle over who's going to dominate the conversation. But to regain control of the interaction, we must step back to taking turns (respectful communication).

Back to Hank and Harriett. Let's say Hank makes a comment or does something that creates a bump in the up-until-then smooth road. The bump could be due to a misunderstanding or it could be an actual issue. We don't know yet. But whatever the case, for Harriett, the impact was a hurtful one. Whether Harriett realizes it or not, she now has five possible avenues to take:

- She can *let it go*, because she's able to truly forgive, or recognizes that it wasn't a big enough issue to actually discuss.

- She can *repress* it - acting like nothing bothered her, when it did (which is different than letting it go, because it *was* a big enough issue to discuss).

- She can *respond* - attempting to inform Hank that what he said hurt her.

- She can *react* - defensively (withdrawing) or offensively (attacking).

- She can give the *benefit of the doubt* - assuming that she must have interpreted it incorrectly, and/or trying to clarify his meaning before she makes a conclusion about the meaning.

Sometimes we *do* need to let the little stuff go. We can't afford to make an issue out of everything. There does need to be room for grace in a relationship, without the expectation of perfection in our partner.

If she represses it, hopefully this isn't a pattern for her where she keeps sweeping things under the rug and it's starting to pile up. If so, sooner or later, things are going to start leaking out around the edges, usually building to an explosion.

Responding is a good choice, because it's attempting to educate your partner of something that you don't want them to repeat. However, it's still assuming that you took their intent correctly.

If she chooses to *withdraw*, it's different than repressing. To withdraw, you're still visibly upset but you're refusing to talk about it. Repression is where you swallow your upset and move on, *acting* like everything's okay when it's not.

The problem with both repressing and withdrawing, if they are never addressed further down the road, is that, if this is actually a misunderstanding, we're walking away with an incorrect assumption of what was meant, and never taking the time to find out if we understood correctly. If this is our pattern, we may have formed some extreme misconceptions of our partner over the years by doing so. Ideally, we should still brave a brief discussion to test the accuracy of our interpretation before we decide to address it or let it go.

If she reacts by attacking, the fight is usually on.

If she gives the benefit of the doubt, she recognizes that there still remains the possibility that she misinterpreted what was said or done, and her first effort needs to be finding out if she took things correctly.

For the purposes of this model, we're going to focus on *reacting, responding* and *benefit of the doubt*.

Scenario #1. Everybody Loses (Reacting).

Let's start with the "worst-case scenario". This is the pattern that *reactive couples* take.

Harriett is upset and so she *reacts*. Reacting (going with instinct) leaves us with the two choices of attacking or withdrawing (while still angry). In this particular situation, Harriett is going to choose to attack.

Referring to the model, the communication has split between her anger (the top line) and her hurt (the bottom line). She's got a choice, whether she realizes it or not, of which way to go.

Between when Hank made his remark and before Harriett first speaks in reaction, she has a split-second conversation in her head about what Hank meant by what he said. She *assumes* a hurtful meaning which leads to her reaction.

By going with her anger, she is *unintentionally* moving the conversation further away from the underlying hurt which is at the root of her upset. If she reacts by attacking, she *thinks* she's expressing her hurt, but it's only the anger that's coming out, diverting her partner from the reason *why* she's angry. While Harriett probably feels that she *is* addressing the issue, she's actually turning Hank's focus to her unwarranted attack. (I say "unwarranted" because, in this situation, let's say that Harriett misinterpreted Hank's actions.)

*   *   *

Now it's Hank's turn to choose between reacting to Harriett's reaction or responding in a way that gets at her underlying hurt. Since Harriett *did* react, Hank will most likely be focused on the unfairness of her reaction, rather than thinking about *why* she is reacting this way. If it's obvious to Hank that she just misinterpreted what he said or did, then he knows that she just assumed the worst about his intentions rather than giving him the benefit of the doubt. And not only did she assume the worst, but she's now inappropriately attacking him rather than respectfully addressing him with her upset.

He has the same choice that Harriett had, to react or respond, but because he's now over-focusing on her negative behavior, rather than thinking about his own, he will predictably react in turn.

With each interchange, the emotion escalates, moving the couple further and further away from the core of the issue and more and more into the side-issues brought up by the reactions.

There's a paradox here in that while each is engaged in a verbal control struggle, *each is actively giving up his control by waiting for the other partner to do the right thing first.* Someone needs to take back control of his own part.

*   *   *

After Hank's reaction to Harriett's reaction, the ball is now back in Harriett's court. Even though it was Harriett who initially verbally attacked Hank, she is still unrealistically expecting a vulnerable, sincere, mature response from him that addresses her hurt and not her anger. She's not thinking about how her reaction just made that very unlikely to occur. So when Hank reacts, rather than seeing what she did that led to his reaction, Harriett now feels even more justified to continue to react because Hank's essentially confirming for her, by his negative behavior, that her initial negative assumption must have been correct.

So Harriett continues to keep the reactive cycle going even though it was actually she who started this fight, not Hank, by failing to question her negative assumption and reacting.

The situation continues to escalate until someone either loses all control, shuts down or storms off. What started out as a simple conversation and a possible misunderstanding quickly escalated into a major incident simply because no one knew how to stop the process.

For reactive couples, 60 to 70 percent of their arguments are potentially due to misunderstandings because they don't take the time to successfully correct the initial assumptions. And even if those misunderstandings *are* cleared up over the course of the argument, it's only after much additional damage has been done.

Scenario #2. Hank comes through (Responding).

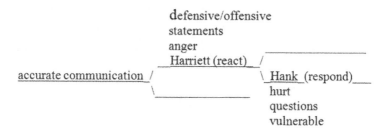

Okay, now let's take the same situation and give Hank some better tools to work with. Hank makes a comment. Harriett misunderstands or takes issue with what was said and, once again, reacts. (Don't worry, she'll do better later.)

This time, however, Hank's got it together and does the smart thing. Harriett's angry response is his cue that something's gone amiss. He knows immediately that, instead of reacting to Harriett's hostility, which is masking or leading him away from what's actually going on, he needs to get to the bottom of it - the hurt that's underneath. He knows that even though her present grievance may be unfounded, the underlying need that's been hurt is legitimate.

So how does he get to the hurt?

He simply, sincerely, *responds* with a question. He *asks*.

Hank says something profound like, "What's got you so upset? What did you hear me say?"

Now if his tone is concerned, or at least neutral, and he really sounds like he's interested in wanting to know, a number of things will be accomplished all at once.

- There is a reason that Hank intervenes with a question rather than a statement. *A question does not attempt to define reality for your partner. It is asking him to define his reality for you.* If your partner has just reacted, which usually is because he has assumed an attack or insensitivity on your part, a *sincere* question indicates that you're not trying to invalidate his experience. Most reactions are expressed through statements, telling the partner what he needs to do or stop doing, or what kind of person he is for having done it. And if questions *are* asked, often they are done in a hostile tone that doesn't invite vulnerability. "I can't believe you could be so insensitive." "You need to shut up." "That's a lie." "What's your problem?"

- Statements are often perceived as attempts to control the situation. "You need to calm down," is the Parent talking to the Child. Your partner may be acting like a Child, but it's not your job to be the Parent. You are trying to help him step back into an Adult role. "What did you hear me say?" or "How did you interpret what I said?" is a pretty smart thing for Hank to ask. It's automatically pointing out that what Harriett heard might not have been what Hank meant, leading Harriett to doubt her assumption. Other options might be "What did you think I meant by that?" or "Why was that hurtful to you?"

- By not giving Harriett something else to react to, Hank is not adding any more fuel to the fire. He is stopping the progression up the conflict ladder and he is also removing himself from the pattern of conflict that they may have had in the past.

- By not reacting, Hank is actually holding up a mirror to Harriett. Hers is the only raised voice. Hers are the only hostile words. If Hank is successful in keeping his cool and not buying into her aggression, sooner or later Harriett's going to become self-aware that she's the only one acting rashly here.

- The most important reason for using questions is because *people can't fully think and feel at the same time.* It involves two different areas of the brain. If I give you a math problem when you're upset you're going to do one of two things: solve the problem because anger took a back-seat, or not be able to solve the problem because your feelings got in the way of thinking it through. One of the two will dominate. The best way to deescalate hurt feelings is to make that transition from feelings (emotional logic) to thought (rational logic). So, if you ask a question, especially one that requires some self-analysis, you're helping your partner move past reacting, and on to *thinking* about what's going on. Why did that actually hurt? You're still asking about feelings, true, but you're putting it on an objective level. You're helping your partner find some emotional distance from the problem in order to resolve the problem, deescalating the tension at the same time.

If this was a misunderstanding and Hank is now able to redirect Harriett to her incorrect interpretation, and correct it, the conversation only strayed but slightly before it was brought back on track, saving the couple from a potentially very ugly interaction.

Hank's response was a *controlled* reaction. He might have still been upset about how Harriett reacted, but he managed his own emotions and kept the conversation focused in a healthy direction.

Scenario #3. Harriett does Good (Benefit of the Doubt).

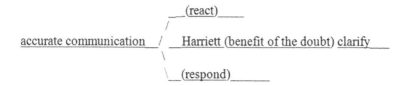

Alright, this last scenario is where Harriett nips it in the bud.

Hank makes his statement that sets something off in Harriett. Harriett finds the statement insulting for whatever reason, but, instead of reacting, Harriett does the most difficult thing. She gives Hank *the benefit of the doubt*. She doesn't automatically *assume* that he's trying to hurt her. She tries first to find out if what she heard was accurate. She recognizes the possibility of her own error in interpreting.

Benefit of the doubt recognizes that what my partner does or says, even if they do it three days in a row, can be for a totally different reason each day. More than that, why we do what we do in any given moment often is not for just one reason but several reasons intertwined. It recognizes our complexity, rather than over-simplifying our behavior into just a single negative motivator.

Level-headed Harriett knows that Hank loves her and wouldn't intentionally do something to cause her pain. (Now if Hank *does* have a past pattern of doing things to intentionally hurt her, with words or deeds, then it's going to be much more difficult for Harriett to give the benefit of the doubt. But it doesn't change the fact that it's still necessary if they want to move things ahead in a healthy direction.)

So Harriett steps in with "Hank, I'm not sure what you meant by that. What I *thought* you meant was (fill in the blank). Is that accurate?"

She just indicated her possible confusion (a vulnerable stance, not a defensive one), told him her interpretation of what she heard him say, and then asked for confirmation.

Hank may say, "No, that's not what I meant at all" and explain himself and Harriett finds out it was just a misunderstanding. And no one has to walk out the door, or manage their blood pressure. All that energy saved because of one simple step.

Note that I didn't even suggest that Harriett *respond* to Hank. To respond would be attempting to educate Hank about how he'd hurt her, but Harriett didn't know yet whether she had a right to be hurt. She first needed to *clarify* Hank's meaning before she would have an idea of where to go from there.

Conspiracy Theories

When the benefit of the doubt goes away, it's often replaced with *conspiracy theories*. Conspiracy theories are the pieces that we put together over time that explain our partner's behavior to us. They are usually based on actual experience, but it still leaves it up to us to make sense of those experiences. Sometimes those theories can be correct, but other times they are wildly inaccurate and only serve to stand in the way of the relationship progressing. Often, they feed our own insecurities, fears or resentments.

The problem with conspiracy theories is that, once they've crystallized, they don't allow for contradictory information. Everything that happens now feeds the theory. If the theory is "He doesn't love me anymore," her attention is only going to be focused on those continuing experiences that fit the theory. And now each of those little experiences is going to provoke a larger reaction from her because they've come to mean something very big.

Even when he behaves in a way that *doesn't* fit her theory, this behavior will tend to be ignored, minimized or distorted by her. So if he does something that's actually loving, her internal interpretation might still be, "He's just doing that because he feels guilty." So the possible negatives get most of her focus and the positives no longer carry any weight.

His experience of this is a "damned if I do, damned if I don't." No matter what he does, it's going to be the wrong thing for her because she's looking for the negative in all of it. He may not even be aware of her underlying theory. He just knows that no matter what he says or does, it doesn't seem to make a difference, or she doesn't seem to believe him.

When a theory exists, it needs both parties involved to dismantle it.

1. The benefit of the doubt has to be re-embraced, where we start to allow for explanations other than the one that's easiest for us to reach for.

2. The person with the theory has to recognize her own theory and stop feeding it, since she will tend to think on it and distress herself with it even when he's not there to fuel it.

3. The person who helped create the theory, has to know what he's doing that's keeping it alive. He needs to either change what he's doing that contributes to it, or do a better job of explaining himself if her interpretation is inaccurate.

The harder theories to dismantle are the ones that were there before the relationship started. ("Women can't be trusted." "Men are only in it for one thing.") These are often underlying beliefs that have formed from previous relationships or what we witnessed in our own homes growing up (maybe even our parent's conspiracy theories that have been passed on to us). The problem with these unhealthy beliefs is that, even with rational evidence to the contrary, since they're beyond reason, they persist and can hold us back from drawing closer.

When it comes to irrational feelings or unhealthy beliefs, *the primary way to weaken them is to choose to live in a way that challenges their truth.* Otherwise, the more I cater to negative feelings, the more I increase the likelihood of a negative outcome. If I become lost in my fear that my partner is going to leave me, the more I will typically do things that push him away and make my abandonment likely. The more I feed my fears, acting like they're true, the stronger a hold they have over me.[9]

At the same time, the more I choose to *act* the part of a loving partner, and *think* loving thoughts, the more likely I will be able to reconnect myself to loving feelings towards him, and incite a loving reaction in him. People often get the sequence wrong. Their feelings dictate their behavior. But for the emotionally disciplined, they have learned to guide their emotions by how they choose to act and what thoughts they choose to entertain.

I don't mean to promote deluding yourself about who your partner is if abuse, chronic deceit, or an affair has occurred. In those cases, you need evidence of change, or evidence of the truth, more than naively just trusting. Here I'm referring to those situations where our perception has become distorted and now it's standing in the way of the relationship working because the benefit of the doubt no longer exists.

The Physiology of Anger

When I referred to how we can't fully think (rational logic) and feel (emotional logic) at the same time, there's an important biological piece to better understanding this.

---

[9]   I'll spend more time talking about this in Chapter 9.

Hang in there with me for a minute, while I get a little scientific. The limbic system, at the base of your brain, is the first part of the brain to develop. It's often referred to as the "old brain", and is where our *instincts* and *primitive emotions* reside.

The neo-cortex, or "new brain", is the top layer of the brain and the last part of your brain to develop (usually maturing somewhere between ages 17 to 24). It's where your *higher reasoning* abilities are located.

When our brain experiences an event, often the information gets filtered through the limbic system first. If the information is benign or nonthreatening, it continues on to be processed by other parts of the brain. If the information is stimulating (in a positive or negative way), it sets off an excitatory response, activating our base emotions - which is why our initial reaction to surprises is instinctive.

At the point the limbic system gets over-stimulated, due to a perceived threat, the information process gets halted, because our primitive brain has gone into "survival mode". This is unfortunate, because what you want to be able to do most in a crisis is think, but that's usually the hardest thing to do in those moments. For the information to be able to go on to the neo-cortex where it can be properly processed (thought through), the alert level has to be lowered.

So when an argument begins and reactions start to occur, limbic systems activating, each continued reaction keeps the "old brain" over-stimulated to the point that nobody's actually thinking anymore, just emotionally, instinctively reacting. In order for rational thinking to prevail, somebody has to stop adding fuel to the fire.

This is why it's so important in heated conversations to buy enough time that each of us can actually start thinking things through. *If we just continue to give each other more things to react to, the necessary parts of our brain never get involved.*

That's why questions are so important in helping us engage on a rational level - they help us start to think.

It *is* possible to train our brains to be less reactive. The brain often acts like a muscle in that the parts we exercise the most result in the best developed neural pathways. It is much easier for someone who regularly exercises the rational part of his brain to manage his feelings. But just because someone may be more feeling-based, doesn't mean that he can never learn emotional control.

When Questions Don't Work (Healthy Exits)

There are times during an argument when questions, even good questions, backfire. At the point that someone is overwhelmed emotionally, to try to engage him in thinking things through can actually agitate his frustration rather than deescalate it. It's like going full-out in fifth gear and then trying to shift into reverse. It's too much of a transition for the brain to make.

While it doesn't mean you should be afraid to try questions, it does mean that when you find it's heating things up rather than cooling things down, that's your cue to shut down the conversation and re-approach it once things have had time to settle.

The term that I use for ending an argument that is becoming out of control, is taking a "*healthy exit*".

There are two rules for taking healthy exits:

Rule #1. Either of you retains the right to end a heated conversation.

Of course, there are good ways and bad ways of leaving a conversation. Throwing up your hands and walking off is not a good way. Throwing out a final insult and then trying to shut the conversation down is also not a good idea. Hanging up on your partner is not the best of choices.

Respectful communication requires stepping back and saying something like, "I need for us to walk away from this for the moment. I'm feeling like things are too heated and I might say something that I don't really mean". You're taking responsibility for your behavior by doing this, and stopping things before bridges get burned.

If you said, "I'm stepping out because you're obviously losing it," or, "I'm taking a walk because you're saying things you're gonna regret", it could incite another reaction. But you could say, "This is getting too intense for me. I need to step away from this and give things time to cool down." Or, simply, "I need to take a time-out."

The couple needs to decide for themselves what appropriate exit lines to use that have the highest odds for success.

The unspoken part of this first rule is that *whoever is asking to end the argument is given the room to withdraw.* Many couples who've turned things into a control struggle will attempt to force the partner back into the conversation by following him through the house or continuing to try to reengage him in the argument. If your partner's already said he can't continue, then you need to respect that. By continuing to push things when he's already said he's at his limit, you're asking for a reaction.

If what you want at that point is to still work things out, you need to accept that you're not going to make any further progress by trying to force it.

Rule #2. Whoever is leaving the conversation agrees to take responsibility for bringing the issue back.

Often the reason why one partner is panicked about letting the other escape the argument is that there has been a pattern of avoidance in the past. Issues are approached and the partner continues to take an escape route rather than work things through.

One way of getting around this dilemma is him being responsible for bringing the issue back to his partner rather than making her feel obligated to have to bring it up again. If she knows that he will treat the issue with respect and assume responsibility to bring it back, he's teaching her that she doesn't have to try to over-control things.

Each side needs to be respectfully handling his part - letting the partner go and the partner coming back on his own.

Often you will need to attach a timeframe to how long the two of you will take to calm down, rather than to just leave it hanging. This is especially true if there's a deadline pending for a decision. It can become a control issue if the withdrawing partner just takes his merry time re-approaching, and doesn't give any indication of how long he is going to need.

Ideally, couples need to try to re-approach within 24 hours rather than letting things linger for days at a time. It depends on how big the issue is and how much thought is required. At the point the couple re-approaches, it should be with some better ideas about how to move through the issue this time.

*   *   *

There is a difference between taking a healthy exit and seeking flight.

Seeking flight is exiting the conversation prematurely. You're allowing your discomfort or upset, fear of potential conflict, or projection that the conversation's not going to go anywhere positive, to make you seek escape before resolution has even been attempted.

Taking a healthy exit is ending the conversation at the point that things are escalating too far, and the conversation cannot be re-directed to a calmer path.

*   *   *

Another dilemma concerning questions is that sometimes your partner, in that moment, doesn't know *why* he is upset, and trying to get at it past the point that he is able to think it through presents a new problem. If your partner doesn't know why he is upset, while you can still take the time to explore possibilities as to what that might be, you don't have to make a project of digging it out if it's only creating more frustration. You can simply agree to give him time to figure it out.

If you know your partner well, you can still help soothe things in the meantime by falling back to whatever his "love language"[10] is.

While the conflict model is somewhat purist in order to simplify the steps, the reality is that arguments are typically not consistently either reacting or responding, but a combination of both. Things may start out well (responding) and then devolve into reacting, or things may start out with a poor delivery and then get corrected. Or it may go back and forth between the two as the conversation proceeds, each partner briefly recovering and trying to do the right thing only to get pulled back in again and the fight once more deteriorates. In other words, arguments are often not a step-by-step progression but a competitive mess. I tend to think of it as a couple trying to dance but who keep stepping on each other's toes. The faster you go with these conversations, the harder it's going to be to catch the mistakes, and get any better at it.

Ultimately, we are trying to learn to be more consistent with doing the things that actually work.

*　*　*

Almost anyone can handle things when they are going relatively well. What distinguishes our character is how we handle things when they're *not* going well. Do we attack, blame, run? Or do we face the test of character, show some self-discipline, and work it through.

Healthy love thinks of the good of the relationship, the future wellbeing of *both* people involved. Unhealthy love tends to be focused on self, and doing what feels good in the moment (yelling, attacking, etc.) at the cost of the relationship's future.[11]

You or your partner may learn to ignore the temper tantrums, or not respond to the hurtful things that are said. That may be how the relationship has survived. But you would be mistaken to assume that

----

[10]　See Chapter 10, regarding Gary Chapman's "The Five Love Languages".
[11]　See Scott Peck's "The Road Less Traveled" for more on healthy and unhealthy love.

that means that everything's okay. Because one person has learned to "take it" does not mean that they will be able to, or even should, continue to "take it" over time. It wears on a person.

Other relationships survive by remaining superficial. They avoid the deeper topics that set off issues, having learned not to rock the boat. But usually this is at the cost of any deeper emotional intimacy.

The secondary damage that is done when we have not learned how to resolve our conflicts peaceably is reflected in our children, the habits that they are going to imitate. If we don't care enough about ourselves or our partner to learn how to temper our angry words, then perhaps we care enough about our kids to model better ways. It all starts with us.

Discussion Questions:

1. **Why is it so hard to extend the benefit of the doubt?** What is the damage done if the benefit of the doubt no longer exists? Do you use more statements or questions when the two of you discuss issues? Are you both willing to believe the answers to questions asked, or do you think you know better what each other's true thoughts or feelings are? How is that not a conspiracy theory?

2. **Which path do you tend to take when issues come up: responding or reacting?** If reacting, do you lean towards fight or flight? Aside from your partner, what prevents you from changing any negative patterns? How much of how you approach an issue depends on your partner's state of mind rather than yours? If you were taking back control of you during those interactions, what would that look like?

3. **What percentage of your arguments do you think are actually based on misunderstandings?** Do you understand that if you aren't making sure your initial assumptions are correct, there may be a whole lot of things that were initially misunderstandings that become issues because they were never clarified?

4. **What prevents you from remaining vulnerable to your partner when you discuss an issue?** What can each of you do to remove those obstacles?

5. **Are you able to stop an argument before it "burns the house down"?** What makes it so difficult to step out of a conflict when it gets that heated? How do you attempt healthy exits?

Chapter 4
When an Issue Exists

**"But now you must rid yourselves of all such things
as these: anger, rage, malice, slander, and filthy
language from your lips."** (Colossians 3:8)

So let's say that when Harriett clarifies things with Hank she finds out
that she took things correctly. It *wasn't* a misunderstanding. So now she
has an actual issue she needs to discuss with Hank. Where does she go
from there?

The guidelines for the conflict model still continue to apply. Harriett
still needs to: speak from her hurt and not her anger, respond rather
than react, explore things with questions, give the benefit of the doubt
as they go.

Let me clarify for a moment what I mean when I say "speaking from
the hurt" when you respond. *In relationships, we typically don't get
angry because we're angry, we're angry because we've been hurt.* The
hurt is the truer emotion. Usually, the bottom line for *why* we're hurt
is because we care and thought that our partners cared about us too.
If we're able to bring our injured heart into the discussion early on, it's
such a vulnerable move that it usually promotes a vulnerable response
from our partners. It invites them in, rather than pushes them away. For

example, "Do you understand that when you say that, it's hurtful to me? It comes off like you don't care about my feelings."

Rather than being a victim to reactions, we need to handle them wisely. In other words, because my partner is taking all of his cues from me as to whether he's going to be reasonable or get upset, I need to handle the control he's unintentionally giving me in a responsible way. By remaining controlled and respectful, I'm more likely to get the same in return.

The ideal progression for conflict resolution, when it involves a deeper issue, looks like this:

1. **Identification**
2. **Validation**
3. **Explanation**
4. **Resolution**

Step 1. Identify the Issue

By attempting a discussion, Harriett is continuing to go *against* her instinct by trying to work things out rather than stepping back to reacting. Sticking with responding, Harriett's going to attempt to educate Hank about why what he said hurt. It may not change his opinion about what he said, but, now, knowing that it is an issue for Harriett, at the least, he will probably be more careful next time. And it may not even be an issue with the core of *what* he was saying, just with *how* he said it, so hopefully he will be left with a better course to take in the future.

Let's say that Hank made a decision without consulting Harriett. Maybe it involved their mutual finances, and he's just now informed her about it. Harriett might choose to say something like this:

"Hank, I have a real problem with what you did. To me, it's saying that you don't care about my opinion or what also belongs to me."

Harriett's accomplished a number of things by the statement she just made.

- She's getting across that she isn't feeling valued by what he did.

- She's also letting him know that it came across as disrespectful using something that was also partially hers without her permission.

- She's letting him know that it's not a little issue for her.

- She *isn't* resorting to using judgments ("You're so selfish.").

Now, obviously, the conversation doesn't stop there. The ball is back in Hank's court. But Harriett's done a great job in just two sentences to get to the core of her issue with him.

Another option, consistent with the conflict model, Harriett could have turned her statement into a question, "Hank, do you understand why I would have a problem with what you did?" If he gets it, then an explanation isn't even necessary.

* * *

The dilemma with "identifying the issue" usually occurs when our *delivery* is a poor one. If we just bring up issues when we're upset we typically haven't thought it through, so while we may just be intending to vent, how it comes across is an attack.

Bringing up issues is often our attempt to hold our partners accountable, but many times our delivery comes across as a judgment, an ultimatum, or a rejection, rather than necessary information.

A useful tool is, when you're not in the middle of an argument, asking your partner for feedback on the ways that are best for you to raise issues with him, in the same way that he needs to know how best to approach you.

Step 2. Validate the Issue

The next part of this, Hank's part, is, in my opinion, the number one "hang-up" for most couples in resolving conflict. Most couples, if they are having a very difficult time in getting to the *resolution* stage, are usually stuck in the *explaining* stage. And they get stuck because they keep skipping *validation*.

If Hank goes right into explaining why he did what he did, then what he's doing unintentionally is *invalidating* Harriett's reaction. She's saying she's hurt and he's basically saying "You shouldn't be." He's still attempting to address it as if there's a misunderstanding, but Harriett already knows what happened and she's not looking for further explanation, *at least not yet*. She's looking for her hurt to be *acknowledged*, and Hank's attempting to dismiss it. He isn't doing this to be cruel, it's just that an explanation is the most visible path for him to take.

By not involving her financially, it gave a hurtful message. He needs to give recognition for her pain ("I understand why you feel hurt, and I'm sorry, I didn't mean to hurt you."), explore it further if he or she feels they need more details (explain), and move on to agreeing on a solution ("In the future, I'll consult you about those kind of decisions before I do anything.").

Hank needs to remember that *often it's in times of emotional pain that we have our greatest opportunities to connect on a deeper level with our partners*. If he skips validation, or going deeper with the bigger issues, Hank's unintentionally communicating to Harriett that he's not "safe" to share her concerns with, and she will not be able to feel truly secure with him.

*   *   *

Let me briefly describe different options for validation.

Sometimes simply *listening* can be validating. By showing respect for our partners and not trying to rush them through their issues, not jumping in with our opinion before they've had a chance to finish, or not trying too quickly to just solve it for them, we're giving them the attention they desire. Further, the more we take the time to explore their issues, to better convey our desire to understand them, to make sure we're hearing them right, the more they'll feel heard.

The visual I attach to this is that of a Rubik's cube. When your partner approaches you with an issue, he basically just dropped a Rubik's cube in your lap. He needs you to take a look at it, turn it a couple of different ways first to be sure you're actually understanding what this particular cube is about, *even if you think you already get it.* ("So, basically, your saying that you're upset because..."). If your paraphrase is accurate, the conversation continues. If it's not correct, the partner needs to restate the issue until you can paraphrase it correctly.

Beyond listening, there's *acknowledging.* Acknowledgement is *not* agreement. It is simply recognizing your partner's perspective. There's almost always a certain logic, at least a partial truth, to his thinking. You need to take the time to understand how he's connecting the dots. True, there may be more dots involved that he's not considering, but it usually makes sense that he's coming to the conclusion that he is with only the dots that are in his line of sight. We need to start with the dots he's focused on, even if we don't agree with what he's concluding from them. ("If that's how you're putting it together, I can understand why you'd feel that way.")

Beyond acknowledgement, there's *apologizing.* That's not to say that you would apologize for something you didn't do. Let's say your partner thinks you intentionally did something to hurt him. You wouldn't apologize for intentionally hurting him if it was actually unintentional. But you *could* still apologize for the pain it caused, unintentional as it was.

For the record, "I'm sorry you took it that way," is not an actual apology. You're saying you're sorry for your partner's mistake, but an apology is at least partial ownership of what *you* did. "I'm sorry it came across like that, that wasn't my intent."

Beyond apologizing, there's *ownership.* Ownership is simply accepting fault or blame. If he was right and you screwed up, the easiest path to resolution is simple ownership of the wrong. "You're right, I shouldn't have done that."

At the same time, *ownership loses its value if we've overly applied it in the past, yet nothing has changed.* More than ownership at that point, we need to talk about what actual strategies or solutions we're willing to commit to, and be held accountable for.

* * *

Some people will sabotage their own efforts to be validated. For instance, someone is angry to the point that he says some very hurtful things to his partner, but then acts surprised and becomes more upset because his pain is not being validated. However, *by expressing his anger inappropriately he just made sure validation was not going to occur.* That's like knocking the legs out from under someone and then criticizing him for not standing.

When I promote validating your partner's hurt, I'm not suggesting you try to validate the inappropriate angry behavior.

* * *

If you feel like you can't validate what your partner is asking you to, find something else in what he's saying that you can.

If he's seeking validation for how he's been managing his money ("I've been doing well with my money this past month, yet you haven't said a thing."), yet you immediately think of all the times this past month that that didn't prove to be true, you could *in*validate his issue ("How can I say it, if it isn't true?"), or you could choose to focus on those times in the past month where he *did* succeed. ("Yes, there's been times this month where you did what you said you were going to do, and I appreciate those efforts.")

Some people will be hesitant with this because it's only a partial truth, and not completely accurate. But this is failing to recognize that you sometimes need to separate validation from a more complete explanation in the same way that you need to separate a compliment from a criticism. Better to say, "Honey, you look great in that dress," and leave it there, than to add, "but I really don't like those shoes." If you combine the two, the compliment never gets heard. That doesn't mean you ignore accountability for what he said he was going to do, but you are careful not to invalidate the small successes along the way. Those successes, and the positive reinforcement that he gets from you for it, is what motivates him to continue to improve in his consistency.

* * *

There is such a thing as *over-listening*, where you're paying too much attention to the details and accuracy of what your partner is saying, and, as a result, are always in disagreement with him. Paying attention to the *content* of what is being said is much more important than the *details* of how it's said.

The majority of the world is somewhat sloppy with their wording: vague, over-generalizing, distorted, etc. If I corrected a couple in couple's counseling for every time their wording was poor, we would never get through the session. And often that's what makes it difficult for the couple to progress in a conversation is because they're too closely monitoring for those inaccuracies.

It's more important to find the points of agreement that support mutual understanding than to over-focus on imprecise small details. Certainly take the time to get a better explanation if your partner's words can be taken different ways, just don't punish them for not speaking exactly the way you want them to.

* * *

A common mistake is that we don't *ask* for what we want during our arguments. We just remain upset that we're not getting it. We're looking to be validated but our partner's caught up in explaining himself. He's operating with good intentions because he's trying to help us understand where he's coming from, but it's not what is needed most in that moment. Rather than staying frustrated, we need to *guide* our partner in the right direction. ("Is there anything about what I'm saying that you can validate for me?")

And even then, sometimes, we need to guide them *specifically* to how we want them to validate. (Listening: "I just need you to hear me out."

Acknowledgement: "Do you understand why that was so upsetting to me?" Apology: "I need a sincere apology from you." Ownership: "Is there anything in what I'm saying that you can own?")

Some people will be hesitant with guiding because they want their partners' response to be authentic rather than something that came from them, but often partners are already trying to validate or resolve, they're just not doing it the way the other is looking for. Rather than to just let the partner flounder, becoming frustrated and angry with his own failed attempts to satisfy his partner, it's kinder to show him the way. It would be a better judge of his lack of sincerity if you led him to what you needed but he refused to provide it.

Whenever I would confront my daughter about something she'd done, she'd immediately defend herself providing all sorts of rationales and excuses. But when I'd sidestep her kneejerk reaction and simply say, "Megan, all I need to hear from you is ownership for what you did," she'd immediately be able to change tracks and tell me what I needed to hear from her. Her ownership wasn't insincere, it's just that up until I pointed out what I needed from our conversation, she was lost in her own perspective.

Remember, you're trying to function as a team, not play mind games with each other. No matter how long you've been together, you will still need to educate each other at times as to what validation path is most desired for that particular conversation. Because we are complex we don't always seek the same kind of validation, so we need to be realistic that our partners aren't mind readers. Help narrow the options for them.

*   *   *

Stereotypically, men immediately try to problem solve when someone brings them an issue, skipping validation. However, many times, for women, *validation is the resolution that they are seeking.* Men will attempt to simplify the process by trying to jump to Step 4, but end up over-complicating things because all they really needed to do was to go to Step 2.

Step 3. Explain the Issue

I say provide an explanation "if necessary" because sometimes an explanation really doesn't need to occur. If you know you were wrong you don't need to waste time explaining yourself - validating by taking ownership should be enough.

For couples that get lost in marathon arguments, *circular explanations* are usually the cause. Circular explanations occur in three different forms, but they keep the argument going round and round, never really getting anywhere because the path to actual resolution keeps getting stalemated.

The first form of circular arguments sometimes occurs because there's an underlying assumption, by whoever the issue is directed at, that there must be a misunderstanding at the root of the issue. The natural thinking is that if our reasoning is understood, the misunderstanding pointed out, our partner will back down and the issue will resolve itself. Sometimes that is the way it works, but other times it doesn't because we're making it about our partner hearing us, when, for him in that moment, it's about us first hearing him.

The experience goes like this:

She identifies her issue by saying, "I'm upset with you because...(she presents her evidence)".

To which he responds (explaining), "You *shouldn't* be upset, because... (he presents his evidence)".

They each go back and forth adding more evidence to make their case, each side seeing the other as being difficult because they're not accepting the explanations.

If she feels that she has a right to be upset, his telling her that she shouldn't isn't going to help move things forward. He just invalidated her. He may actually have a valid point, but it's not going to be heard until he validates her first. Remember, validation does *not* mean agreement.

Second, for couples who play "the blame game", the circular argument is where each keeps pointing the finger back at the other.

For a couple that's been together for any significant period of time, each has a good deal of examples of where each has fallen short in the past. The blame game can be an attempt to balance our partner's perception by pointing out that he does the very thing he's accusing us of - that there's a double standard. But this natural tendency to counter our partner comes across as a deflection, which it may very well be.

An out-of-control blame game, where we keep piling on each other's faults to prove who is worse, ends up overwhelming the situation with issues that may not even be issues. And we have no idea how to start sorting it all out. And all either side feels is rejected.

You can't fairly address two issues at the same time. Whether or not your partner does what he's accusing you of, doesn't change the fact that, if he raised this issue, it's his issue with you, so he needs to have it addressed and resolved. Then it can be your turn, making the resolution that you agreed to with him into a rule for both.

* * *

Third, for the bigger issues, couples go back and forth because the issue requires a solution for *both* partners. The struggle is over whose side of the issue gets validated and resolved first.

By raising the issue, she's making the issue about what she needs from him, which leads him to automatically think about what his need is of her with the same issue. And the reality is that the solution is going to have to address *both* needs, so it's going to have to have two parts.

She starts with, "I need you to be more caring."

To which he responds with, "Well, I would be more caring if you were more sensitive."

To which she counters, "Well, I would be more sensitive, if you were more caring."

To step out of the stalemate, *each* person's part of the issue needs to be addressed and explored, but *it starts with whoever brought it up to begin with.* She initially has the stage and her side needs to be validated, processed, and at least partially resolved, before it switches over to the partner. At which point, the partner's side of the issue takes center stage and now he gets his validation and resolution. One side at a time or it turns into a competition.

If they don't take turns this way, her experience of their conversation will be, "It's my issue, I raised it, but you keep making it about you."

Step 4. Resolve the Issue

Does there always have to be a solution? No, not really. As I said in Step 2, sometimes validation is a resolution in itself. But, if the situation is a recurring one that requires change, more than just validation, specific problem-solving needs to take place if the cycle is to stop.

Just remember that you don't have to have all of the answers up front. It is more important to stay open to finding solutions together, and asking each other for help when the right words can't be found.

The biggest part of resolving the issue is focusing on *two-part solutions*: what she needs from him and what he needs from her.

In a relationship, there is no such thing as an individual issue, because his or her issues become *our* issues. Even if I'm the one with the anger problem, there are still things that my partner can do to help or hinder my issue. By trying to identify things that *both* of us can do to help whatever issues arise, we are staying with a team approach, avoiding the blame game.

By accepting joint ownership for the issues that arise, we are communicating the message, "I am not your enemy. I am your partner. We'll work this out together. We *each* play a part in the solution."

*   *   *

Many people avoid conflict because they hate the discomfort of dealing with their partner's pain, or their own. But what they need to realize with avoiding going deeper with their conversations is that they're also losing emotional intimacy. As I pointed out earlier, you can't feel secure in a relationship if you know your partner can't handle your pain. The relationship develops a superficial feel to it. By avoiding validation and explanation, we lose a very important opportunity to better understand our partner's perspective. It's also an opportunity to show *them* that we understand it, respect it, and can still support them even when we don't completely agree with it.

Emotional intimacy may have been created initially by sharing the good times, but the foundation of a relationship is significantly strengthened by the intimacy gained when we're able to go through the difficult times and still remain respectful and considerate of each other.

DVDs and Blu-rays

I will often suggest to couples to think of approaching the 4-step process with a DVD remote in your hand (or, for the tech-savvy, a blu-ray player). Unless it's a minor issue, you don't want to hit the fast-forward button, but you do want to feel free to hit the rewind button as much as is needed. I don't say this in order to suggest that you keep rehashing an issue, I mean rewinding back to the point in the conversation where things went wrong and attempting a do-over.

If the delivery was bad, you hit the rewind back to that point. He says, "Can you put your issue out there again but this time try to do it a little more gently, because it's hard not to take it as anything other than an attack." If she's so out-of-control that she can't do so, maybe now is not a good time to have a conversation (unless you're willing to give her the room to vent and the two of you can come back later to process it).

If validation is absent, it's hitting the rewind button again. She says, "I don't need you to solve this for me, I just need you to take the time to hear me out."

We're leading each other to the things that need a chance to be restated rather than just expecting them to get everything right the first time through.

Sometimes it's hitting the rewind button for ourselves. "Okay, let me start over. That was a crappy way to start the conversation, I admit it."

The Best Relationship Question Ever

One of the most effective questions that is both validating and resolving is, "What do you feel that you need from me right now?"

You want to be careful that you don't use it too early in the conversation, however, because you don't want to convey that you're doing "the guy thing" and just trying to skip past the validation and processing piece of the conversation to solve things.

And you need to ask it with the right tone and sincerity, not with impatience and frustration.

"What do you *need* from me?" addresses the likelihood that if this issue is that upsetting, it is likely impacting a need, and you're willing to tend to that need.

"What do you need from me *right now*?" addresses those issues that have a history. Many times the current infraction is being connected to past events or old patterns of similar infractions. We are sometimes being loaded down with not only what just happened, but with things that happened weeks, months, or years ago that we can do nothing about in the moment.

He reacts with, "What I needed from you was to not have embarrassed me at that party *6 months ago!*"

To which we respond, "Yes, I understand that. But since I can't change history, what do you need from me *right now,* so that we can start moving forward again?"

By doing this, we stay focused on the present moment, the only thing that is actually in our control to do something about. For couples that get lost in over-exploring issues, or are stuck in circular explanations, it's a nice refocusing tool that can get couples back on a positive track with where the conversation needs to go. Solution-focused versus problem-obsessed.

Replays

I said at the beginning of this chapter, "the ideal progression for conflict resolution, *when it involves a deeper issue,* looks like this", because sometimes it *doesn't* involve a deeper issue and to get into a major discussion ends up making something small overly complicated, and mistakenly bigger than it is.

Part of knowing when to go deeper and when to stay on the surface comes back to attaching a value to the issue.

Let me use an example. Sometimes someone will be walking out the door of a relationship, fed up, and the partner is looking on in total surprise having no idea that things were that bad. It wasn't that the person walking out had never said anything, it was that she had never really attached a value to her issue. She had complained, yes, but it kind of sounded like all of her other complaints. So it got filed away in "the complaint drawer". It left it up to her partner to attach his own value to her issue. In his mind, "She's just complaining. She'll get over it."

I'll often ask couples to start attaching a value to their issues using a 1-10 scale. One being minimal and 10 being a deal-breaker. If either says an issue is a 5 or greater, then it's likely going to require a deeper discussion. If it's below a 5, then they can probably just do a *replay.*

Replays are solution-focused. It's not going to be a deeper discussion, it's simply going to be, "If we had to do it over again, what would you have needed differently from me?" And then, "This is what I needed different from you." Alternatives are identified, different approaches agreed on, and back to living life. For the smaller stuff, it doesn't have to get any more complicated.

The Reactive Couple

There are two extremes when it comes to mental illness: taking on too much emotional pain (depression, neuroses) or avoiding it altogether (character disorders, psychoses). The reactive couple is doing a little bit of both: taking on too much pain by actively looking for offense with each other's behavior, and yet not taking responsibility for their own behavior (considering their own fault).

For the reactive couple (the couple that reacts to each other's reactions), there's a special dynamic that develops over time. Normally when a couple is having their first few arguments there is a gradual escalation to the negative emotion. It starts at neutral but then changes to frustrated. Frustrated raises to agitated. Agitated turns into angry. Angry moves to raging (if it ever gets that far). Usually when this negative pattern is starting it takes many encounters before it ever gets to the "raging" level.

But because the reactive couple is now quite practiced in moving through this negative emotional ladder, the over-familiarity with the pattern leads them to begin skipping steps. The normal course of escalation is now greatly accelerated because they go straight from neutral to angry. Because of how quickly it becomes intensely emotional, it leaves little opportunity for an actual intelligent conversation.

The reactive couple no longer takes turns with the tennis back-and-forth interaction, and so things quickly become chaotic and competitive. Prior to this you usually see some attempts to balance conversations. He's upset so she soothes, or vice versa. But when things have become reactive there is no longer any balance, *both* are going with instinct and fall into attack or angry withdrawal mode.

When the relationship has deteriorated to this point, the couple has to intentionally start *slowing the conversation down* again in order to have more opportunities to think about what the partner is saying, and what they're about to say - taking back control. So long as it remains the fast paced no-holds-barred approach, there's no time for anything to be constructively edited or thought through.

One tool for restoring a sequence to the conversations (taking turns) is to use an identified object, such as a pillow. Whoever is the holder of the pillow "has the floor". When he's done with what he has to say, it gets passed on. If the holder of the pillow is being a Child, he may refuse to give it up. Or, if he's being the Parent, he may try to turn the pillow privilege into a lecture, or a monologue. But you're trying to work at being Adults, so be nice with the pillow and share.

Reactive couples need to have conversations in terms of approach-retreat: taking time before they jump into an issue to think things through, focusing on staying with the issue and managing their own reactions (not the partner's), and taking a healthy exit if things start to get too intense. Then they try again. The initial goals are simply to keep it slow, regain some control of the reactions, and know when to step away. Baby steps.

The Avoidant Couple

The opposite of the reactive couple is the couple that constantly *avoids* conflict (those who withdraw or seek flight). It goes counter to many people's sensibilities that in order to find happiness in your relationship you need to be *willing* to experience pain. The avoidant couple avoids the pain of perceived conflict, yet also takes on too much imagined pain for how their partners *might* react.

Perhaps they never saw their own parents argue. Or perhaps that is all they saw and so their way of dealing with the pain they were exposed to as a child was to retreat altogether. But *the ways we coped with life as a child will not usually work as an adult. Adult life works by different rules.*

The avoidant couple often avoids conflict because they see "raising an issue" as being synonymous with "starting an argument". For them, approaching conflict is being intentionally hurtful, and they don't want to be mean. So while their actions frequently come from good intentions in the moment, the "kindness" of their withholding, in the long run, actually ends up hurting the relationship, just not as openly.

They typically recognize only the two extremes: *passive* (I lose but you win) or *aggressive* (I win but at the cost of you losing). To be aggressive is seen as selfish (one putting his own needs first), and neither wants to be selfish. But they fail to recognize that there is an ideal middle ground called *assertive* where we can respectfully address our issues, and *both* sides win.

Even if they do recognize that assertive exists, the projected discomfort of walking that verbal tightrope is enough to keep avoidant couples from trying.

On the surface, the couple that actively seeks flight can look very healthy. The *absence* of conflict is automatically assumed by many to indicate things are going well for them. For the couple themselves, this *illusion* of health can be enough to maintain the relationship for quite a while, because of their own need to see everything as okay.

It makes sense that this kind of couple usually takes longer to reach a crisis point, and longer to get to the point where change is seen to be necessary, simply because the relationship is about maintaining peace at all costs. The reactive couple is much more likely to bring things to a head in a much shorter time. Their constant conflict, if not resolved or given space, naturally leads to a crisis. The avoidant couple, however, is working actively to prevent this from happening. Any crisis is soothed by the act of silence, minimizing or denial. It's unusual since sometimes it is not just *one* person withdrawing and the other resenting him for it, *both* sides can often be in a sort of collusion to maintain the peace.

I'm not referring to those couples that have learned to accept each other's petty differences (which is a healthy thing), but rather those couples whose needs aren't being met who just pretend they're okay when they're not.

Seeking counseling for such a couple is often unlikely since the idea of talking about private things openly, things that could possibly be painful, is actively stepping out against the tradition of the relationship. This is why at least one person in the relationship has to have the insight to recognize that avoidance is not working, and that they very much want the relationship to work - enough that they are willing to risk the pain of honesty and vulnerability.

One of the underlying dilemmas with the avoidant couple is that, because they *don't* share uncomfortable information, they are still making assumptions of each other but never attempting to find out if those assumptions are accurate. As a result, their understanding of each other can become quite distorted. Their positive behavior creates a sense of closeness, but because the verbal intimacy that does occur is only a partial truth, they can still be growing apart without even realizing it.

If they can come to understand that conflict doesn't have to be a negative, that there is such a thing as *constructive criticism*, they're more likely to start venturing into that fearful but necessary territory. The approach-retreat ritual that the reactive couple takes becomes the same path for the avoidant couple. They practice sharing necessary information in a respectful way, seeing that they can do it safely without the imagined harm, and learn to find their own voice in the relationship.

––––––––––

There's a lot of information in this chapter and the last. I understand that it can be overwhelming the first time through. If I had to summarize it, it would come down to these five key tools of conflict resolution:

1. Remembering to give the benefit of the doubt, rather than to assume or feed a conspiracy theory

2. Staying with sincere questions ("How did you interpret what I said?", "Why was that so upsetting for you?", "What do you need from me right now?")

3. Taking the time to validate (listen, acknowledge, apologize, own)

4. Working towards 2-part solutions

5. Knowing when to take healthy exits

For the majority of couples who do not reach workable solutions, it is usually due to at least one of these five points being ignored or forgotten. Try to view them as tools to bring into play when you're trying to work through things with your partner. If you're getting lost in an argument, stop for a moment and ask yourself which of these tools would be the most helpful. Even if you don't know which one might be the best in that moment, at least you've got options you can try.

* * *

The next four chapters are going to go into more detail on the four stages of moving through an issue (Identify, Validate, Process and Resolve). Each has particular strategies that overlap to a degree with the other stages. What I would suggest is taking a look at the "ABC's for a Fair Fight" in the Appendices at the end of this book. This is a summary of the 26 points that will be covered in those four chapters. What some couples will do is identify for themselves which of the 26 points are their own trouble areas, and then focus on the corresponding sections as they go back to the reading.

Discussion Questions:

1. **Where does your relationship get stuck? Identifying, validating, explaining or resolving?** How do you plan on improving those blind spots?

2. **Why is validating so difficult to do, and so easy to forget?** How are you going to do a better job of remembering it?

3. **How actively do you work towards two-part solutions, where each person accepts a part in the solution?**

4. **Why is it important to attach a value to your issues?** What is the difference between a replay and the 4 steps?

5. **How is emotional intimacy gained by taking the time to validate and process?**

Chapter 5
Identifying the Issue

"My dear brothers, take note of this: Everyone should be quick to listen, slow to speak and slow to become angry." (James 1:20)

The tools for conflict resolution are deceptively simple and it is perhaps because of this simplicity that they are often overlooked. Just because many of them are basic does not make them easily remembered, or easy to use in the heat of the moment. You can say, "Well, of course, I know that listening is important", and you may feel that you do it all of the time, but do you do it in a way that helps your partner feel that he's really been heard?

Identifying an issue is that delicate territory where we have to decide how we're going to bring up an issue to our partner. Not just letting him know we're upset, but *why* we're upset. Of course, many of us don't give it too much consideration. Something upsets us and we launch right into expressing our emotions, never stopping to think about what we're going to say or how we're going to say it - like putting a car into "drive" before we've even given ourselves a chance to get behind the wheel.

So let me make a few suggestions for what to consider *before* you start the car.

Betty walks into the room upset. Bob's sitting on the couch reading the newspaper. Betty says, "Bob, this is really bothering me. Whenever I try to talk to you, you don't listen. I'm trying to communicate with you and you're off in your own world, acting like you're listening when you're not."

Bob, looking up from the newspaper, responds, "Honey, you're *always* wanting to talk! There's no way I can possibly listen to all of it. Even when I do listen, it never seems to be enough. I don't know what you want from me!"

Betty says, "Well, I want to feel like you care enough about me to listen!"

Rule #1. Choose your battles, and battlefield, wisely.

You've probably heard variations of the phrase, "What good is winning a battle, if you lose the war." For relationships, it makes the point that sometimes we get so caught up in winning the battle, the fight at hand, that we fail to see the long-term impact that these battles are having.

Ideally, the goal of winning a war in the real world is to restore peace. For a couple, the goal of the "war" is the survival of the relationship: to win your freedom from unhealthy past alliances (emotional baggage), to quell whatever rebellions start within the ranks (the struggles over self), and to unite your forces for a common good (working as a team to have a godly relationship). To "lose the war" is to destroy what keeps the couple connected: letting history get in the way of the present, self come before "us", and circumstances distract and divide.

The war is *not* against your partner. It's against everything that threatens or can harm the relationship. Because sometimes it *is* your partner, or you, that is endangering the relationship, some of the battles will be between you and him, but the war itself starts out with the two of you on the same side. Thinking in these terms, it's important that when we approach these "battles", the focus is on restoring the healthy alliance, not pushing our partner further into the role of enemy.

We need to take the time to consider the weight of our issues before we just let off a cannonball volley at our partner. Is this something really worth getting into, or are there better things for us to be focusing on?

Often, in the moment, what seems like an issue isn't that big a deal a day later. In the scheme of things, it would have been better to let it pass by as the temporary annoyance that it was, or maybe to mildly educate your partner rather than to initiate an attack.

By saying this, I'm not promoting neglect. I'm not saying ignore voicing your needs. But I do want to caution you not to make every little thing into a big thing.

Some people are critical by nature, and part of their everyday conversation is to judge and critique. To them, doing so may be considered nothing, just a passing observation of something that they noticed. They could just be into improving the relationship and see another area for potential growth. But to their partners, this chronic "complaining" can have a very negative impact, wearing away at their peace and creating resentment. To them, the critic is never satisfied, never content.

In deciding on our battles, we need to be *thinking* consciously of the big picture rather than becoming lost in the *feeling* of the moment. And if we're so close to it that we can't see the big picture, usually it means that we need to take some time to step back from it so that we can.

For Betty, she'd had a lot of time to think about things. There was a recurring pattern going on with Bob that needed to be addressed. The issue was relevant in terms of the quality of their relationship, both now and for the future. The "battle" was a necessary one.

* * *

In terms of battle*fields*, before we start discussing an issue, we need to take a moment to consider the setting - the "where" and the "when" the conversation is to take place.

Bob and Betty's setting is in their home, in the living room, a natural place for a discussion to occur. The "where" is okay, or is it? The TV may be on, or the radio, kids may be running through the house.

Sometimes people have a tendency to bring up serious issues in the wrong places: where there are distractions, kids who don't need to be exposed to the intimate details of the relationship, friends or family embarrassed. We don't need to interrupt a positive activity and ruin it by raising an issue. Some people want to deal with issues as they occur to them, regardless of the setting, and they need to rethink this habit if they want to get positive results. *If you want focused attention, choose a place where you're most likely to get it.*

What about the "when"? If you asked Bob, in the middle of reading his newspaper, it probably wasn't a good time. (Of course, Betty might respond "Well, there's *never* a good time for Bob.") I didn't say whether it was on the weekend or during the workweek. If Bob was just relaxing, unwinding after a day at the office, it probably would have been better for Betty to wait until later in the evening. The reason for this may not be so obvious. If Bob's repeated experience of coming home is that he gets hit with problems soon after he gets through the door, Betty's shaping Bob to dread coming home.

While Betty's needs *are* important, it's just as important to pick a time when those needs are more likely to be heard. Bob's still mentally dumping the problems from work and trying to get some space from his day. Bob's trying to de-stress and Betty's putting more on him. Now, I'm not trying to make Betty the bad guy. She may have had a hard day too. But rather than finding out first if now is a good time to talk, she jumps right in. If she wants to be heard, she needs to find out first if now is a good time for Bob to listen.

If Bob has a tendency to say "not now" but "later" never happens, then he's asking for Betty to force things. Otherwise, asking is a simple sign of respect. And the person asking needs to be shown respect in return. If "now" is truly not a good time for Bob, then he needs to commit to a time that *would* work, rather than just leave the issue hanging.

Another time people often pick to discuss issues is just before bedtime. While some people just *have* to talk about an issue, because if they don't they won't be able to sleep, they need to choose a time where there's less need to rush through the conversation. Besides, usually if you're ready to sleep, your mind is not at its sharpest.

Of course, there are times when it's just not convenient but things still need to be said. You may have to settle for not getting the full attention of your partner. Or he may have to drop what he's doing out of respect for your need. The point that I'm trying to get across, however, is that if you have the luxury of being able to think ahead, choose the time and the place carefully if you want an optimal solution and optimal responsiveness. If the issue is an important one to you, you want to approach it with the greatest chances for success.

When we get to Chapter 10 on healthy routines, having an accountability routine where the couple regularly sits down and discusses both the positive and the not-so-positive becomes a platform to regularly voice concerns. Having such a routine provides a place for the couple to discuss their issues so now issues don't have to creep into all of the other conversations. There's a time and a place reserved.

Rule #2. Identify the purpose of approaching a conversation to your partner. Don't assume that he knows it.

Rule #2 addresses the "why" we're starting an issue. Looking at Betty and Bob's conversation, note that nobody's actually being hostile. Nobody's trying to hurt the other. Betty's sharing a concern and Bob's responding. Nobody's abusing anybody. It's a relatively harmless interaction with no grievous errors. But let me make a few comments about this conversation. Betty *does* want more than just a listening ear. Betty probably wants different things at different times. While some times it is probably just about being heard, other times she probably wants assurance. Sometimes she may want resolution. In this instance, she probably wants a variety of things but, mainly, she is seeking a resolution to a recurring problem.

The greater error with just jumping into an issue without knowing what we want is expecting our partner to know what we want when we don't know it ourselves.

More often, we have an *intent* but we don't flag it for our partner. We just expect them to know what it is we're looking for. One word for this is *egocentric* - when we assume that others are aware of what we mean because *we* know what we mean. If we're able to let our partner know what we need from him up front, he won't have to be put in the position of being a mind-reader.

It's more important that the initiator express what he needs from the conversation rather than complaining about what he doesn't.

She says, "Don't solve this for me."

He responds with, "Okay, you *don't* want a solution but what *do* you want?"

Betty needs to identify for Bob what she is looking for from him with this particular conversation: a listening ear, help with a problem, support, ownership, whatever. Let's say she does it "by the book". This time she starts with "Bob, I've got a concern that's been bothering me and I need your help in resolving it."

She's letting him know she needs more than eye contact and a nod. She isn't starting off with an attack. She is inviting his input and needs a resolution to the issue.

If Bob's doing his part in this, he now has some sense of direction. He can reach for those problem-solving skills guys like to wield so often. If Bob only apologizes but a plan is being sought, then Betty needs to let him know she needs more than just an apology. If Bob complies but only offers a plan that says what Betty can do different, then she's going to need to let him know that she needs something different from him as well.

When couples are in sync, you don't have to point out what you need every time. However, if you notice you're either not being heard correctly or your partner is trying to help but missing the point, take the time to stop and explain what you want rather than walking away frustrated.

Rule #3. Confrontation is based on facts. Don't confront based on fears and doubts.

With inappropriate confrontation, we are telling our partner what they have done, *without* the facts to support it. We are going on a hunch, a fear, a guess, a possible pattern of behavior, or a leap of logic. But if we are tempted to confront based on our fears and doubts, then *what we need to do first is seek information in order to get our facts straight.*

What we often really need is *assurance*: about love, trust, fidelity, etc. However, because this is seen as a position of "neediness", or weakness, it is often avoided.

One of the basic principles for dealing with any situations where our concerns are based on fears and doubts, not facts, is to identify them for what they are. We don't need to keep them to ourselves, but we also don't need to approach our partner as if our fears are realities.

If we accuse him of something he didn't do, but we're *afraid* that he might have, then we are essentially calling him a liar and directly attacking the trust of the relationship.

If we express it as a fear, "Honey, I don't know if this is just me or what, but I'm feeling like you're drifting, that you're losing interest in us", then we are identifying it as a feeling, not saying it's a fact, giving them the *benefit of the doubt* and inviting assurance if it's not true.

If we find that we continue to need frequent assurance *despite* no further evidence for our fear then, hopefully, we will start to see that our own insecurity is the problem.

Now some people would say that this is being naïve and leaving the other person to take advantage simply by saying "Oh, no, honey, everything's fine" when it may not be. While it's true it does leave us open to be taken advantage of, this is our partner we're talking about. Part of the definition of any significant personal relationship is the willingness to be vulnerable (the willingness to risk out of trust). It's choosing to take the moral high road. Better to trust and be wrong than to not trust and, as a result, never have a relationship where you can be truly close because you are unable to risk being hurt.[12]

*　*　*

Confrontation, when it does take place, works best if it is done in a loving manner, not a judgmental one. It is not done to hurt or to punish. *It is done to hold your partner accountable to his commitment towards the relationship.* Part of the process may involve sharing your pain over the wrong done, but its' intent is not to commit an additional wrong by attacking.

The approach I like the best is the "Columbo" model, taking the Peter Faulk role of confused detective. You take what your partner's saying and you share your confusion over the difference between two contradictory statements or the discrepancy between something he's done versus what he's said. It's usually phrased like "I'm confused. You said this, but this is what you actually did. Help me understand how those match up...?" You're not making any accusations but you're letting him see you're noticing the discrepancy. It's then up to him to own up to things or provide an explanation, but it's done in a way where you've pretty much led him to the water and it's now up to him to assume responsibility for taking the drink.

What Betty did with Bob was a mild confrontation. She called him on the times that had occurred when he had failed to attend to her. This was based on actual past occurrences, not her fears that at some point he may not listen. She did start to make some inferences from this about his not caring which started to miss the mark, but the initial confrontation was over factual events.

---

[12] There *are* people who continually choose bad relationships and trust all the wrong people. For those folks, discretion and evidence should play a more central role in their relationships than the norm.

We have to be careful about generalizing a *pattern* of problems too broadly when we are pointing out a problematic "theme" to our partner. While we may not share the same specific problems that our partner has, *when we start to broaden the scope of the problem that we're addressing, often it will start to encompass areas that we ourselves have difficulties in.*

For example, let's say we are approaching our partner about not being disciplined enough in managing the finances, essentially creating a threat to our financial security. It would be a mistake to address it as a lack of discipline, rather than a *specific* problem with managing the finances, since we *all* have areas where we're not disciplined.

*   *   *

There is a particular phenomenon that occurs sometimes when we question our partners. The more we question them, the deeper we go with an issue, we may start to get different answers of explanation. Sometimes this is because we've exposed a lie, but sometimes this is because we're starting to discover the complexity of the issue.

If we start with just a surface conversation, we get a simplified explanation.

He says, "You didn't get home when you said would last night."

She responds with, "I lost track of time. Sorry about that."

So her simplest explanation is that she was late due to being distracted.

He presses, "So what was going on?"

"When I was out shopping, I added some things to my list that I hadn't initially thought of."

So now the explanation is both distracted and a longer shopping list than expected.

"You didn't tell me you were going to go shopping," he replies, a little upset. "You said you were running late with work."

"I was," she defends. "And on my way home, I thought of some things we needed."

So now the reasons are: 1) distracted, 2) longer shopping list than expected, and 3) running late from work.

"So you lied to me," he insists. "You never told me about the shopping until now."

"You didn't ask for details until now," she says, getting upset herself. "Why should I have to tell you every little thing I do? We're adults! Are you saying you don't trust me that I was actually shopping?"

Obviously he has his own conspiracy theory about the real issue, and maybe there's a history of her withholding information. But without such a history, this is simply a matter of finally having a more detailed conversation about what happened last night. The more in-depth the conversation gets, the more details will come out. No one detail has to be the whole truth. Each detail can actually be part of what makes up the whole.

Remembering that each of us, and our situations, can be more complicated at times than we give credit for, if we can hang on to the benefit of the doubt, we can handle the likelihood that the deeper we go with an issue the more factors we're going to uncover that contributed to the issue. Rarely do we do any one thing for just one reason.

When it comes to lies, the things we're concerned with is when there's *contradictions* when more details are added.

"Wait a minute, you said you were at Susan's last night. Now you're saying you were at Sarah's. Which is it?"

* * *

Part of learning each other's personalities and "language" is learning how to confront so that the other can receive it. And what that looks like from couple to couple will differ. How we discover the styles that work is through trial and error and through asking our partner for his help with the ongoing education. The error is in the extremes: when confrontation is avoided at all costs, or when it occurs so frequently that it loses all meaning or becomes constant rejection.

Rule #4. Attach a priority to issues, so there is some sense of how important or unimportant an issue is.

As I mentioned last chapter regarding replays, in those situations when one partner is walking out the door of the relationship that the other suddenly starts to pay attention, the problem can sometimes be the *overly familiar pattern of confrontation.*

If your partner becomes used to you regularly complaining, after a while, the issues tend to take on a similar drone to him. If you complain about everything to the same degree, not identifying for your partner which issues are big and which ones are small, it leaves it up to him to assign his own priority to them. They all go into the same "complaint drawer".

When the partner is finally walking out the door, the one being left suddenly becomes attentive because it isn't until then that it was made clear to him just how important her issues were for her. Prior to that, while he probably did notice when she was venting, he still thought that the relationship itself was secure.

In the same way that as parents we need to teach our children what wrongs and rights are more important than others, we also need to accurately communicate what issues are priorities for us in our relationships. ("On a scale of 1 to 10, this is an 8 for me.")

Betty attempted to let Bob know that her issue was an important one to her. ("Bob, this is really bothering me.") Bob, by explaining himself, was attempting to get her to understand his side of the problem, but he was failing to validate things for Betty. She would have to go on to let him know that her issue required a solution more than a defense. (She might say, "I understand there're complications to this, but this isn't something I can just accept as not going to change. We need to talk this through to what we can do differently. It's that important to me.")

If our partner feels that our issue is over "nothing", then we need to be able to identify that it may be "nothing" for him, but definitely "something" for us.

We need to recognize that all issues aren't created equal. Some issues are minor, and others are big. We don't want our partner thinking that all our issues are big ones or we become deserving of the label "high maintenance". If just about everything *is* "something" for us, then we might need to learn to get a better perspective on what is worth getting that upset about.

Some will hesitate to label minor issues "minor", thinking that if they do it will continue to be ignored. But, as with needs, the couple should have a clear sense of what issues are more important for each person.

Rule #5. Bringing up the negative past during an argument should be done only if the problem is continuing to occur.

One of the biggest "beginner" mistakes in communication has to do with how couples handle bringing up the past. Typically, the past is used as a tool to punish rather than a tool to gain understanding. How can we keep a positive environment in our relationship if we are using attack strategies? And how can we develop a mature relationship if we are engaging in childish mudslinging?

Let's say something has happened in the past, maybe several years ago, that has been traumatic to the degree that it has wounded the relationship. One partner seriously wronged the other. Let's also assume that the same situation has not occurred since, but trust issues continue to be a significant part of the relationship. Maybe the trust issues now are around finances, or taking each other at his word. It would be predictable, but unwise, that when issues become heated that that past traumatic event will ultimately be brought up as "the big gun", since it is connected to the damaged trust. In this situation, *the traumatic event becomes a way for the injured partner to always be in a superior position.* There is nothing that the other can do to erase the past and so he is always helpless to defend himself. But to continue to use this as leverage in arguments undermines any act of forgiveness that hopefully occurred concerning the past wrong.

Now we may say that the past event *was* connected to the other issues because it is all trust-related, so why not bring it up again? But even if that is where the trust issues originated, usually both sides are so aware of its having happened and the pain it involved that *there is no need* to bring it up again. Everyone knows where it started. Continuing to bring it up only turns the focus of attention off the current issues and onto you for being "harassing" or "unforgiving".

Continuing to resurrect old issues for ammunition in the present is working against the relationship moving forward by anchoring it to the past.

* * *

Bringing up the past can often sidetrack the current issue. The conversation is going along well, both sides taking turns and hearing the other out, when suddenly somebody references something that happened a couple months ago. It automatically shifts the attention away from talking about the present issue and leads the other to believe that this other event needs worked through as well. So now we're not just dealing with what happened today, but the other month, too. We're starting to stack up issues or events. And the conversation starts to get overly complicated. It might be helpful to stop and say "Wait a minute. Is that something that still needs worked through too or are you just using it as an example?" in order to clarify what the other's wanting.

* * *

Using the past frequently can give a negative sense of record-keeping to the relationship. Record-keeping gives the message that we are not being forgiven for our past mistakes. It makes us feel like we are living with a disapproving parent who is keeping lists on us. Now if we *are* acting like an irresponsible child in the relationship, expecting there to be no accountability, then maybe we are forcing our partner into this role.

Typically, lists go along with judgments. We use them as barrages to overwhelm our partner about what a horrible person he is. She calls him a "failure" or "lazy" (insert insult of choice) and then goes into her long list of past wrongs to substantiate just how much of one he is. As we'll discuss later concerning judgments, we are operating in delicate territory when we attack our partner's character as it leaves little room for a positive outcome and a continuing relationship. If we want to be effective in motivating change, we need to be more selective in how we use the past.

Betty identified to Bob that the problems had been recurring. However, she did not go into detail about when and where, *and there was no need to*, since Bob wasn't arguing the point. He did counter her issue with a rationale, but he didn't deny that her perception was accurate so there was no need to reach for more evidence. *Don't go for overkill to make a point if the point has already been acknowledged. Focus on working out the resolution.*

* * *

Let's define some of the specifics of "only if the problem is continuing to occur", or when bringing up the past is justified.

1. If the significance of a problem is being denied or dismissed, we can use past events to support the point we are trying to make, showing our partner that it is not just a current, isolated event but something that has happened before. The intent is to create a basis for our argument. Note that much of our success in getting this across will have to do with our tone, our body language and our delivery.

2. Using the past is most helpful when our partner is requesting examples in order to better understand our issue or concern.

3. *Always* feel free to bring up the past in order to give recognition for things done well or things appreciated. It's much more beneficial to the relationship to be keeping a list of the successes rather than the failures.

———————

Each "rule", used well, requires a good deal of restraint, humility, and emotional maturity. It's tough to swallow pride. It's difficult to think when we're upset. It's hard to refrain from verbally striking back when we've been hurt. It ain't easy!

Successful application of the rules requires practice, and they need fine-tuning to fit each relationship, but they get better results than if we ignore them and just go with what comes naturally. Doing the work of using the "rules", choosing the more difficult but mature path, allows us to retain our integrity during times when integrity tends to be lacking.

Discussion Questions:

1. **Of these first 5 "rules", which ones do you have the most difficulty with?** Why?

2. **How are you going to put the rules that are most often ignored on such a conscious level that they are being applied when issues are being discussed?**

Chapter 6
Validating the Issue

"From the fruit of his lips a man is filled with good things as surely as the work of his hands rewards him" (Proverbs 12:14)

Validation is the most frequently missed step in the resolution stages, and so couples go back and forth between restating the issue, and re-explaining their sides.

Reactive couples have this angry, verbal ping-pong match going on where the only thing they take turns with is finding new ways to be offended. Each person keeps making the issue all about them rather than taking the time to focus on one partner's issue at a time. Validation, a respect for perspective, is absent from the conversation.

Validation attempts to move us out of our reactive mindset and think beyond our own internal perspective, restoring a balanced focus.

Peter and Patty were in their mid-20's and had been dating for 8 months. Their concern was that there was a recurring theme of doing marathon discussions with the few problems the relationship had encountered. They were concerned that even though the problem count wasn't very high, they weren't able to resolve the few problems that there were.

"We just keep rehashing the problem," said Peter. "It's not like we don't spend the time talking it out, it's just that we don't get anywhere."

"Peter doesn't hear me," said Patty. "I'll explain to him my concerns, but he thinks I should just get over it."

"I don't expect you to just 'get over it', but I want you to accept what I say in return," responded Peter.

"For example?" I asked.

Peter looked to Patty.

"We were at a picnic last weekend," explained Patty. "And I was feeling like Peter was in a bad mood. He wasn't saying much and he didn't seem to be trying to spend much time with me. I thought he was angry at me, so I approached him about it, and he denied it. So I let it go, but he never came out of it. I approached him again later, and he denied it again, but I could tell he was upset with me for continuing to ask. So I let it go, but the rest of the day was ruined.

"I tried to talk about it again the next day, but Peter just acted like I was the problem and I should have just not said anything after the first time he said he was okay."

"I'd had a hard week at work and I wasn't really feeling sociable," said Peter. "I'd told her before that I didn't really feel up to going to the picnic. But I wasn't angry at Patty. She kept pushing me, insisting I must be angry with her, when I wasn't. Finally, I did become angry at her."

"I told you, you didn't have to go," inserted Patty.

"Yes, but I knew it would have disappointed you if I'd stayed at home," said Peter.

"It didn't make my day any better by you going and moping around," added Patty.

"And that's just it," replied Peter. "Part of my issue with her is that no matter what I do it doesn't seem like it's good enough."

Rule #6. Balance the negative with the positive.

Think, for a moment, on how your parents motivated you as a child. Typically, it was based around consequences if resistance was encountered. If you did not do "such and such", something bad was going to happen: whether it was your father was going to be told, privileges were going to be removed, spankings would occur, disapproval and guilt were going to be handed out, lectures would occur, etc. Most children grow up learning that, to motivate another to do something, there need to be negative consequences attached. And so, as adults, we try to motivate each other by attaching punishments, lectures, and judgments in order to get compliance. In other words, we use parenting tactics.

We initially attract others through our unconditional regard and approval of who they are, only to later push them away through our rejection of the things we now voice our disapproval of. But *our primary focus needs to remain on reinforcing the positives, the small successes, as they occur.* If the relationship has deteriorated to a great degree, finding and reinforcing the positives can be difficult since we may first have to retrain ourselves to see where the positives still exist.

Since our initial response to criticism is usually to explain or defend ourselves, it's a positive strategy to enter into the conversation already providing for our partner's defense. When you approach him about an issue, try to think of a few positives to share first so he can see that you recognize there are good things happening too, and that you understand there are reasons for his behavior (though that doesn't excuse the behavior).

One form of this is trying to think about what some of your partner's reasons may be for his part of the problem, and validating them.

Patty, upon finding out that Peter had a hard work week, and really had made a personal sacrifice to come to the picnic, could have used that at some time during their discussion later. For example, "Peter, I do appreciate the fact that you were already stressed from work and still came to the picnic. I understand that you were doing that for me, and that means a lot. You're right, part of my concern was that you were angry with me, and it's good to know that that wasn't the case."

Since Peter's relating he doesn't feel appreciated for his sacrifices, Patty's validating that for him by recognizing his sacrifice as being important to her. She essentially just took part of his argument away from him, and, at the same time, did a half-decent job of not attacking.

She could have also reached for past successes. For example, "Peter, we've had many times together in the past, socially, where you were wonderful. Because this time was so out of character for you, it stood out to me and made me concerned."

Not only in this statement is she giving him credit for typically *not* being a social problem, she's also bringing her heart into it by expressing her reason for concern, rather than judging him for his behavior.

Patty can then move on to tell Peter what she's needing from him.

Unless Peter is paranoid and suspects a hidden agenda, he will probably respond positively to this approach. The difficulty, of course, is in being able to maintain this non-adversarial role throughout the rest of the resolution process.

*　*　*

In couple's counseling, if someone is stuck in his own perception of an issue, counselors will sometimes have the couple switch roles and try to argue the point of view from the partner's perspective. While this can get twisted and used as an opportunity to bash the other, it can also be a very positive opportunity to think through what the logic and feelings of your partner might be. We are all too used to seeing things from *our* point of view. How potentially educational to try to reason from someone else's.

*　*　*

It's an interesting phenomenon that, in healthy relationships, we tend to automatically try to create balance in a relationship when it's being threatened. If you are pointing out the negative about something, the natural tendency for your partner is to try to balance it by recognizing the positives, and vice versa.

If you are really irritated with a family member, upset by something she said, and share that with your partner, it's natural for him to try to alleviate some of your irritation by presenting a less negative perspective ("She probably didn't mean that." "Maybe she was just having a bad day.") rather than to feed into it. But you have to be careful with this because, *in an effort to balance each other, you can often unintentionally be invalidating.* If your partner is wanting to vent about a family member and you try to rationalize the family member's point of view, the message you may be giving to your partner is that you're not supporting her. This goes back to Rule #2 to identify what you're looking for ("I don't need an alternative viewpoint right now, okay? I just need you to let me vent and be supportive.").

This natural tendency to balance works when you verbally recognize your partner's strengths. It frees him to examine his own weaknesses.

She says, "You really did a good job with putting me first last night. I appreciate that."

He responds with, "Thanks. I know I need to be more consistent with doing that."

By us defending or supporting our partners, they don't feel as much of a need to self-protect. Because they see that we're paying attention to their successes, they don't feel that they have to point them out. You are setting a positive pattern for the relationship - one of support, inspiration and growth that has a ripple effect into the other areas of the relationship.

Couples who get caught up in chronic arguments often reactively over-focus on making counterpoints to everything the partner is saying, or over-correcting.

He says, "When I came home after supper..."

And she quickly steps in with, "It wasn't after supper, it was at least 8 or 9..."

If the debate isn't about when he got home, then why even go there? It just interferes with the normal progression of a conversation and makes the partner feel like they have to be overly accurate with everything they say, and that their partner is only looking to find fault.

While this may be an attempt to broaden his perspective, or an example of balance that's gotten out of control, we have to recognize that what we need to be trying to do is find common ground, or *points of agreement*, in order to move forward. The more we stay focused on differences, or petty inaccuracies, the further away from resolution we get.

Rule #7. Own up to your contribution to the problem first, and it will open the door for your partner to examine his part.

Change typically starts with us.

If a pattern of hurtful behavior exists in a relationship, each partner is a part of that pattern. We may not be the *cause* of that problem, but we often will do something that plays a part in helping or hindering it. We can even be doing the "right" thing to deal with it, but it's still the wrong choice for what would actually work with our particular partner.

Changing our own part is particularly effective in situations where the "problem" is occurring as a *reaction* to what we're doing or saying. If we change our approach, then, predictably, the reaction should change since our reactive partner's behavior is dependent on us. It may not get the desired reaction, but at least now we're approaching it by looking at what is in our control first.

Even if it is a character or personality issue in our partner that has occurred in past relationships, we still play a part in assisting with the solution. Even if it is just a *supportive* role, how we choose to be supportive can make a big difference. It is part of being a team rather than giving the rejecting message of "It's *your* problem. *You* deal with it."

If your partner is owning the problem but isolating himself ("It's *my* problem, *I'll* deal with it"), then he's also missing the opportunity to draw closer by exploring how his partner can help him overcome whatever his struggle may be.

If we have already wrestled through what we may be doing that has maintained, created, or worsened the problem, sharing our efforts with our partner can open him up to examining his own end. If he is able to see that we're not putting it all on him, that we are already recognizing that we play a part, we are sharing the burden of responsibility for the relationship from the very start. There is then no need to point the finger or pass judgment because it is a shared problem.

*   *   *

Some couples get hung up on apologizing - that to apologize is taking *all* of the blame and they're not going to do it. Again, they are operating by extremes: taking *all* of the blame or *none* of the blame. Why not just apologize for your *part* of the problem?

Some couples have to itemize what percentage of the problem was theirs: 45%, 83%...92.5%. This seems ridiculous but I see it frequently, couples who get so nitpicky about every little thing.

In working towards a strategy for resolution, it does become important to examine what each person's part of the problem is, but not for the purpose of assigning who is the most to blame. The purpose of examining each part is to give each side strategies that they can use to help fix the problem.

In the example of Peter and Patty, at the picnic Patty was trying to explore Peter's upset but he wasn't giving her much to go on. Patty *did* press Peter past the point that he asked her to let it be, but, on Patty's behalf, Peter really didn't do a good job in the moment of letting her know what was going on with him. Because he didn't fill in the blanks, she kept coming back for more information. He was denying his upset with her, but he *was* upset about being at the picnic. Peter was focused on Patty letting him be, rather than recognizing that he was giving off noticeable signals that a caring partner wouldn't ignore. He was acting withdrawn and moody at a social function.

What Patty could have done a better job at while at the picnic was expand on her reasons for being concerned about Peter. By focusing just on was he angry with *her*, he did answer her question by saying "no". Peter was being concrete, something that is stereotypically male. By her continuing to press the *same* concern repeatedly, it was like calling him a liar. What she needed to do was broaden her line of questioning regarding the possibilities of what was going on with him, or possibly share her observations of how he was coming across to others at the picnic to raise his awareness. Maybe those paths would have been more productive.

How Patty could approach it might be something like this:

Patty says, "Peter, when I see you withdraw like that I don't know what's going on. The only thing I know is to try to ask questions. You're saying I should just leave you be, and I understand needing space, but you're also telling me now that you *were* upset, just not with me. What could I do different in the future that wouldn't shut you down, but also get the information I need to be able to let it go?"

She's sharing with him her frustration at not being able to be more successful at being heard, and this is honest since part of her frustration is not just with him but with her own lack of success with this problem.

Up until this point, her way was to press him with questions until he became angry. His way was wanting her to let him alone without a decent explanation, which just distanced him from her. *Neither individual strategy worked for the relationship.*

By putting it on herself, what she could do differently, Patty's not pointing the finger at Peter, yet she's still pulling him into the resolution process.

Because she's remaining vulnerable, the odds stay good that he might start to own some things that he could have done differently. But even if Peter just provides some solutions for her part only, Patty doesn't have to back off. She can ask for more, but she needs to make sure she doesn't undo what she's already accomplished. So it could look something like this:

"Okay. I'll try to hang onto your suggestions. It's good to know there's something I can do to make it better. But I'd like to balance this out because the other part of this is what I need from you when this happens. Can I make some suggestions?"

Notice that she's not making any accusations. She's essentially thanking him for what he's offered, and then she's moving on to let him know that her needs have not yet been met. She doesn't start making demands. She asks him *can* she make some suggestions (Rule #19).

She's not assuming an overly submissive role by doing this. This is the same role I'd suggest for a male. She's giving him the benefit of the doubt and she's showing him respect by requesting his attention, asking for the opportunity to give some feedback. This is good manners, folks, the same way we'd hopefully treat our best friend!

If he cares about her needs, which most partners will say they do, he'll *invite* the suggestions. If he says he's not interested, and this is the pattern, then you've got some serious things to consider concerning the future of the relationship.

How well he listens may be a reflection on his listening skills and the priority he places on the relationship, but much of it also has to do with the *delivery* of those suggestions.

Granted, there are unhealthy individuals out there who would have no problem with letting everything be our fault, but what I am discussing here is a method we can use to defuse a potential conflict by validating an issue through ownership. The fact that we are acknowledging our own contribution to the problem validates our partner's perception that it's not a one-sided issue.

Rule #8. Take turns talking and listening.

You say, "Well, of course, we're going to take turns". But remember, over a period of time in a relationship you naturally start to take shortcuts. Part of how we take shortcuts is that we no longer take the time to completely hear the other person out. We finish his sentences for him. We speak over him with our own point. We try to "cut to the chase". We motion him to move on with it instead of dragging things out. We're overly focused on thinking about our response before he's even halfway done with his. As a result, there are times when we don't give each other enough room to be heard.

If you look at the conversation between Peter and Patty, they weren't interrupting each other. They seemed to be taking turns. But neither was really *listening* to the other. Each was stuck in his own perspective. Patty was focused on how Peter ruined the picnic. Peter was focused on how Patty kept pressing him even though he told her he wasn't angry with her, and how he could never get credit for his efforts.

This is a very typical scenario. It isn't that they are incompatible or that this relationship is doomed.

For many couples, in the early part of the dating process, you took the time to talk. You focused your attention on hearing each other out and responded rather than reacted to each other, giving the message that you, maybe more than anyone else, understood where the other was coming from. You weren't in any rush to get through the conversation. (Yes, I'm making assumptions about your dating life here.) But, now, you don't put that kind of energy and patience into it anymore and, as a result, you don't get the positive response you used to get.

If an argument is going nowhere, couples have to slow the discussion down to where one partner is saying his piece, and the other is taking time to understand it and validate it before the couple moves on. Because each is now feeling heard, they are able to move forward with the conversation. There is a heightened awareness of what has already been said, so there is not as much of a need for repetition.

*   *   *

Take some time to look at the Listening Exercise at the back of the book (Appendix). It walks you through a step-by-step interaction, teaching couples to relearn how to take turns responding to each other and validating as you go. There are several reasons for this exercise.

- It often comes as a surprise to a couple just how difficult it has become to "take it slow" and take turns, and how much work goes into really focusing on hearing, clarifying and validating what the other person is saying rather than automatically turning the focus to you.

- It's often immediately rewarding if you or your partner have had little success in the past with feeling heard to discover that it is still within your ability to meet this need for each other. It's not some major leap of logic or perspective that is necessarily required to convince someone he has been heard and understood.

- It also helps you learn to separate the emotional reaction to what your partner is saying, since your focus is now outward, not inward. You are learning to view what your partner says as information, rather than continuing to look for any potential offense.

- For couples who are overwhelmed with the whole process of changing how they communicate, this exercise cuts things down into nice simple steps. It can be reserved for those times when there's been no progress because emotions are too involved, or the discussion has become too complicated.

For some people there is resistance to this exercise because they feel it overly structures a conversation into "baby steps". But by breaking a potentially emotionally-overwhelming conversation down into do-able chunks, we're able to walk through it relatively unscathed, without becoming distracted by side-issues or our own reactivity.

Do you always have to slow things down to this degree? No. But for the important things, and the issues that have a lot of emotional baggage attached, keep it in mind.

*　*　*

For most arguments, there are two contradictions that we participate in that involve the extremes of under-listening and over-listening.

1. In terms of our partner, while we often are *under-listening* to the actual content of what he is trying to share, we tend to *over-listen* for the words he is using that contain potential offense for us.

2. In terms of ourselves, while we are often *over-focused* on explaining ourselves or our viewpoint, we are completely *under-focused* on the actual words that we're using (*how* we're expressing ourselves).

Rule #9. Be respectful of your partner's perception of an issue. Don't define reality for the other.

"Defining reality" is telling your partner how he thinks or feels. It is not talking about how you yourself think or feel. It is making assumptions about your partner's thoughts and feelings and doesn't invite an actual conversation. It is a statement, not a question, so it doesn't leave room for debate (though it certainly creates a whole lot of debate as a result). Why should I even attempt trying to explain myself if you've already filled in all of the blanks for me and are unwilling to question your conclusions?

Patty starts defining reality for Peter when she says "I'll explain to him my concerns, but he thinks I should just get over it." Unless he has actually told her to "just get over it", which he denies, she is deciding for him that that is what he thinks. It would also explain why the discussion at the picnic became so problematic if her pattern was to chronically assume that he was angry with her, even though he was denying it.

Note that Patty made a statement a little later, saying that, "…I was *feeling* like Peter was in a bad mood." This is *not* defining reality for Peter. She's saying that that's how she felt, which allows that she might be wrong. It is, after all, a feeling, and we each have a right to how we feel.

Some people will say that this is just semantics, but it makes a major difference when we actively use this in conversation. To say "I *feel* like she doesn't care about me" versus "She doesn't care about me" is not saying the same thing. In the second version, I have already concluded that she doesn't care. How can that be argued if it's already been concluded?

A decision has been made. But if I say "I feel like...", then there's room for debate since I'm allowing that that's just my perception. I haven't assumed the role of mind-reader.

Understand, I'm not saying it's okay to say something like "I *feel* like you're a jerk." While this may not be defining reality, it is still very much a *judgment*.

*   *   *

A particular style of counseling that's often used by the media to make fun of the counseling profession is where the counselor spends a lot of time asking questions about how the client "feels". "Tell me how you *feel* about your dog dying." "How does it *feel* when he rejects you like that?" And, of course, the obvious answer is "I feel horrible! How do you think I feel?!"

When counselors *do* focus on clients talking about their feelings it's usually because the client is intellectualizing and detaching from his emotions, and so the counselor is trying to get the client back in touch with them. What I'm suggesting is that people use better terminology in their conflict resolution that doesn't *assume* what the other thinks or feels. How they go about doing it is up to them, I'm just pointing out one of the simplest methods.

A humorous misunderstanding occurred around this distinction when I was working with a couple in their second or third session.

The wife started off in a resentful tone with, "Well, Bob just feels that I should have two fulltime jobs, a career and be a housewife all at the same time."

Bob's eyes are shooting daggers, teeth clenched, as he responds with, "That's not true! I only come off that way because she feels that a man is supposed to make all the money so she can go spend it!"

We'd already talked about not speaking for each other, so I stepped in to make a comment on their wording and each looked at me with a confused expression. I asked them what they didn't get and the husband replied, "I thought you said for us to talk about our feelings!"

They thought that because they were no longer telling each other what the other *thought,* but now telling each other how the other *felt,* that they were doing what I had suggested. What I had meant was for them to talk about their *own* feelings, not each other's. They were still continuing to define reality for each other and feeling just as upset by doing it.

* * *

There was a simple experiment I was victim to in my high school psychology class. The class was just starting when, suddenly, a stranger walked into the class and "mugged" the student who was closest to the door. (Keep in mind this was back in the 70's when there was greater leeway to do such "experiments". The whole event was planned and the mugged victim was in on it.) After it happened and the stranger ran out, everyone's jaws were hanging, either out of shock or not knowing what to do. The teacher came back into the room, having pretended to chase after the mugger, and started to interview the class on the details of what they'd seen. Every recount of what just happened was different: different accounts of what the mugger looked like, how he was dressed, even what had just happened (some more accurate than others).

It's important to remember that there are *two* people in a relationship. Even though we may be going through the same events, our experiences of those events and how we interpret them for ourselves are very different. *We cannot put ourselves in a position of saying that our interpretation of the event is the only right one. We can only say what our experience of the event was.* Especially in times of stress or strong emotion, our ability to interpret events accurately has greater likelihood of being impaired because we tend to only remember the pieces that are most relevant, or hurtful, for us.

This is why it is so problematic in a relationship when I elect myself as the only one who sees or understands things accurately. I do have the right to say what I did or didn't mean by something. I don't have the right to tell my partner what he did or didn't mean, think, or feel. By doing so I am saying that my viewpoint is the only one that matters in this relationship.

Part of understanding this rule is accepting that even my *own* perception is slightly removed from reality. My own history, insights and perceptions filter all information that comes into my brain from the outside world.

I am *not* saying to question your own judgment to the point that you can never take a stand on anything. I *am* saying we need to learn to give each other the "benefit of the doubt" - that we may be missing something that the other person sees, hears or understands that is important for us to consider in order to balance our picture.

*   *   *

Let's talk briefly about how to best respond to an "I feel" statement, where your partner has been successful with wording things in a way that doesn't define your reality for you. She could have said "You don't care anymore", but, instead, she says "I feel like you don't care anymore". If you respond with a simple "That's not true. Of course I do", you may feel like you're correcting her perception but you've actually just *invalidated* how she feels. Bear with me a second.

Patty confronted Peter about being angry with her, which he simply denied ("That's not true."). By leaving it at this, Peter was unintentionally being invalidating. If he was paying attention, he should have moved into a better explanation of what *was* upsetting him. ("I'm not angry at you, I'm just having difficulty letting go of this horrendous work week.") That would have been validating for her that he was, in fact, upset, just not with her. Her *observation* that he was upset was accurate. It was her *assumption* that was wrong. As I said before, with validation you are often, in that moment, ignoring the points you disagree on, and just focusing on the ones that you can support.

If a perception or assumption is incorrect, you will still want to correct it at some point in the conversation. But the validating part is the time you take to explore *why* your partner has that perception, or made that assumption, and being respectful of it, even when you disagree with it.

Rule #10. Be willing to be wrong.

Ownership is validating. But to apply ownership we have to be willing to admit when we're wrong.

Most of us have a lot of past baggage attached to the words "right" and "wrong". When accused of doing "wrong", we react with anger, resentment, defensiveness, bitterness, guilt, or anxiety. Any number of very powerful feelings that often have only a little to do with the current situation. It's sometimes more about what being wrong *means* to us, rather than the actual wrong we may have just committed.

Pride, control and competition all play a part in being unwilling to admit fault. Some people, even though they can see that they're wrong, will still not give their partner the "satisfaction" of admitting so. Yet, if you are not able to accept responsibility, then why do you expect it of your partner?

A relationship should not be about competition. It's not about being better than the other person or always being in the right. That goes against the whole definition of a team: being partners. If you've accepted that you're both going to be "missing the mark" at different points in your relationship, then learning to admit wrong isn't about fear of judgment or attack. It's just owning up to your part of the problem in order to better the relationship.

*   *   *

The person who is not afraid to admit his faults shows greater strength of character than the person who has to constantly hide or deny any shortcomings. How freeing to be able to say, "You know, you're right. That wasn't the best choice for me to make, and I can see how it could have hurt you." Suddenly, I've changed the whole battleground. It's no longer a battle because I'm not participating in the struggle. I've admitted to some fault in the situation. I've validated my partner's perception. And I've remained humble in the process rather than turning things into a blame game.

Hopefully, I'm also setting the stage for my partner to own up to his own mistakes. As in a support group, where one person starts to admit to some personal issues, suddenly it's okay for everyone else to talk about faults in front of the rest of the group and to not feel judged.

By putting ourselves above blame, we automatically set ourselves above our partners. Granted, some mistakes are more detrimental to the relationship than others, particularly when they aren't "mistakes" at all but things done intentionally to hurt. But what I am referring to is the common ground you should be trying to create in your relationship where honesty is rewarded and being vulnerable is welcomed rather than rejected. You are admitting to what didn't work in order for things *to* work.

Sun Tzu's classic "The Art of War" was about military strategies for the fighting samurai. In it, the warrior who has to hide his weaknesses lives in fear of them being discovered and used against him. The man who has owned his vulnerabilities is at an advantage because he is hiding nothing. His weaknesses can't be used against him because he has already acknowledged their existence.

* * *

Keep in mind what I said earlier about ownership. Being willing to be wrong and admit it is great, but sometimes resolution requires going past ownership and being willing to agree to new strategies if things are going to actually improve. Repeated ownership without meaningful change loses its value pretty quickly.

Rule #11. It's okay to disagree.

Part of understanding validation is recognizing that you don't have to agree with your partner's perception in order to validate it. For people who need others to constantly be in agreement with them in order to feel at peace, agreeing to disagree can be tough.

There are *interest* differences. He likes sport shows and she likes home improvement shows. Each doesn't really care for the other's preference, but they can live with the difference so long as no judgments are being attached ("That's a stupid show.", "That's a waste of your time.").

There are differences around *routine* where she would prefer him to clean up the house to her standard, but ultimately has to accept that he's not her. Usually, in these situations the key is that the partner *is* accepting responsibility for getting the job done, but there is room for him to do it his way.

There are differences in *skills* or *personality type*, where he has to accept that what he is asking of his partner is an area that is a natural strength for him but not for her (such as, where he may be naturally social but she is not). They still need to try to stretch to accommodate each other, being open to learning new skills, but expectations need to remain realistic - that he's not using himself as the standard of what is acceptable.

There are differences around *core beliefs*. If you're a Christian and your partner's Jewish, you need to be mindful that your job is *not* to convert him. Your influence is stronger when shown by your respect for his faith, not your judgment.

Peter could have agreed with Patty that he was upset. But he couldn't have agreed with her that he was upset with her when he wasn't. Her trying to force his agreement of something that was inaccurate, didn't work for either of them.

In seeking a resolution to the situation, in this particular situation, Peter and Patty needed to do more than just agree to disagree. If there was to be a better outcome, they would have to decide on better future strategies to make things work. They were each holding out for the other to adopt their particular solution, and nobody was budging. They needed to be more realistic that the solution had to be something that would work for the relationship, and would probably require a small stretch for both. Patty needed to stop defining reality for Peter, and Peter needed to be more open to discussing Patty's concerns.

*   *   *

Ultimately, in seeking resolution, learning to agree to disagree, to live with the things that aren't going to change, comes down to whether the issue is *need-related*. If these are core needs that are not being met (security, significance and fun), then you've got a problem.

There are couples who have stayed together because at least one partner stopped looking to have core needs met by the other and has coped by developing a life outside of the relationship (getting security and significance through friends, family, work, and his spiritual life). While some relationships can survive like this, more often the couple has learned to simply coexist rather than having any emotional intimacy.

If these are *preferences* that are not being met, then it's more a matter of learning to accept and live with it, recognizing that the more important needs *are* being satisfied. The message we often give to our partners by pushing our preferences, past the point of educating them about our likes and dislikes, is not only "You need to be more like me and less like you", but "There's something wrong with you for not being more like me".

At the same time, if *enough* preferences go routinely unmet, at some point it may actually impact a need.

––––––––––

The biggest predictor for successful change in a relationship comes down to the couples' state of *readiness* to change. Those couples that are willing to do whatever it takes to have the relationship they both want, are more likely to be successful in creating it.

You won't get the relationship you want based on good intentions or desire. You have to act on it and live out that commitment to seeing it through. Part of it is being willing to die to self, your way of doing things, at least to a degree, for the sake of the relationship. Part of it is remaining open to learning and adopting better approaches. Part of it is taking forward steps, even when you're not completely feeling it (which is okay, because the feelings will typically follow).

Discussion Questions:

1. **Of the validation "rules", which ones do you have the most difficulty with? Why?**

2. **How are you going to put the rules that are most often ignored on such a conscious level that they are actually being applied when issues are being discussed?**

Chapter 7
Processing the Issue

**"Reckless words pierce like a sword, but the tongue
of the wise brings healing."** (Proverbs 12:18)

So you've already brought your issue to the table and you're working on providing mutual validation as you go. The next stage is called *processing* the issue, where you and your partner are taking the time to examine the issue from different sides in order to better understand each other's perception and insights into the problem.

While I addressed them in separate chapters, validation and processing are very much intertwined. As you and your partner discuss and explain, you're also validating as you go by continuing to respectfully hear each other out.

Jim and Janet have been married for fifteen years. During the first couple years of their marriage, things seemed to be going pretty well. When they started to have kids, however, the business of the day distracted them from continuing to attend to each other's needs and they slowly drifted apart without even realizing what was happening. At the point that they have come in for counseling, they are both feeling very stressed and at a loss as to how to change direction.

In response to being asked why they are coming for counseling, Jim steps in first, saying, "We've gotten to the point where we've actually been talking about separating. Neither of us wants this to happen, but we can't seem to work anything out. Janet seems to get upset about the least little thing that I say and will blow up at me, and then I'll retreat. We're locked in a stalemate and keep going through the same routine."

Janet is tight-lipped while Jim is talking, nodding on occasion and looking very serious. They're sitting on the same couch but there's noticeable space between them. Janet's arms and legs are crossed tightly. Jim seems a bit more relaxed.

"Jim's right," she says. "It *has* gotten to the point where separation comes up. And he *does* run away from conflict. As far as my blowing up at the 'least little thing', I have a lot of stress on me and I feel like I'm not getting much help around the house. So, yes, I do 'blow up' at him."

Janet's tone is becoming more strained as she continues to speak. It's obvious she's fighting a desire to "blow up", even now.

Jim counters, "My job involves a lot of responsibility at this point. I can't manage the load I carry during the day without some of it coming home at night. Janet gets upset when I have to back out of helping with the kids sometimes because there's work to be done that can't wait."

Janet responds, now avoiding looking directly at Jim, "I work part-time on top of taking care of the home. I can't do it all! Sometimes I feel like he's just using his work as an excuse to not have to deal with the rest of us!"

"If that were the case I wouldn't be coming home at all. I'd stay at the office!" Jim is quick to reply. He's becoming more emotional, but there's more hurt in his voice than anger.

"You may as well stay at the office!" Janet shoots back. "I doubt the kids would even know you were gone!"

"Don't bring the kids into it!" he reacts. Now the anger is coming. "I can't stand it when you try to use guilt to get me to give in. Stop trying to be my mother and manipulate me into doing what you want by using them!"

"Don't you dare compare me to your mother! I'm nothing like her!"

"I said you were *trying* to be my mother. I wasn't comparing. Besides, *she* doesn't have temper problems, so it wouldn't apply."

"Then why don't you marry someone more like her?"

Jim starts to say something and catches himself. He visibly steps back from the argument, withdrawing. He looks at me with a shrug. "You see," he says. "This is exactly what happens at home."

Rule #12. Keep in mind the goal of the conversation.

It seems that one of the hardest things for couples to do when discussing an issue is to keep from getting sidetracked. It's so easy to bring up additional issues when trying to explain yourself. But when you do this, your partner automatically tries to address the extra issues and, before you know it, no one can remember how things got started. You've overwhelmed each other with so many different problems to be addressed that you're left with the feeling that if this much is going wrong there's no hope for the relationship. The initial topic goes unresolved and the issues continue to pile up.

Jim and Janet started off agreeing, for the most part, on why they were there for counseling. It didn't take long, though, before the kids were brought into it, then Jim's mother, and things were getting pretty far off-track from where they started. The direction of the conversation was lost and so many other things were being added to the mix that it quickly became impossible to sort it all out or resolve everything that was being brought up in one sitting.

Once you've already identified to your partner what you're wanting (Rule #2), it's helpful during the ensuing conversation to be asking yourself "Is what I'm about to say going to help us move closer to a resolution or just complicate things?"

If it's a problem you're discussing and there's something that needs taken into account in order to better understand the situation, then it probably needs to be brought into the picture. Just be careful not to bring things into the conversation that are just going to add another layer of issues.

Women, stereotypically, tend to explain themselves by making emotional associations. They see the connections between how this makes them feel, and how that overlaps with how this other thing makes them feel. And they try to bring all of those connections into the conversation thinking that it is adding depth and relevance to what they are trying to say. Yet, for the man, who is more compartmentalized, he is likely to get easily overwhelmed by all of the additional threads his partner is trying to add. It *isn't* helping him understand her issue. He's now going to start debating the validity of the associations she's making, getting things even further off-track.

The same holds true for partners who like to monologue. They spend too much time talking without taking time to give their partner opportunities to interact. They need to learn to talk in *pieces* of information, making sure the partner is still "with them" as they go, rather than trying to give the *whole* story in one big chunk and losing their audience in the process.

If, historically, there is great difficulty with staying on task with issues, you might want to consider starting to write the initial issue down on a sheet of paper. Then check it from time to time during the conversation to make sure you're sticking with the original topic.

When a side issue is brought up, ask your partner "Is that issue important enough that we need to address it as well?" Often times, if the other person really thinks about it, he will realize it really wasn't something else he wanted to get into. It was just that the one issue set off others.

If something else is brought up that *is* important and needs to be discussed, write it down as well and come back to it *after* you've dealt with what's first on the list. The practice of staying focused like this helps with learning awareness of your *own* communication style and how you contribute to your own frustration by getting off the subject.

* * *

Sometimes there is no "goal" to a conversation other than to vent. Now that one partner's essentially "burned the house down" with an emotional outburst, he's satisfied because he got the emotional release he sought. But, often, there's a cost to doing this.

There are many cultural stereotypes (Italian, Greek, etc.) where venting is routinely practiced in the family. Because someone was raised in such a home where emotions would openly flare and subside, they learned not to take it personal. It's just what you did. Losing your temper wouldn't impact anyone's security because no one took it to heart. They knew it was just an outburst, and once the outburst was over the wave would pass.

Yet we typically don't choose partners who come from the same kind of family that we grew up in. And, so, if we have this inherited practice to just openly vent without any filter attached to what comes out, it will likely have a negative impact on our partner. It *will* do damage and effect the security of the relationship.

Realistically, we are going to have to learn how to manage our words better, rather than expect our partners to just learn not to take it too seriously when it happens. What we see as "just venting", for the partner, can be closer to being a deal-breaker if it shows no respect to whom it is being said. It will be viewed as a Child throwing a tantrum.

* * *

Reactive couples have many bad habits in their communication. They just can't help but throw another barb into the conversation. One more put-down. One more jab. One more complaint.

They've developed this punishing behavior with each other that is totally purposeless other than to hurt, or to make the partner feel "less than". And it is in total contradiction with any goal they may have to reach a resolution.

You can see them actually reach a resolution, but then have to throw some last comment in that totally undermines the progress they just made.

"So we're agreed then?" he asks.

"Yes," she says. "Let's just hope you can follow through this time."

Why?! What was the point of that? She just undermined his motivation to make it work. Maybe there's a history of him not following through, so she feels justified in saying this, but her actually saying it *is not helpful*. She is now sabotaging their progress.

At some point such people have to take ownership for their bad habits, and stop it, if they are going to regain control over their communication. Many people do it and don't even recognize that they're doing it because it's in a blind spot. Which is why they have to become more conscious of it in order to get control of it.

* * *

Sometimes it is difficult to remain goal-focused because you are feeling so emotionally overwhelmed by the content that you can't adequately explain yourself or reason things through. At such a time, finding a resolution may not be possible but it doesn't mean you shouldn't approach your partner at all.

The goal in such a situation may be to simply educate your partner about what you're going through and maybe some of the reasons why, so that he doesn't misinterpret your behavior in the meantime. Further, a goal may be to express to him what you need from him while you're going through whatever it is you're wrestling with, even if all you're asking for is some space to sort things out. That way he's not "in the dark" and having to resort to guesswork.

Rule #13. Exercise loving accountability. Avoid value judgments.

A *value judgment* is when we are making a judgment about someone else's character (the kind of person we think he is).

Words that would commonly express such a judgment might be "lazy, slob, selfish, childish, evil, sick, perverted", etc. And, of course, the majority of curse words have all sorts of weighted judgments built into them if they're directed at us. We may not say these judgments out loud but, often, when we see another's negative behavior, we automatically attach a judgment to his actions.

Looking back at Janet and Jim, at the start of their conversation they did a fairly decent job of avoiding any *stated* value judgments. Usually, at this point in a relationship, however, even though the statements may not be *openly* stated, they are often being *implied*. For instance, Janet says "I feel like you're just using your work as an excuse to not have to deal with the rest of us". Jim may automatically interpret this in his head as, "She's saying I'm selfish and don't care about my own family." If Jim doesn't communicate his inner dialogue to Janet with a question ("So are you saying I'm selfish and don't care about any of you?"), then things can get heated pretty quickly without any surface reason for why offense is so intense.

When Jim accidentally mentions "mother", there are obviously all sorts of negative judgments that Janet has with this, though Jim stated none. But you can't avoid every implied judgment. You can't control how your partner is going to read into everything you say. But you *can* work at clarifying his interpretation.

It's interesting to note that, at this point in Jim and Janet's relationship, when things *do* get close to character judgments, the couple retreats. They still have some sense of boundaries as to what's "going too far" and, when that line is about to be crossed, they back off (or at least Jim does). However, for some couples, the character attacks start before the third or fourth sentence is said.

It is difficult enough to work on issues when you are just focusing on specific behaviors that need changing, but when you take it to the level of a judgment, how can you work out compromises around that?

"She said I'm 'a piece of trash'. So what's to work out? Does she want to live with trash? If that's how she sees me, then why is she still here? And why would I want to continue to stay?"

Judgments are not only an attack on the character of a person, they also undermine the core of the relationship (which is supposed to be based on trust, acceptance and commitment). If I am making a negative judgment about my partner's values or character, *I am rejecting the person that he is*. That creates a dilemma for the relationship since how can I continue to have a relationship with you if I've just told you I don't even like who you are?

No relationship can handle character rejection for very long. When a relationship is no longer working well, it has to be able to fall back on the friendship to catch its breath, because the friendship still provides for some degree of acceptance. If the rejection runs that deep, to the point that there is no longer even a friendship, then the relationship is in dire straits.

*   *   *

People tend to jump to conclusions and judge their partners based on *pieces* of information before they actually understand the *circumstances* behind what was said or done, often missing a vital piece of the picture. Take this court scenario:

- a man is in court for the shooting of a clerk in a department store
- witnesses testify they saw it happen
- the man accused of doing the shooting has admitted to it

On the surface, this sounds like an open-and-shut case. Are you already forming a judgment about this man and what might have happened? But let me add a few more facts first.

- the shooter has no criminal history
- the clerk is in the hospital but he'll live (the shot injured his shoulder but it will heal)
- the shooting occurred in the sporting goods section of the department store

Is your picture changing yet? Okay, let's add some *circumstances*.

- The "shooter" was in the store looking at guns in the sporting goods section.

- The clerk was giving the man pointers on cleaning and loading a gun.

- The gun was not supposed to be loaded.

- The shooter was not intentionally aiming the gun at the clerk when it went off.

- The court hearing was around who was negligent in this situation.

Do you see the shifting that occurred in how you would naturally perceive this case based on simply the surface facts versus the circumstances? Often, when we judge our partner, we do not take the time to discover the circumstances around what's going on. We simply judge based on the surface information.

If he is acting upset towards us, do we take the time to explore what's going on first, or just jump to a quick conclusion that he is unfairly rejecting us and, therefore, "cruel, mean, evil"? There are countless possibilities as to our partner's motives, but we tend to reach out and draw a quick conclusion. If we do that often enough, over time, the message that we are giving is that we automatically assume the worst about him (that we don't trust him, that we don't give him the benefit of the doubt). And then he starts to form his own judgments of us for our quick assumptions of him.

* * *

Though God may look at all sin as the same, it's important in our relationships that we separate the big from the small. Obviously, if we treat a moment's harsh word the same as an infidelity we have lost perspective.

In addressing each other's mistakes, we all need to learn the best paths to exercising loving accountability. Some partners will respond to *any* criticism of their behavior as depriving them of their freedom because they feel that demands are being made of them. Others view accountability as simply being responsible to the relationship, and an opportunity to demonstrate the strength of their love by respecting the partners' request for change.

Many times we get a negative response from our partners when we are approaching accountability because we are doing it in an overly punishing or judgmental way. We may even be using the right words, but our tone and expression can be conveying many other contradictory messages that aren't being said.

There are two terms I want to use that will shed better light on the distinctions I'm trying to make between being accountable and being judgmental. *Conviction* is when my accuser (whether it be myself, circumstances, or someone else) is pointing out my mistakes in such a way that I am able to hear it, respond to it, and be motivated to make the necessary changes so that the mistake will not continue to occur. Conviction is a *positive* thing because it *inspires* change. If I feel convicted of something in a relationship, then *I'm* the one who has accepted my own guilt at having done something that's harmful. And *the response to a feeling of conviction is a desire to correct the error, setting the wrong to right.*

Condemnation is when my accuser (whether myself, circumstances, or an individual) is pointing out my mistakes in such a way that I am overwhelmed with feelings of judgment or rejection. While I may be able to hear it and, on some level, recognize the truth of it, it is unlikely that I will know how to respond to it because of all the emotions it is setting off in me. I am being presented such a negative picture of myself that it is doubtful that my motivation will be in a positive direction for change. In some individuals, where condemnation has become a regular part of their lives, ultimately they come to accept themselves as "bad" people, and, as a result, lose any motivation to try to do better.

Try to think in terms of conviction as being equivalent to *accountability*, and condemnation as equivalent to being *judgmental*. The Holy Spirit *convicts* us of our sin. Condemnation is a *corrupted* form of conviction.

Accountability is a part of any healthy relationship where a commitment to respecting the relationship has been made. When things are happening that are a threat to the relationship's present or future, accountability comes into play. If my partner, knowingly or unknowingly, is doing something that is harming the foundation of trust or respect of the relationship, I am responsibly accepting my part of the relationship by approaching him about it, just as I would hope he would do the same with me. I need to do this in a way that conveys respect and love, even if it's damaged respect and love, separating the sin from the sinner.

Accountability is also where I or my partner have promised to do something and failed to follow through on it. We are gently reminding each other of the commitments that we have made.

Holding someone accountable is usually done by:

- focusing on the problem *choices* and *behaviors*, not the person's character
- staying focused on expressing the unmet needs, not giving in to anger or attempting to punish
- not yelling
- being specific and not using overgeneralizations (example: "always/never")
- finding strategies and solutions for change, which also include any way *you* can assist the change
- attaining a commitment and specific plan for follow through
- sharing the dilemma that's created when they fail to follow through

If you have difficulty knowing the difference between accountability and judging in how you communicate, ask for feedback.

"How do I come across to you when I have an issue? Do you feel like I judge you?"

"How do you prefer that I approach you in terms of accountability?"

"How can I talk to you about this without shutting you down?"

"If how I'm approaching you is pushing you away, how can I approach you in a way that doesn't, yet also addresses my concern?"

Accountability is applied by both partners, so it is a mutual struggle to find the best approach for each. What works best for you, might not work well for your partner.

Rule #14. Approach the conversation with options, not ultimatums.

Making judgments automatically sets the stage for *ultimatums* to occur, but I strongly suggest you *don't use ultimatums unless you're ready to act on them*. If someone continually threatens to leave a relationship but keeps backing down and staying, ultimately he loses any respect from his partner because of the false threats and seeming attempts at manipulation. If you're not really going to go, then you shouldn't make the threat in the first place. There's better ways of letting your partner know you're upset.

You may be trying to attach a priority to the issue for your partner, letting him know that it's a deal-breaker for the relationship if the problem continues, but you should be trying to deliver this as information, not a threat.

I know very few people who respond well to ultimatums because it comes off as an attempt to control without compromise, and has a degree of rejection automatically built into it.

By staying with options and potential solutions, we are keeping our partners focused on their *freedom and choice*. Ultimatums are about *forcing* a choice.

When Janet starts to react with, "Why don't you marry someone more like her", she's getting close to an ultimatum. The fact that separation has been brought up in the past indicates that possibly there have been ultimatums used before. Both are focused on their own personal dilemma, rather than options to make the difficult realities easier, even if that means just accepting the fact that the workload at present is very stressful for *both* of them.

* * *

At the same time, for some issues there is no compromise and an ultimatum *is* required. These are the situations where the behavior is either self-destructive or destructive to the relationship to the degree that there can be no further toleration. For instance, I am not suggesting that you compromise around such a thing as an affair. I've seen some relationships where the "compromise" for someone staying in the marriage was that, unbelievably, a spouse got to keep his mistress on the side. This was incredibly degrading to his partner and an insult to the marriage. Such a situation would call for an ultimatum: choose the mistress or choose the marriage, but you can't have both.

Rule #15. Try to treat emotionally-weighted words as information rather than attacks.

In the same way that being too emotionally distant can be a problem in a relationship, it can also be a problem to be so close that we've now fallen "under the radar" (so close we can no longer see ourselves or our partner clearly). We need to be emotionally available to our partners, but we also need to keep enough perspective that we don't take everything too personally. If friends disappoint us, we may be hurt but we can often move past it because of any number of reasons:

- it might have been a mistake
- we know they care
- they have so many other good qualities
- it was an isolated event
- it's their issue, not ours

We can separate that event or statement that was hurtful because our relationship boundaries are intact, our filters in place. For people who have poor boundaries or fragile self-esteem, almost everything becomes personal. Even something that a stranger did or said to them is difficult to separate from who they are ("What is it about me that made them say that? Why do they not like me?").

In a romantic relationship, where we have supposedly made ourselves vulnerable to this other person, we are automatically more sensitive to any signs of rejection. We can't minimize that they wouldn't have done or said such a thing if they knew who we really were because, supposedly, they *do* know. So we have to turn to other defenses, most of them being rather primitive. If I'm being rejected, then I reject back! So there!

For those who are too emotionally *close* to a problem, they need to gain enough emotional distance from the problem so that they can get a better perspective on it.

For those who are emotionally too *distant*, they need to learn how to lower their emotional walls, and empathize more effectively.

For the purposes of Rule #15, we're going to be focusing on emotionally distancing yourself from the problem in order to gain perspective.

*   *   *

In terms of visual imagery, consider the simple image of water rolling off of a duck's back. Ducks' feathers secrete a type of oil that prevents water from soaking in, so instead it rolls off. The negative words that your partner occasionally aims at you is the dirty water and your job is to let it roll right over and off of you rather than to let it sink in, staying focused on what's going on *beyond* all those words.

Reactive words are only the surface layer and can often be very misleading from the actual hurt going on underneath. Your concern is with what's *creating* those words, and how to get to it, *not what's actually being said.*

If I can recognize that my partner's being reactive, or that I must have just stepped on one of his emotional wounds[13], then it should be easier for me to not take whatever happens personally because I understand that, at that point, it's no longer really about me. It's the wound talking, or maybe the wounded child striking back. I need to accept that when someone gets that upset they don't mean half of what they actually say.

Your image doesn't have to be a duck. It can be whatever represents the same thing to you: an island, a calm pool, an armored tank, whatever. The idea is to choose something that is protected but not so closed off that you are no longer connected to the conversation. Then your personal gauge becomes, "Am I still this calm pool or am I allowing myself to get stirred up?"

If you're getting stirred up, then you need to focus on whatever you need to do to calm yourself down. If you *can't* get calmed down then you don't need to be participating in the conversation any further. Take a healthy exit. Excuse yourself or let your partner know that you're too upset to try to get any further with the issue at the moment.

*   *   *

We don't get upset by events, or what people do or say to us. We get upset because of what we tell ourselves about those things.

Jim coming home late is a neutral event, just a fact. Janet doesn't get upset about Jim coming home late. She gets upset because of the things she tells herself about him coming home late. She makes the mental leap from "He's late again" to "I can't stand it when he does that" to "Once again his job's more important than us" to "I don't know how much longer I can put up with this".

While we can't altogether "shut off" our self-talk, we *can* work on replacing it with statements that are not so disastrous or destructive. Of course, we have to become aware first of what our self-talk says.

---

[13]   Harville Hendrix "Getting the Love You Want."

I'm not suggesting you lie to yourself by trying to pretend that something's okay when it's not. But, in situations where the emotion is outweighing the actual event, you need to be able to talk yourself through it. Just as when your partner's reaction is over-the-top, your internal questions to you need to be, "Where's this coming from?", "Is this possibly a misunderstanding?", "Why is this bothering me (or him) so much?"

By asking ourselves questions that help us think things through, we're applying the same logic to why we ask our partners questions: to move them to thinking rather than lost in their emotion.

If our heads are full of thought distortions fueled by our emotional logic, we have to be able to doubt our own conclusions knowing that we tend to gravitate towards distortions when we're upset. You need to have some reality-based thoughts that effectively counter your own distortions to help keep you grounded.[14]

*   *   *

The majority of emotional arguments in a relationship revolve around loss of perspective. As a counselor, what I am constantly doing is trying to help move couples back to a larger perspective of what's going on with them in the moment. That larger picture restores a sense of control over what's going on, and gives the couple a better sense of what they need to do to make it work. Having stepped back from the intensity of the situation, they can start to see other options than just continuing to react.

---

[14] David Burns' "Intimate Connections" is a good resource for exploring, and correcting, relationally distorted thinking.

That is where knowing some of the tools (questions, benefit of the doubt, healthy exits, validation, 2-part resolution) comes into play. Because the couple knows that introducing these tools can have a positive impact, they are stepping back for a moment to consider what tools they might be overlooking, and start re-introducing some of them.

Rule #16. Remain vulnerable.

Being willing to be wrong is about being able to acknowledge *fault*. Being willing to be *vulnerable* refers to a general *attitude* towards your partner.

It goes against our nature to put ourselves in situations where we know pain is likely. Our own instinct for survival wants to protect ourselves from possible pain and death. Yet, the only way that we can have a relationship where we have achieved the closeness that we desire is to be willing to show our flaws and trust that our partner will respect that confidence, knowing there will be times when those ideals aren't met.

Because we are all initially children in relationships, it takes time to learn how to respect each others' flaws. In school, flaws are usually made fun of by our peers, so we hide them. As adults, we have learned to put on different fronts of "having it all together" both to impress and to protect us from criticism. But, ultimately, we cannot hold a double standard, demanding honesty and vulnerability from our partners yet being unwilling to give it in return.

The defenses that we use to survive in the world around us will actually stand in the way of an emotionally intimate relationship if we also use them at home. We have to redefine our definitions of weakness and strength. To let down those emotional walls with our partner takes strength. To be vulnerable with our partner takes courage. To show our hurt and tears is an act of trust. To admit fault and a need for personal improvement is being willing to model true Adult behavior. To express our need is acknowledging to our partner that there are things we rely on him for, part of what makes him feel significant. These are all things that need to be supported and rewarded when they occur.

Even in the animal world, where instinct is very much a natural part, there are models for what I would suggest. Let me call on all the dog lovers out there. Have you ever seen two dogs fighting? It may be play-fighting or not. The dogs will growl at each other, bark, maybe pace around each other looking for an opening. Often, they're trying to establish dominance, which makes it completely surprising that, at some point in the middle of this struggle, one of the dogs will inevitably roll over on its back, exposing its most vulnerable areas - the throat and belly. Why would it do that? It knows it's being attacked, yet it's intentionally making itself vulnerable to be hurt.

Well, if you continue to watch, the next odd thing that will usually happen is that the attacking dog will start to back off! It doesn't go for the jugular when it so easily could. Why? Because, *by being vulnerable, the prostrate dog has established that it is not a threat.*

Now, I'm not saying that we're animals. I'm not calling you a dog. I'm not saying that you should roll over on your back in the middle of an argument (though that can defuse things pretty quickly). I'm trying to point out the simple fact that being vulnerable removes you from the position of being perceived as the enemy. And *it sets an example for your partner and the relationship that you're willing to risk.*

Not only are you changing the attack mode of the conversation, you're putting it on a different level, a much more mature one. While it is often the *weaker* animal in nature that rolls over, with humans it's usually the person who has more emotional discipline that is able to do so.

By being vulnerable you aren't acknowledging your partner's dominance over you. He hasn't "won" anything. You're showing the greater insight and self-control by being able to defuse the situation by stepping out of the fight.

Now, when that dog first rolled over, the dog left standing may still keep barking for awhile. It may feint and bluff to see if the dog will stay on its back or start to attack again. It may not automatically just assume that the threat is gone. If you suddenly move to a position of vulnerability in your conversation, your partner may not initially trust that. He may suspect a manipulation, or a trap. He may try to test it. But if you remain consistent and can maintain that stance, you'll prove your sincerity.

What will often happen in arguments when one person attempts to remain vulnerable, if the partner does not initially respect this and continues to attack, then the vulnerable one will give up their vulnerable stance and jump back into attack mode as well. *Our choosing to remain vulnerable cannot be dependent on our partner's willingness to be vulnerable in return.*

It is important to note that all dogs are not alike, and there *are* some sick puppies out there. There are those dogs that are cruel at heart that will go in for the kill. And there are people out there that will take advantage of your vulnerability and step all over it. But that's useful information too. If this is a pattern, it potentially tells you something about your partner's character that they are willing to continue to attack someone who has chosen to be defenseless.

We need to examine how we, intentionally or unintentionally, sabotage the vulnerability that we desire from each other. To remain open enough to say "I don't know the answer...," "I'm afraid that...", or "I need..." can invite undeserved criticism or ridicule. Because we are often brought up to value strength and despise weakness, we often step on perceived acts of weakness in our partners when they, in reality, may have been taking a step of faith in being vulnerable with us by sharing something very personal.

In the example with Jim and Janet, both were sharing valuable information about their perspectives and needs. Both had good points to make about the realities of their situation. The job situation itself was a valid problem. The job *did* make heavy demands on Jim, and Janet was also feeling overworked. It was a difficult situation. The problem didn't have to be one of selfish motivations on either side. Both were putting a lot of work into maintaining the home through maintaining their jobs.

It didn't have to be turned into a battleground by attributing the causes of the problem to selfish motivations.

*　*　*

We have to have the freedom in relationships to be able to admit our *need*. Some people cringe at the very word. When I use that word I don't mean being an emotional leech that clings and smothers. Being able to express your needs in a relationship is being willing to expose at least a small degree of dependency to your partner. You *do* need acceptance, to feel valued, loved and trusted, and you do need help to make the relationship work. If you cannot humble yourself in order to express these needs, chances are, if they're not being met, they're not going to be met.

The word "humble" is appropriate since often our avoidance of being vulnerable, aside from our instinct at self-protection, has to do with *pride*. Pride can say, "I'm not the one who's in the wrong here", or "I don't need any help". Yet there's great validity in the proverb "Pride comes before the fall." Pride stands in the way of a relationship. It makes compromise extremely difficult. Pride pushes us into a rigid position, at a time when flexibility is what's needed most.

My frustration with much of couple's counseling is that people often don't come for help until it's almost too late, often due to their pride (like the stereotypical male who won't stop and ask for directions until he's utterly lost). On occasion I will meet incredibly wise and foresighted people who recognize that things are moving in a dangerous direction and they want to prevent a possible crisis by seeking help now rather than later. It's so much easier to intervene at that stage rather than when things have gotten so emotionally entangled that the only way to achieve safety and perspective is through physical distance.

*　*　*

Being vulnerable is a two-way street. It's us being willing to be vulnerable with our partners, and welcoming them to do the same with us. It would obviously be unfair to share our fears, concerns, and needs with our partners, yet be rejecting of them when they attempt to do the same. Also, it would unbalance the relationship to welcome our partners' disclosures, yet never open up and trust them with anything personal of ourselves.

Rule #17. Don't negatively compare your partner to others.

Often during arguments there will be this temptation to compare a partner to someone who is modeling better behavior (be it friend, family or foe). Yet, longstanding relationships with friends and relatives have been undermined this way, though that was not typically the motive for the initial comparison. Whatever the intention, making comparisons gives the impression that you are looking at somebody else more desirably than your own partner, which is a problem for the relationship, especially if this is a pattern.

Jim wasn't making comparisons, but Janet automatically heard one when he brought up her acting like his mother. He didn't literally mean *his* mother. He was referring to her attempt at parenting him through the use of guilt. This might have indicated a deeper insecurity on Janet's part, being sensitive to comparisons, or maybe Jim's mother had been an issue for them in the past.

Of course, you're put in a bind if your partner *asks* you for comparisons ("Am I like that?"). While this may be a simple opportunity for a compliment, assurance or education, now it's possibly catering to their habit of comparing. And it's a potential trap in the same way as, "Honey, do I look fat in this?" is.

If you know your partner well enough that you know they are simply seeking information and can use the honest feedback in a helpful way, then this might not be a problem. But if their self-esteem is poor and they are constantly feeling "less than" through their comparisons, then it's probably not helpful to participate in the comparison game. You can still provide assurance or be complimentary without having to cooperate with continued comparisons.

Rule #18. "Never" and "always" need to be stricken from the couple's vocabulary.

The words "never" and "always" fall into the category of "black-and-white thinking" or "all-or-nothing thinking". They are extremes.

"You *never* help me clean up around here."

"You *always* have to have the last word."

Well, sorry, but, for a relationship, there is no such thing as those two words.

It may feel to you like it's never or always. But it is likely that now and then there is the occasional success. You may feel that, in comparison, the desired behavior hardly ever happens, but you're not allowing credit for it when it does. And when a relationship's at the point where everything is focused around things going wrong, giving credit for what's going right becomes vitally important.

Better to put things in terms of "I appreciate the times where you have gone out of your way to help, but I still need more of a consistent effort with cleaning things up." It goes back to Rule #6 ("Balance the negative with the positive"). If your partner is feeling like they have been "helping clean things up", but not in a way that is significant to you, you may need to better define what you mean by "cleaning things up". It may be a simple matter of two different definitions that is confusing things, and if they had a more exact idea of what you meant you might see better results.

Using "never" and "always" in an argument comes off as a blatant exaggeration. It puts you in an extreme light for using that terminology - that you're blind to your partner's attempts to help or change. It also undermines the partner's motivation if he feels he doesn't get any recognition for the times he *has* tried.

We're not just trying to be careful to use more accurate words in our conversations, but also in our own minds. Even though I may not be saying "always" and "never" openly to my partner, if my *internal* dialogue is constantly hanging onto those distortions, then I'm still viewing the situation unfairly.

Jim and Janet's conversation didn't involve "always" and "never". There was still enough conscious control that words like "I feel like", allowing for personal perspective, and "sometimes", a healthy qualifier, were still being used. But you could also see how it was getting close to Janet feeling like Jim was at the office "*all* of the time", and her having to handle "*all* of the work" at home.

You may feel that minding your wording is a petty thing, but it can make a very big difference. You may say, "He knows I don't really mean always or never." But I've rarely seen a couple that was so laid-back that there wasn't an underlying negative impact from the regular use of those words.

Rule #19. Make requests, not demands.

As I mentioned earlier, personal boundaries (what keeps me able to see my partner as separate and "other" from me) deteriorate with familiarity. In times of stress, the filters we use to monitor our own behavior are likely to get dropped. In such times, it's important that you don't forget the simplest methods for showing respect to your partner, such as making requests, not demands.

Since it wouldn't be healthy to be the Parent dictating over your partner, or the Child making pouty demands, you're trying to maintain an attitude of freedom and choice in the relationship, rather than turning it into being all about obligation, responsibility and a long list of "to-do's". You're *asking* him for compliance with certain things, trusting that if he cares, he is taking your request into account. *It doesn't mean that if he loves you, he'll do everything you ask.*

It also doesn't mean that you assume he heard you the first time and is ignoring your request, if you're not seeing results. There's no harm in following up a request with seeking further information, or providing a reminder. And there's no harm in doing some problem-solving with your partner if there are things that are getting in the way of satisfying that request.

Jim and Janet's conversation didn't offer any solutions, so it was unclear if "requests versus demands" was a problem for them. The only demand of note was Janet forbidding Jim to compare her to his mother, which she could have done in the form of a request. ("Jim, I'd really appreciate it if you didn't bring your mother into this, or make those kinds of comparisons.")

The obvious dilemma that comes with making requests is when the request is understood but still being refused. At that point it comes back to is this a preference for you, or a need? If it's a preference, you may simply have to learn to let this particular request go if there's no compromise that can be worked out. If it's a core need, then accountability comes into play, and the partner needs to be approached in a considerate way that directly addresses his accountability to the relationship.

Especially when trying to work out resolutions to issues, there's fine wording involved in trying to avoid being demanding. "I need more help around the home", even though said as a statement rather than a request, accurately identifies the need without coming across as "You'd better start helping more", which is a threat.

Ideally, you are working toward phrasing things in terms of questions, "Could you please find more time to help me out around the house?" This may sound painfully nice, but it is also choosing to address your partner with humility and respect, something you're wanting in return. You may feel their behavior doesn't deserve either, but to put things on a demand level before it has really reached a point where accountability needs to be brought into it, is choosing to turn things into a hostile power struggle.

Some people will automatically feel like they have the right to make demands because this is, after all, *their* partner. But even just saying it in those terms makes it obvious that they are looking at their partner in terms of property, which they aren't. This is another separate human being with feelings, thoughts, needs and desires of their own. They aren't yours to order around. They are yours to express your needs to, but not yours to control.

While couples often work hard to keep the relationship from getting to a crisis point, sometimes they need to embrace the crisis rather than run from it. The discomfort of a crisis often gives us the motivation to make the necessary changes. Avoiding getting to a crisis delays that change. If you can be proactive and do something to reduce any need for that crisis to ever occur, that's wonderful. But for those who just live in toleration and misery rather than approach change, a crisis is usually what has to occur to get things moving again.

Keep in mind that the problems of the relationship tend to expose the weaknesses of *each* individual in the relationship (the things they need to get better at). The positive piece of any crisis is that, if the relationship is to improve, it will usually mean that each person in the relationship changes in a *necessary* way.

Discussion Questions:

1. **Of the processing "rules", which ones do you have the most difficulty with?** Why?

2. **How are you going to put the rules that are most often ignored on such a conscious level that they are actually being applied when issues are being discussed?**

Chapter 8
Resolving the Issue

"Do not let the sun go down while you are
still angry..." (Ephesians 4:26)

The final stage of conflict resolution is actually *resolving* the issue, if validation wasn't enough. This is where you and your partner are taking the time to arrive at a solution, or possible solutions, that best meet *both* sides' needs.

Often when people are looking for solutions, they are trying to identify "the one right answer" to the problem. Well, in the same way that there is usually not just one thing that caused the problem, there is usually more than one solution.

The initial act of seeking resolution strategies is brainstorming *possible* solutions. People can get so overwhelmed with trying to seek for something deep and immediately impacting, when the initial part of the process of brainstorming is just getting into problem-solving mode. *Any* possibilities at the start, no matter how ridiculous, are at least getting the process rolling.

A sense of humor, if not distracting from the goal, is almost always helpful in keeping perspective while seeking an answer.

The solutions that don't work might need to be tossed aside, but sometimes they may just need to be fine-tuned. Sometimes they didn't work before because they weren't tried for long enough, or weren't attempted consistently.

Nancy and Nate had been married for about 7 years. The first two years of their marriage seemed to go pretty well while riding on the momentum of their infatuation for each other. During the fourth year, Nate had had a brief "fling" with a girl from work who is now no longer working with his agency. Several people from his office had gone to a workshop in a neighboring city and had spent the night. Apparently Nate and the girl in question had been drinking and things went too far. Nate had confessed the one-night affair to Nancy. They had separated for a month and then got back together, neither wanting to lose the relationship over one foolish night. There had been no further infidelities. They talk about having kids but wisely want to work through their current issues before bringing children into the picture. Neither relates their current issues as involving the affair.

They've been in counseling for a couple sessions and are at the point where they're trying to work out actual strategies to put their relationship back in balance since both feel things have gotten off track.

Nancy is explaining the current impasse. She is very matter-of-fact. "We've been taking the time to sit down at least once a week and that seems to be helping to keep things from getting overwhelming, but we're having problems with agreeing on specific solutions.

"You'd suggested we start putting some priority on spending more time together just having fun, rather than talking about the problems all the time. So we started to talk about the things that we could do together and, while we came up with a couple things, there wasn't anything on the list that we both liked to do."

"Nancy's really into her craft stuff, and I'm not," said Nate, joining in. "I like to watch my sports games or actually go see a game, and she could care less. We used to go to games back when we were dating but I guess she just went because I wanted to."

Nancy nods. "That's true. I really don't have the patience for that kind of thing anymore. We made a list of movies that are out, but we couldn't find one we both liked. He likes action and comedy, while I like dramas and romance. We both like movies, we have that in common, but not the same ones."

"So we didn't get anywhere on that one this week," added Nate.

Rule #20. Some of the best solutions are the old ones. In seeking solutions don't try to reinvent the wheel.

One of the easiest ways to find possible solutions for the present is to think back on your past history as a couple and identify those things that you have done in the past in similar situations that worked. Often, couples were doing positive things during the dating period because the relationship took priority and there were fewer distractions. Or the marriage had some initial golden years before falling into a routine. Now that the focus has drifted to other demands, the couple has stopped doing those positive things. So now they need to think back and pull some of those activities or habits back into the present. And it can simply start with the question, "What did we used to do? When we had more success with this, what was it that we were doing different?"

The current issue may not be relevant to any prior history, but the starting place is always to go back to old successes first, for guidance in the present.

Nancy and Nate's history was being labeled as outdated. They had come to a point where neither was interested in the things that they used to do, at least not in continuing to do them together. What had changed was that they were no longer doing things simply because the other person was doing them. It was now about how interested they themselves were with the activity. But does that mean you should *only* do things together that are just as much fun for both? Ideally, it would be nice if those activities existed. But you need to be careful that the relationship isn't gradually becoming about self, rather than "us", which leads to the roommate relationship. If healthy love continues to be a motivator for the relationship, then sometimes a shared activity is done just because it's shared. For example, how some couples will find fun ways to share in getting the chores done, or a home project. The chore or the project itself is secondary.

What Nate and Nancy needed to bring back from the past was engaging in mutual activities just for the sake of being present with the other. Having fun not because of what they were doing, but because they were doing it together.

*   *   *

Solutions don't have to be restricted to the history of your current relationship. Other prior relationships provide keys to success as well, even relationships that you weren't in yourself but witnessed in others.

The important part here is to be very careful about making continuous comparisons (Rule #17). Sometimes one person will have had a fairly healthy childhood and he keeps using that as the model for the relationship. However, the partner has come to where she has started to resent the other's parents, because they are constantly being used as the example of what to do. While they may actually be a good model, overusing them as a verbal reference has created a sore spot. It would be better for further suggestions to not include the source.

You also have to be careful that you not use any one relationship as the sole template that dictates the way your relationship should be. Your relationship is *your* relationship, not anyone else's. It needs to be a combination of what works for both of you, and not an exact replication of somebody else's life.

Especially if you are looking at prior romantic relationships, it is *not* suggested you keep telling your partner "Well, my ex and I used to do this, and that really seemed to work…" You don't want to be giving an unspoken message that another romantic relationship was better than your current one.

This is just using discretion, being tactful with what you say, attaching a healthy filter. It's the same kind of filter you use when you're editing your anger, still expressing the hurt but weeding out what would be destructive.

Rule #21. If you have already given some thought to possible solutions before you "come to the table" with the issue, it will move the process more quickly to a solution.

Rule #7 suggested you consider your part of the problem first before discussing an issue. Rule #21 is the follow-up to this, with thinking through *possible solutions* ahead of time. It assumes you've already decided that you're looking for more than just an apology, or a listening ear, and you need some actual changes made.

You might think that because you're coming with solutions *before* the discussion that this rule should be under "identifying the problem". However, you still will often need to go through the steps of identifying, validating, and discussing the issue, before you start to unload the options you've thought of.

Thinking of it in terms of the strategies that are used in business, typically, most bosses are not inspired to change after being given a list of the things that are wrong with how they manage things. They are usually much more responsive to suggestions on how things can be improved when it is obvious that the changes will benefit the company. While a couple is not a business, they are both based around relationships. And, usually, real people are more open to a solution-focused approach than problem-oriented.

*   *   *

While it is fine to voice your *preferences* for a particular solution, the idea in approaching resolution is not coming into it with "the" solution where it's simply a matter of you dictating what's going to happen.

Your solutions are *suggestions* to be discussed, examined and worked through. Your partner may have some solutions of his own.

If none of the solutions are good enough, you don't just give up and walk away. You take one or two of the ones that have the most promise and fine-tune them until you have something that may be a bit of a sacrifice for both, but will ultimately meet each other's needs.

In Nancy and Nate's case, they may have actually spent the time thinking about what to do together prior to discussing it. Their mistake was not in preparation, but with their focus. They focused on what *wouldn't* work rather than on what *would*. In other words, they continued to focus on the differences. They should have been focused on finding common ground, and, if none could be found, creating it.

Rule #22. Solutions should be tolerable to both sides, not an imbalance of one side constantly "giving in". Try to avoid black-and-white solutions.

Rule #22 has already been stated in many ways in the content of prior rules. However, it also needs to stand on its own. You are trying to avoid developing a pattern in the relationship where one person is usually getting his way and it is creating resentment in the other. You are also trying to avoid thinking in terms of only "his way/her way" since this can turn competitive and doesn't give couples practice with actual compromise.

Nancy and Nate were stuck in thinking of "his way/her way". They couldn't yet think in terms of finding the middle ground where they were sacrificing a little and getting something back. There were the things he wanted to do and the things she wanted to do, and neither showed much interest in the other. And so, the resolution process stopped short with nothing accomplished except for a greater awareness of how far they'd grown apart.

If you are rolling your eyes and saying an exasperated "Fine!" when you agree to something, you probably have not reached a satisfactory resolution. Often couples will give in for the sake of avoiding a hassle but just as much damage can be created in the long run by those who constantly take a backseat in the relationship. They may be doing it out of not wanting to create more conflict or because what their partner wants is more important to them than what they want, but, ultimately, if this is an ongoing pattern, they are practicing having a passive identity in the relationship, where only one voice dominates.

You may be a passive person but the relationship needs *your* voice just as much as your partner's if it is to retain a shared identity.

*   *   *

The most common solutions come down to:

1) *Let whoever has the greatest need in the situation, or the greatest competence, assume responsibility for that particular thing.* For example, someone who wants the clothes folded a particular way becomes responsible for folding the clothes. Or, whoever is the best cook assumes responsibility for the meals.

For those people who have a particular way of doing *everything*, however, this can create a dilemma since obviously they can't assume responsibility for everything. They will have to prioritize and assume responsibility for the things most important to them, and be willing to let the things that fall to the partner be completed in a way that falls slightly short of mirroring their own.

Ideally, the partner who is less "particular" will still give an effort that stretches a little beyond his comfort zone in trying to reach his partner's standards, but it needs to be accepted that the goal of every task is not to perfectly meet that higher standard.

2) *Agree to a compromise, where the standard is set somewhere between the particular expectations.* You want to go shopping for three or four hours while he only wants to go for one, so you agree to two hours if you're going to go together. Or you agree to balance the places you're

going to go to so that each person is getting to go to places they're interested in. Or he only accompanies you for an hour or two, and you do the rest on your own.

One person wants to work on the yard, while the other wants to go to a matinee. So the moviegoer helps out with the yard work to make it possible for both to catch an early movie.

3) *Agree to disagree.* Some issues are not important enough to have to work through to a compromise. Sometimes we get caught up in petty arguments simply because we have the need to be "right", or have our way, and don't let up until someone gives us that recognition or we drive them away. Recognize that it's unrealistic to expect that your partner's opinion has to reflect your own.

It would be unrealistic to expect that your partner should accompany you every time you went to a movie. Or that every time you do yard work, your partner should be there to help. It's okay to do things separately as well as together. The problem is always with the extremes, when *everything* has to be done together, or *everything* is done separately. Or when *everything* has to be done a certain way.

"Agree to disagree" usually comes down to whether the issue is a preference or a need. Preferences don't require agreement. Needs typically require some type of action or some degree of change.

4) *Try both ways.* If it's a his/her impasse, sometimes a nice workaround is to take a few weeks doing it his way, then a few weeks doing it her way and afterwards, with the new information of what it was actually like doing it both ways, they can sometimes have a better discussion and both agree on one particular path.

Rule #23. To forgive does not mean to forget.

We've all heard the phrase "forgive and forget". When I hear this I automatically think of the counter, "He who forgets the past is doomed to repeat it". If we forget the mistakes we, or others, have made, we lose the opportunity to learn from them. And we typically set ourselves up to repeat them.

If we are in denial about a problem, pretending that it doesn't exist, then we will not be taking steps to avoid the problem as we would if we were owning up to it.

In relationships, while it is vital that forgiveness occurs, forgetting is not a part of that process. This does not mean that you badger or punish your partner about the past, or hold a grudge against him. It is quite possible to forgive while not forgetting, and yet not be ruled by the negative feelings associated with the memory.

Part of forgiving is learning to exercise grace in relationships, knowing that in the same way your partner has issues, faults and imperfections, that you too have your own collection.

People will often learn to forgive through learning empathy for the offender. We can see how there was a misunderstanding. We can see how the circumstances of the day were affecting his behavior or thinking. We are able to see how that person's past has led him to be who he is. We can understand the negative influences on his life that may have twisted or damaged his heart. He had a series of bad relationships. He never learned how to share his feelings. And so, through this empathy, we can learn to let go of the pain that that person caused, because we've come to understand it better. We've "normalized" it.

However, *sometimes forgiveness means letting go of something that was wrong no matter which way you view it.*

As Christians, in the same vein as, "judge not lest ye yourselves be judged" there is also **"For if you forgive men when they sin against you, your heavenly Father will also forgive you."** (Matthew 6:14) By hanging on to un-forgiveness, it leads us to sin ourselves by harboring those angry thoughts against others, and distances us from God.

We automatically seem to expect justice or fairness even though our experience in life may be that we seldom get it. If we have been done a wrong it seems only natural that someone should be punished for it.

Yet real life says that wrongs occur on a daily basis and that they often go unaddressed or with punishments that don't come close to fitting the crime. Yet, *if we don't let go of it, at some point the issue becomes our own because the anger that is attached to the wrong begins hurting us, rather than the wrongdoer.* And that anger enters other areas of our lives, feeding into bitterness and negativity. If we don't at some point find ways of exorcising it from our minds and hearts, it will become poisonous to our physical and emotional health as well as to our relationships.

In the situation with Nate and Nancy, you couldn't help but wonder if there was not still some underlying hostility at work because of the affair. It had only been three years ago, and, just because it was no longer discussed or labeled as an issue, did not mean it had actually been resolved. Neither was openly hostile towards the other in sessions. There was a lack of the subtle putdowns and cuts that often continue to go on as backhanded methods of payback. But you had to wonder why there seemed to be this lack of desire or motivation to arrive at specific plans of action. Each had done a good job of establishing his own interests but the relationship had grown apart. Eventually, if the resistance or procrastination continued, they would have to start exploring the reasons for that resistance and find out if forgiveness was still an issue.

*   *   *

It is very difficult to let go of something when we never get the apology that we desire, or the acknowledgment of guilt or fault. If I have learned that a person has wronged me and is unrepentant about it, then I have potentially learned something about that person's character, and I have some decisions to make based on the following:

- How serious is the wrong?
- If it is truly serious is this someone that I am willing to keep in my life, knowing that the wrong is likely to reoccur if he sees no problem with his actions?
- If this is someone that I can't, or won't, remove from my life, how am I going to learn to deal with this, knowing what I know about him? How am I going to adjust my expectations

of him for the future? How am I going to adjust the things I am willing to trust him with?

Relationships are based on *degrees* of trust. It's not as simple as "we trust" or "we don't trust". We learn over time who we can trust with what. So when someone routinely fails us in a particular area, our experience tells us this person is not as safe as we thought. That doesn't mean that he's not safe with *anything*, but it does mean he's not safe in that *specific* way that he proved untrustworthy. It doesn't necessarily mean that we have to totally cut this person out of our lives, but it does mean we need to be realistic about how much we extend our trust again, especially in that particular way.

On the other hand, people will many times avoid forgiveness thinking that if they do forgive they will have to allow this person back into their life, even though they know he's not "safe".[15] But forgiveness does not always mean reconciliation. You can forgive, letting go of the anger, while still respecting the new boundaries that you've drawn between you and him.

When it's our partner that has failed us, regaining trust is often based on consistent evidence of change. But whether there is change or not, the core of the need for forgiving still comes back to what it does to *us* if we don't.

If our partner is unrepentant and essentially refuses accountability for his actions, we still have to weigh out how grievous the wrong is. If it's something he is unwilling to change, yet the behavior is that destructive (to us or the relationship), it brings the future of the relationship into question.

If I have been wronged and my partner *is* repentant, and takes consistent steps to not repeat it, then if I still refuse to forgive him, at some point *I* am now the one working against the relationship.

Yet, you can't *demand* forgiveness of another. And you shouldn't say you forgive someone before you're really ready to.

---

[15] Henry Cloud & John Townsend's "Safe People".

Sometimes forgiveness is a lengthy process that requires letting go of your hurt more than once. Events, conversations, or people will stir the memory of what happened before, and in that moment you may have that old pain overwhelm you again, and have to once again go through the process of letting go. But once you've let go the first time, the path becomes a little more familiar when you have to walk it again.

You have to be realistic that a painful memory will retain its pain. It leaves a scar. When you think back on it and still feel pain, it does not mean that you haven't forgiven. Forgiveness is better measured by whether or not you've been able to move on.

* * *

Forgiving does *not* mean an absence of consequences. Yet we need to understand the distinction between *punishment* versus *consequences*.

Punishment is usually focused on intentional harm or attaching a negative cost in order to reduce the likelihood of an event reoccurring. An example might be when one person has an affair because his partner first cheated on him. So now the punisher has sunk to the same level as the other (or even lower if the initial affair was not intentionally done to hurt). Punishment often involves vindictive behavior: hurting someone because they hurt you. An eye for an eye. But if it wasn't okay for them, then it's not okay for you to do it as payback. Punishment is an easy indicator of a lack of forgiveness.

Consequences would be the damage to the trust that that affair has now created for the relationship. We're not consciously choosing to be hurtful by not trusting, it's just that realistically trust can only be regained over time with actual evidence that it's okay to trust again.

For some, the reason why they engage in punishment is that they feel if the partner doesn't experience visible emotional or physical pain, that the consequences won't be real enough for him, and so the problem will continue to occur. But we are trying to step away from parenting our partner, and move them toward a more Adult role where accountability still applies, but we are no longer engaging in methods that result in even more problems for the relationship.

Rule #24. Try to resolve issues as they occur. However, each person should also retain the right to put off discussing an issue (not indefinitely) until they feel they can handle their part responsibly.

The longer anger or resentment festers, the greater the damage to the relationship. Ideally, it is best to try to resolve your issues when they happen so that they do not accumulate.

Mental health is all about how people do or don't handle their emotional pain. We can't allow our degree of discomfort to decide whether or not we try to work something out.

Whether or not we approach an issue often has to do with the expectations we attach to the likelihood of our success in resolving it. If you haven't had a lot of practice with addressing issues, you need to be realistic that you will need practice. The fact of the matter is that you may not be successful in resolving things the first or the second time out (or maybe even the eighth or the ninth), but, hopefully, from each failed attempt you're learning more about what doesn't work and getting a clearer picture of what does.

* * *

If it is not possible to resolve an issue within the day that it happens, then at least call a truce with a commitment to re-approach later on.

Sometimes just learning *how* to shelve an issue and set aside those feelings temporarily is a skill in itself. The temptation is to continue to throw a verbal barb out here or there, or use your upset with your partner to keep you from doing anything kind or loving until the issue is resolved to your satisfaction (which is punishment). But mismanaging the situation this way can end up creating a new set of issues. What you are trying to learn how to do is set boundaries between an issue that is on hold and everything that is not a part of that issue.

If the relationship is a healthy one, then both a friendship *and* a romantic relationship should exist. This is where the unconditional regard of the friendship comes into play. The romantic relationship may be stressed by the issue at hand, but you should still be able to exercise respect for your partner by stepping back to the "friend" boundary that should still be intact.

The situation with Nate and Nancy was not an openly hostile one. If there was any anger there it was well hidden. They seemed more than willing to shelve the idea of dating for another week. Neither was pressing the issue. If anything, it would have been desirable if there were *more* passion there, which might have inspired them to be more aggressive in pinning down options for a night out.

There are situations that *do* require time for the best resolutions to occur, and some people are not good with quick responses or solutions and need time to sort things out (whether it's to figure out what's really going on with themselves, what a fair solution might be, or even just how to accurately express their own perspective).

Just be sure that the issues aren't put off indefinitely. A few days at most should be enough so that putting things off does not become a recurring tactic to avoid issues. If your partner can see that by giving you the room to cool down, or think things through, he is more likely to get a better outcome, he'll be more patient next time.

For those that insist on an immediate audience upon demand, despite an awareness that their partner's not at a point of readiness, and where it isn't a situation of avoiding the issue, forcing the issue rarely provides a best-fit solution. Instead, it becomes about control and immediate gratification at the possible cost of your partner's respect.

Rule #25. Decisions made from strong emotion are not going to be good decisions.

People often have difficulty distinguishing between what is an emotional thought versus rational thought. Thoughts such as "I can't stand this anymore," "I hate him," "This is impossible," are based in *emotional logic*. They feel like clear thoughts that are directly connected to the situation, but what they actually do is fuel the fire for whatever feelings of upset are already stirring, clouding the issues.

Emotional logic can be either positive or negative. The emotional thought can be just as much "I love her" and still have little root in reality because the person may be experiencing infatuation. The point is that *the stronger the emotion the further removed from reality our judgment can become.*

Part of what makes being human so enjoyable is the range of possible emotions we can experience. Emotions are what add a level of quality or depth to our lives that would not be there were we solely rational individuals. But *while feelings can be useful guides, they tend to be poor decision makers.* (Sorry, all you romantics out there.)

Think of the people who got married a day, a week or a month after they met. Think of those folks who have a major blowout and they instantly separate, only to get back together when the dust settles. *In the moment,* the decisions made seemed like the right choice, but, when time passed, it became obvious that the thinking was not clear at all and rash choices had been made.

I know that much of what we hear in books and movies is to "trust your feelings" and "go with what your heart tells you", but, frankly, I have heard very few success stories in relationships based on this philosophy. There are times where "going with your heart" works, such as a life direction for a career. But when such a philosophy is used in relationships, affairs occur, divorces, quickie weddings, becoming sexually involved before you're emotionally ready, and the list goes on.

One way of telling if you are being led by your feelings is if your conclusions go back and forth, since feelings change from day to day, moment to moment. This is why people who make most of their decisions based on their feelings typically have chaotic lives.

The core of being "conflicted" is usually the struggle between what we rationally know versus what our feelings are telling us.

At the same time, reason is not automatically above error. Common sense is not found in equal proportions between humans and neither is the ability to think logically. What may seem logical to me may be some incredible leap of irrationality to the next person.

With Nate and Nancy, the feelings were calmed down, but to an extreme. It may have seemed quite rational to them to just ignore what had happened with the affair and try to move forward, not realizing the long-term effect such a strategy would have on the relationship.

The affair itself was an example of making a stupid choice based on momentary impulses with the assistance of alcohol. The fact that alcohol was present did not erase Nate's responsibility in the matter. He should not have allowed the situation to develop as far as it did. The emotional consequences of the situation resulted in a one-month separation where each gathered some emotional perspective on the situation and decided that the relationship was worth hanging onto, despite what had happened. But a lack of passion was now evident in their relationship. Maybe there was an unspoken fear that if passion was allowed to come to the surface again, negative feelings might come out as well.

That is why it is so important that, especially when we are considering making big decisions (whether it is regarding our work, our relationships, or our lives in general) that we seek wise counsel and don't rely solely on our own judgment. Like the hermit who has lived on the island for years by himself, his perception of the real world may be incredibly skewed because he has only his inner world from which to form his judgments.

*   *   *

Strong emotion is usually based on the small picture of what you want, or fear, most *in this moment*, distorting any projection you may have of the future. When emotion is overriding reason, the future doesn't matter as much compared to what you think you need or want now.

Reason is usually able to take a more accurate picture of what's going to happen to my future if I do this today.

On occasion, in couple's work I'll hear a client say, "I'm done," in regards to the relationship. In that moment, he has gotten to the point where he's emotionally overwhelmed. He's exhausted. He doesn't feel like he has any energy left to continue trying to work on things. So, in that moment, if you forced him to make a decision about the future of "us", he'd say that, yes, he was done.

The partner who's lost in the emotional moment says, "So you're done? It's over? Just like that? How could you?! You quitter! After all I've done for you. I'm getting an attorney. I want you out of the house!"

The big picture voice of reason says, "Wait a minute. That's just how he feels *today*. In this hour. In this moment. That doesn't mean he's going to feel the same way in the morning. He needs to have some room, some time, to feel what he's feeling without being forced to make any decisions, just to be able to move through the emotion and see where things are when the emotional dust settles down." It recognizes that what we feel in the moment is colored by the emotion of the moment, and we can't afford to treat each other's emotions as the total truth of what's going on, just a partial truth.

Some people experience "emotional waves", whether the emotion is anger, anxiety, depression or happiness. If that emotional wave is a negative one, the partner will often try to fight the wave when it hits, or control the wave, or react to the wave, rather than recognizing that it's just a wave, and letting it pass. He takes that wave very personally, and treats what is said during that wave as cold hard truth rather than just the passing wave that it is. He fails to recognize that his partner's "type" is one that has waves.

While we need to take each other's emotions seriously, we also need to recognize that emotions come and go, that we do and say stupid things in the heat of the moment. If we're exercising grace, then there's room for emotional upset, while we wait out each other's feelings in order to get back to a place of reason.

Ideally, what is said in those moments of emotional recklessness doesn't cross the line of being completely inappropriate, or a deal-breaker for the relationship, or now it's no longer an issue of "letting the wave pass", now it's a matter of accountability that needs to be addressed.

Rule #26. Be sure the solution is clear to both sides and specific enough that it can be immediately applied.

If a couple is successful in acknowledging a problem, accepting responsibility for it, and committing to doing better at it, they are still only partway there, because they are still operating only on *intention*. If there are no specific strategies in place, change often does not occur.

With two-part solutions, not only does each person have something to work on, there is continued loving accountability in terms of how each side touches base with the other regarding how they're doing. By giving continuing positive feedback and fine-tuning the implemented strategies, the couple stays on top of the issue.

For many couples, this is where they learn how to be positive in supporting change with each other, recognizing the small successes, rather than overly criticizing how things may still be falling short.

Couples need to have the discussion, "How can I best help you maintain your end of this change?"

*   *   *

Sometimes it is fine for one person to assume responsibility and say "I'll take care of it", or "It won't happen again", and then you wait and see if the problem reoccurs. If it does reoccur, this is a good indicator that it's time for a more specific, and maybe joint, solution.

Let's take Nate and Nancy's situation a step further. Let's say that they actually agree on a particular activity together. So Friday night comes around and they know what they agreed on doing, but nothing has actually been planned. They meet a dead-end because no reservations were made, no one actually chose the particular restaurant or movie. Already the evening's half over...and so they default and do nothing for that night. Again. All because of a failure to be more specific about who is going to do what.

People don't want to be bothered with the details, but there's a cost for ignoring them. It may seem like overly tedious work to plan things to such an extent. However, if your history is that it doesn't happen otherwise, then you need to take the time to plan.

Congratulations! You've gotten through each of the four areas for conflict resolution: identifying, validating, discussing, and resolving the problem. If you made the effort to read through each of the sections, you should have some food for thought and, hopefully, some new tools to use the next time you approach a potential conflict.

Much of this may seem like common sense, but for many it may feel overwhelming. Keep in mind, this isn't about having to remember everything I've written, or do everything I've said. It's about starting to improve in whatever small ways that you can. The point of identifying so many different options is to give you any number of ways and choices to approach issues with better tools.

For those who may look at all of this as too much work, nobody ever said relationships were easy. And if you want the benefit of the rewards that come from being a healthy couple, it's completely worth it. Luckily, most of the work is on the front end. The more you master healthy resolution styles *now*, later on the tools become second nature.

If this is going to have any lasting impact on your life you will need to review these tools on occasion. It's one thing to know what they are. It's another to be focused enough on them in your discussions that you actually *apply* them. That's why there's a short version of the "rules list" included in this book (Appendix) to use as a prompter when you're preparing to approach an issue.

At the start, you may need to look at the rules list in advance, then check yourself after you've made an attempt at resolution. You probably need to focus only on the tools that you continue to struggle with the most.

Invite your partner to assess which ones you still need work with. Your errors may be so natural to you that you don't even notice them when you're doing it.

If you have a video camera, it can be very helpful to tape yourselves working things out and then go back and critique it, noting both what went well and what needs improvement. It allows you to examine your own body language, facial expressions, vocal tone, and overall resolution style. Seeing yourself from a distance like this, having a mirror held up to your own behavior, helps create a perspective impossible to gain any other way.

In terms of rules versus guidelines, for those who need rules, because without them they'll be ignored, you might want to consider treating the 26 points I've itemized in these last four chapters as rules. For those looking for pointers to enhance an already functional relationship, treat these as guidelines that help keep you on the right road. The reward for using them is the greater likelihood of having a relationship unhampered by faulty communication and poor problem-solving skills. If you really want a healthier relationship and a happier you, there's your motivation for doing the work.

Discussion Questions:

1. **Of the resolution "rules", which ones do you have the most difficulty with?** Why?

2. **How are you going to put the rules that are most often ignored on such a conscious level that they are actually being applied when issues are being discussed?**

Part III

Strategies for Change

Chapter 9
A Model for Change

"If you really change your ways and your actions and deal
with each other justly, if you do not oppress the alien, the
fatherless or the widow and do not shed innocent blood in
this place, and if you do not follow other gods to your own
harm, then I will let you live in this place, in the land I gave
your forefathers for ever and ever." (Jeremiah 7:5-7)

For relationships that have existed for a while, negative patterns can
create their own special kind of "rut" for the couple. Think of it in terms
of the ox cart that has gone down the same path time and again, making
a deep groove in the dirt road that the wheels automatically fall into.
When you're trying to create a new path for the relationship, the hardest
transition occurs during the initial efforts to step out of that well-worn
"rut". But, with consistency and persistence, a new and healthier path
can be created that also becomes routine in time.

The overall process involves: 1) recognizing the need to change, 2)
deciding specifically what changes are going to take place, 3) making
those changes and then 4) maintaining them.

I'd like to share a conceptual model that I use to assist clients who want
to form a specific strategy for change. At the point that an individual

issue has been identified within a relationship, this model is ideal in helping to break down the separate parts and map out a solution.

The Three-Part Solution Model

The basic concept behind the model is that for any problem there are potentially three different aspects, or layers, that need attention. That doesn't mean that *every* problem involves all three aspects. It just depends on how deep the problem goes.

The first aspect, and usually the easiest to address, is the *behavior.*

Using alcohol abuse as an example, the obvious problem behavior is the drinking. Many people will oversimplify the issue and think that the solution is just as simple: stop the behavior and you stop the problem. So the abuser stops drinking alcohol for a day, maybe a week, maybe more, but then something happens (boredom, stress, extra money to burn, friends who want to party) and they're back to drinking again.

Part of what distinguishes substance *abuse* from *misuse* has to do with the presence or absence of consequences. Misuse is using something for other than what it's intended, but *without* experiencing consequences for the misuse. Or, if consequences *are* experienced, then the misuse stops. In terms of drinking then, for someone at the point of misuse, it is often possible to stop after that first experience of a noticeable consequence. The cost, or potential cost, becomes real enough that the behavior is no longer attempted.

Abuse is a different creature since misuse continues even though we have knowledge of the cost to us or others. We continue to use *despite* consequences. Something's not right about that. To intentionally do something again that we know has hurt us in the past is potentially self-destructive. It goes beyond a mistake and indicates an actual deeper problem may exist.

If we continue to engage in negative behaviors that are costing us, or those close to us, there is usually a deeper need that we're trying to meet by hanging on to them. If we remove a problem behavior, such as drinking, the need it was attempting to meet, no matter how unsuccessfully, is still going unmet.

Since our core needs are always legitimate, we can't just pretend that they don't exist. If the need for this particular drinker was relief or escape from his stress, the unspoken message from his friends who tell him to stop is that he should be okay with remaining stressed. In reality, *he needs to replace the unhealthy behavior with positive ones that adequately meet the underlying need.*

The particular replacement behaviors that he chooses need to be a good fit for him, not just what works for somebody else. If he's decided on exercise as being an alternative, he needs to choose a type of exercise he actually enjoys or it won't be a meaningful replacement.

Also, he needs to come up with a number of different alternatives. If his only alternatives depend on other people, then he's "up a creek" if no friends can be found. Or if he chooses an exercise solution such as running on an outdoor track, what does he do on rainy days, or when it's too inconvenient to get to that track? The more workable options he has the better.

* * *

Sometimes, however, even when we replace the negative behavior with positive ones, the problem still persists. Usually, this is because the problem goes deeper than just the behavior.

The second layer to the solution model is the *thinking*.

It is the thoughts that we tell ourselves (our self-talk) that create, nurture or maintain the problem. Whether it's denial that we've got a problem, minimizing the problem, or how we rationalize continuing to engage in the problem, our problematic way of thinking allows the problem to persist.

Problematic thinking usually starts with just a truthful observation (neither good nor bad) which progressively deteriorates into a distortion, emotional logic, or a conspiracy theory. If he sees that his partner is upset with him, then the initial observation is simply "She's upset with me". But it doesn't stop there. That thought then leads to, "I hate it when she complains" which continues into, "She's always complaining," and on to, "Why can't she ever be happy?" concluding with "Whatever I do it's never going to be enough for her."

Staying with the alcohol issue, the logic path may start with just the initial observation of "I'm stressed", which leads to "I need a break", which continues into, "I deserve a drink". Understanding the thought progression can often lead to other important pieces to the solution. In this instance, we just learned that, for this person, drinking is more than just his stressreliever, it's also his personal reward. He feels entitled to it, or that he earned it. That's one way how he rationalizes his choice. So we need to step back to the positive behaviors and make sure that some of those positive choices he's come up with will also serve as credible, noncostly rewards for him.

So the initial step is just to track the different logic trails he engages in that justify his decision to drink. And then he needs to come up with positive counters, or redirects, to those thoughts that will help move him back to making better choices.

If he's stressed, he's stressed. You don't want him to lie to himself about it. And if he's been responsible with work and getting things done at home, he probably does get to the point of needing a break. So far he's still within the realm of reason. But it's when he makes the leap to "I deserve a drink" that his logic suffers. And that's where the replacement thinking needs to occur.

Instead of "I deserve a drink", the replacement thought would be "I deserve..." and fill it in with any of the positive behaviors that he's already identified that he also views as rewards.

Often, someone who struggles with substance issues will use his friends or sponsor to help redirect his thinking for him because, in the moment, he's too close to the problem to be able to think it through for himself. The 12-step program slogans such as "one day at a time", or "first things first", are all thinking strategies that symbolize a deeper concept, and are designed to restore focus. However, by mapping things out like this with the solution model, actually writing these positive redirects down, even if he's alone he can still walk himself through the process of refocusing.

This is where, for the Christian, inspirational scripture can play a valuable part. When it comes to anxiety and stress, the Bible has many great cognitive redirects that help us get our head back under control.

"For God has not given us a spirit of fear, but of power and of love and of a sound mind." (II Timothy 1:7)

"Be of good courage, and He shall strengthen your heart, all ye that hope in the Lord." (Psalm 31:24)

"I can do all things through Christ, who strengthens me." (Phillipians 4:13)

If the problem doesn't go any deeper, and both unhealthy thoughts and behaviors are consistently managed and positively redirected, the situation starts to self-correct.

* * *

If a problem *still* persists, despite sound behavioral and cognitive interventions, it's probably because it goes even deeper, to the third layer. The third aspect to the solution model is a combination of how we *feel* and maybe even what we've come to *believe*. The problem with each of these, and why they are the most stubborn aspects to deal with is that they can both be *beyond* reason.

The connection between feelings and beliefs is that one is a progression of the other. Unhealthy feelings can start out somewhat unformed, without any particular identifiable thoughts attached to them, but then develop into irrational beliefs if they go unchecked (if we continue to feed them).[16]

Let's use fear as an example. Fear is about the expectation of a negative event (whether it's an "it might", or "what if", or "I'm afraid that…"). If I

---

[16] So, too, beliefs can be conclusions from rational thought, but for simplicity's sake I'm going to focus on the beliefs that form from emotional thinking.

act as if my fear is true, that what I'm afraid of will actually happen, I am now treating it like a belief more than just a fear. I'm no longer treating it as "it might". I'm now behaving like "it will".

With the thought progression I just used a few paragraphs back that started with "She's upset with me" and ended with "Whatever I do it's never going to be good enough for her", that last part was actually his underlying unhealthy belief (as well as an emotional distortion and a conspiracy theory). If he treats that belief like it's a truth, then there's no way he will be able to be happy in that relationship since, as far as he's concerned, nothing will ever be good enough for her. By taking it to that extreme, he's just destroyed his own motivation to continue to try.

When someone feels conflicted, typically the conflict is between what they think versus what they feel: two different parts of the brain. We may know that what we feel is unreasonable, yet still be unable to give up feeling it. We may logically know that our partner is faithful, yet still have difficulty shaking the irrational fear that he's cheating.

Going back to the example of the alcohol abuse, it may not matter that he's stopped his drinking and replaced his thinking if he hasn't addressed the underlying feelings or beliefs that are sabotaging his progress.

The most identifiable *feelings* he experiences that contribute to his drinking are probably stress, shame or guilt.

In terms of the emotional thinking behind those feelings that develops into a *belief*, sometimes with self-destructive behavior there is a buried self-destructive fear or belief, such as "Failure is inevitable", "I'm weak", "I'm never going to amount to anything", or "It's only a matter of time before I screw up again". He may live in denial of it. He certainly doesn't want to believe it. But it can still be at the root of his issues. He's *afraid* that it's true. Maybe it was a negative message that was thrown at him when he was younger (via friends, siblings, or parents), or maybe it was just his own internal doubts and fears that he's harbored over the years.

In terms of "the chicken or the egg", maybe it was his initial negative behaviors that led to him feeling this way, or maybe it was the feelings that led to his behavior. But, at this point, the problem is that his underlying destructive feelings and beliefs continue to steer him to live in a way that only serves to feed and strengthen those fears and beliefs. Basically, his feelings are now dictating his choices.[17]

The difficulty with this level of a problem is that *you can't just replace a negative feeling with a better one.* I can't get up in the morning feeling lousy and just tell myself to be happy. I'm going to have to *do* something, or start *thinking* about something (telling myself something), that allows my emotions to shift.

When it comes to unhealthy, negative emotions and irrational beliefs, *you have to be willing to live in a way that challenges their truth.*

For the person who's afraid of heights and now chronically avoids bridges, escalators, and tall buildings, he has to start going somewhere high again. He wouldn't do something overly traumatizing such as skydiving, but he might want to start with gradual approximations of situations that set off his anxiety, continuing to stretch past his comfort zone, weakening the fear and ultimately disproving the belief.

For the depressed individual, even though he doesn't feel like getting out of bed, he has to force himself to in order for the depression to start to lift. The longer he allows the depressed thoughts to dictate what he does, the more he feeds and strengthens the depression. It doesn't mean that it goes away immediately, because he may have fed that depression for a while. It will still take time to weaken and starve it, but at least now he knows what he needs to do to start getting better.

That's not to say that for the alcohol abuser he needs to regain confidence by going to bars and proving he doesn't have to have a drink. He needs to remain realistic about his limitations and personal triggers with alcohol. But now, he will also start to focus on other need-fulfilling positive

---

[17] Which also happens to be the definition for lack of emotional discipline, or "emotional immaturity". That's not to say that everyone who struggles with controlling his emotional logic is emotionally immature, which is a generalized issue. For many, where their emotional discipline is being tested can be limited to just a specific area.

activities, and ways of thinking, that can allow him to experience a greater degree and frequency of success.[18]

So the ideal positive feelings that he's trying to achieve are: peace, self-respect and confidence.

The ideal positive beliefs he's working at embracing are: "I *can* make good choices." "I can feel worthwhile if I treat myself so." "I'm just as capable of success as failure." (Though you don't want to create unrealistic positive beliefs such as "I will always succeed.")

*   *   *

In terms of relationships, let's apply this to the emotionally disconnected couple. The feelings are a lack of passion or desire, a sense of distance, maybe boredom. Maybe there's a belief stirring around that "Our relationship was a mistake", or "This isn't going to work." The couple became overly involved in the roles of the relationship (raising the kids, paying the bills, building the careers, and getting the chores done). But the emotional intimacy, the connection, was neglected. As a result of that neglect, the positive feelings have faded and they now feel like roommates. So the current problem is that those not-so-positive feelings that now exist are pushing the couple to continue to do things that widen the gulf, to make the disconnect even greater (such as no longer spending one-on-one time together, or attempting deeper conversations). The negative feelings are now leading them to make negative choices.

The disconnected couple is waiting for the feelings to return, or waiting for their partner to create those feelings in them, rather than looking at what each can do themselves to restore those feelings. Often, this is because many people look at feelings as something that are either there or they're not. If the love is gone, it's gone. But that's not really true. If love was there before, often it can be restored.

---

[18]   I want to be careful here to not oversimplify addictions. I recognize that there are different causalities to the disease and, for substance dependency issues in particular, there is also the physical dependency piece, not just the psychological dependency. That's why I specifically referred to *abuse* issues, *not* dependency.

The solution part of this model (the *ideal* behavior, thinking, feeling/beliefs) operates on the exact *opposite* dynamic as the problem part. With the problem part of the model, feelings dictate the choices. But with the solution part of the model, *the need-fulfilling actions and the healthy, rational thoughts are what guide the emotions.* The feelings are now in their proper place, and gradually we step back into being in control of ourselves again because we've regained emotional discipline.

For many, when you first start to implement the plan for change, you have to approach it in terms of "fake it to make it", because the negative feelings and beliefs will still be in the way, sabotaging your efforts. "Fake it to make it" (a 12-step program slogan) doesn't mean to lie to yourself or others. It means that, at the start, while you're trying to make those initial efforts to create this new identity, or restore an old one, *you have to step into the shoes of that successful identity before you're actually feeling it.* The desired feelings don't come first, they come *after.*

So for the disconnected couple, the "fake it to make it" leap is recognizing that if they want to rekindle those feelings they first have to start *behaving* in a loving way again, doing those things that a connected couple does to maintain their connection, such as restoring a courtship. And at the same time with their thinking, they need to doubt their negative conclusions by embracing loving thoughts that challenge those negative fears and beliefs ("Maybe we *can* make this work.", "He does have his positive qualities.", "This *has* been a nice time together today.", "We *can* still show each other love."), allowing for room to actually experience something that is emotionally positive.

The more we over-focus on forcing the emotional piece, however, analyzing every encounter for a better emotional outcome in ourselves, the more we can short-circuit the process, since emotions occur naturally, not artificially. Our focus needs to be on the doing and the thinking, trusting that the feelings will follow without trying to force them. It's the same thing with sleep issues. Our body already knows how to fall asleep. The more we try to force it to go to sleep, the more we're getting in the way of something that our body already naturally knows how to do.

*   *   *

Are positive behaviors more important than positive thinking? Both have their place, but it usually depends on the particular person.

Because irrational beliefs are, by definition, beyond reason, trying to reason with them directly sometimes isn't as effective as simply doing something positive that breaks us out of that emotional spell.

Many times people will over-think a situation and talk themselves out of doing something healthy. They need to adopt the Nike slogan of "Just do it" and not give themselves any more time to think, since "thinking" for them just means becoming emotionally overwhelmed. Their focus is on behavioral strategies.

At the same time, for many people who struggle with emotional issues, often there is an *absence* of rational thought. And even if rational thinking does occur it's usually *after* the problem behavior and not before. So their focus is on learning more thinking strategies that restore a big picture perspective to their situation.

Staying with the substance abuser, it can be a simple process of him *feeling* stressed so he goes for a drink. No thought required. He has that drink because *he never took the time to actually think about the consequences.* He may make many choices along the way from getting to his house to the store or the bar, but he isn't actually thinking about what he's doing. He's just following the path to making it happen. He never considers "What am I doing?", only the next step to acting on his emotional impulse. For him, the new strategy becomes introducing *more* opportunity for thought to occur.

*　*　*

We naturally label negative feelings as being bad, but, in reality, negative feelings actually have a healthy component. It all depends on what we do with them.

Healthy anger occurs when we've been wronged. It gives us the courage to take action and say or do something about the injustice (so long as we do it in an appropriate way).

Healthy guilt exists to convict us and move us to take responsibility for something we should or shouldn't have done.

Healthy fear serves to make us think of potential consequences for our behavior, or to come up with a better plan for something we're concerned might happen in the future. In its most primitive form, fear is our survival instinct attempting to protect us. If our fear register *didn't* kick in when we were about to do something dangerous, we could seriously harm ourselves.

At the point fear becomes unhealthy, it:

1) grows so extreme it emotionally paralyzes us

2) makes us over-focus on the things beyond our control

3) keeps us from taking healthy action on the things within our control

4) keeps us from experiencing peace even though we've already assumed responsibility for the things in our control

For the Christian, fear is the most common place where our faith gets tested. Where there is an unhealthy, overpowering fear there is also, predictably, an absence of faith. Remembering spiritual warfare, I need to be cautious that I'm not giving a foothold to the wrong team. Unhealthy fear ultimately leads us to forget that God is our Source and Protector.

What makes it hard to totally dismiss a fear, or an irrational belief, is because it usually has some small element of truth to it. For instance, there *is* always the possibility of failing at something. There *is* always the chance that our partners may not prove faithful. But *focused in a positive direction*, that discomfort hopefully inspires us to do our part to keep it from happening. Though we're aware of the potential to fall short, we continue to focus our energy on succeeding where we can. If we're aware our marriage isn't affair-proof, then we continue to take steps to keep it healthy. And we leave the rest to God.

* * *

In the same way that negative feelings have positives, positive feelings have negatives. With unhealthy love, we can get lost in doing things that make us feel good, but are killing us, or our relationship, in the process. If we are tempted by an outside relationship, we can start entertaining unhealthy, positive beliefs ("She's my soul mate."), which will make it incredibly difficult to redirect ourselves because now we're magically viewing this outside relationship as "meant to be".

———————

The end result of the solution model process is having mapped out the *ideal alternative*: a specific plan for the solution that will replace the problem. Once you've worked out the plan, the focus is now on the ideal identity you're working towards, not remaining lost in over-obsessing on the problem identity.

That specific plan becomes your daily personal accountability system (your focus at the beginning of the day, your review at the end of the day), keeping the solution on a conscious, applicable level.[19]

Discussion Questions:

1. **Do you struggle more with problem behaviors, thoughts, feelings or beliefs?** What strategies do you use for correcting your areas of weakness?

2. **Can you recognize an underlying need to whatever your particular issue may be?** What other positive ways can that underlying legitimate need be met?

3. **Is there anything you find yourself conflicted about with the relationship?** Are you able to separate out the rational voice from the emotional one?

4. **If you have any unhealthy fears, irrational beliefs, or conspiracy theories, what would "living in a way that challenges its truth" look like?**

———————

[19] If you're interested in developing a specific plan using this model, go to the Appendix at the end of the book and refer to the 3-Part Solution Model Exercise. It leads you through the process of how to personalize this to your situation.

Chapter 10
Healthy Routines

"The soul of a lazy man desires, and has nothing; but the soul of the diligent shall be made rich." (Proverbs 13:4)

One big problem with positive change is how do you maintain it over time? Or how do you hang on to the good thing that you've already got? Usually it comes down to looking at the routines in your relationship that either lull it to sleep, or keep it awake and thriving.

There are three important rituals, or routines, that every long-term romantic relationship needs:

- a courting ritual
- an accountability ritual
- a forgiveness ritual

The Courtship Ritual

One of the first things to go in a marriage is a consistent dating routine. And when the couple does go out, they bring the kids, the relatives, or the friends. But the marriage has to continue, at times, to take center stage. If other relationships consistently come first (even the kids) the marriage will suffer.

Our ability to function as a team is what allows us to manage all of the other responsibilities. In viewing everything as energy, we only have so much to burn and every responsibility uses some of it up. Our "alone time" with our partner should be time to recharge our batteries, enabling us to handle all of the other things. But if that alone time has become just another responsibility and not something we look forward to, something has gone amiss.

Dating is supposed to be time out of the regular routine to let us live a little. You're not *adding* to your list of responsibilities. You're taking a *break* from your responsibilities together.

When communication starts to break down, time alone with each other often becomes avoided. While we are conserving energy by avoiding conflict, we've inadvertently managed to cut ourselves off from one of our most important resources: each other.

We need to continue to keep the romantic sparks alive if we wish to continue to experience passion in our relationships. We can't assume that just because we love each other the desire will always be there. It stays if we continue to nurture it and keep it alive. Just because a married couple still has a sexual relationship does not mean that the romance is still alive. While courting *enhances* the sexual relationship, a good relationship consists of more than just the physical.

Men are more likely to feel emotionally connected to their partners so long as the sex life continues, however, women typically depend on the emotional connection to motivate them to have a sex life. If the courtship now only consists of the physical relationship, women are the most likely to lose the emotional connection first because the sex is not what sustains them.

The reality of our modern world is that there are time demands from our jobs, children, and ourselves. We do not have limitless amounts of energy to lavish on each. But we did make our partners a priority at some point in the relationship that convinced them of our love, and it is only natural that, if that priority shifts or diminishes, their experience of our love towards them will also diminish.

The courting relationship shouldn't be a one-sided experience. This isn't an opportunity for the woman or man to just sit back and expect the other to exert all the effort. It is a *shared* effort to continue to show each other in thoughtful ways that they are valued.

A good romantic relationship provides for all three of our core needs.[20] A loving partner lets you know that you're valued by giving you continued recognition for the efforts you put into the relationship (significance). He shows you his commitment through his continued efforts taking care of the relationship, and his willingness to be respectful of your pain when issues are being discussed (security). And, through the courting relationship, the two of you remember to still have your fun.

Dating is only one piece of a courtship. It's also thoughtful calls during the day just to say hello, to express appreciation about something, or to say that you care. It's an unexpected card, something extra picked up at the store while you were out, or a backrub that didn't have to be requested. It's being creative and continuing to do nice things just because you know how it makes your partner feel.

It isn't having to do conscious acts every single day to the point that you're exhausting yourself. Often the best surprises are the unexpected ones. The flowers received every so often may have much more of an impact than flowers given every day.

Here are some suggestions for your dates:

- Don't always do the same thing (the same restaurant, the same type of food, the same types of movies, the same hangouts).
- Take turns planning dates. One week, let her plan it. The next, let him. This way no one has the "burden" of having to do all of the planning.

---

[20] Though this doesn't mean that *all* of our needs are met by our partner; it's more like *portions* of each need.

- Explore doing some of the things you have talked about doing in the past but never got around to.

- Take an evening class, a workshop, or read a book together - a shared learning experience.

- Go deeper with your conversations than just the business of the day (such as where you'd like to be five years from now, what your dreams for the relationship are).

- Try to find new territory/experiences to discover together, bringing out new aspects of your personalities to explore.

If the relationship has gotten to the point where neither cares for the play activities of the other, then put some energy into finding new ones. Chances are when you were dating you did things with your partner just because you wanted to be with him. It wasn't about whether you were doing something you enjoyed just as much as he did.

It's all about attitude. If this is the person you say you love and want to spend the rest of your life with, why is finding time together such a chore? At what point in time did visible evidence of your affection stop being important? Usually, that shift is because we've become lazy when it comes to "us", and our feelings are telling us we don't have the energy.

If you don't have a lot of money to spend, find things that don't require money. Picnics, walks, sports/exercise, volunteer activities, church activities, and local festivals - all of these can be either inexpensive or free.

Don't keep looking for reasons why you can't make it happen and figure out how it can.

If children are in the picture, don't allow their presence to prevent you from finding time for the two of you as husband and wife. You are still treating the kids as a priority by valuing the marriage relationship, because you're also modeling for them what a healthy balance looks like. Do you want them to eventually go into their own marriages thinking that a normal relationship is one in which the parents neglect each other?

For those with younger kids, often the dilemma for the parents is lack of resources. Family isn't close by, or they don't know other couples that they can tag team the kids with, or they don't know any good babysitters, etc. But the more in-balance our lives are, the more resources we have at our disposal (the more likely we are to have a peer group to rely on). Because the couple has over-focused inward with raising the kids, and possibly become more isolated, they have detached themselves from the potential resources outside of the family.

Realistically, the courtship will take some "hits" during the initial first two or three years with having a child, or when starting a new career, or when job demands are increased. But the challenge remains as to how we continue to reincorporate the intimacy needs *despite* these changing priorities.

Part of the reason for continuing to court is keeping an atmosphere of playfulness alive, since one of the gauges for how far a relationship has deteriorated is by how little laughter there is. Laughter allows us to keep our perspective. It allows us to not take each other, ourselves, or our lives, too seriously. When a couple is no longer able to laugh together, typically, perspective has been lost and the relationship is in trouble.

One of the only "rules" for dates is that this is not time used to further discuss issues. We need to draw safe boundaries around this time together, and not allow the problems from other areas to corrupt it. It's supposed to be an opportunity to continue to share positive experiences together that can continue to keep the relationship healthy and fit.

*   *   *

Part of enhancing a courtship is knowing and speaking each other's "love language". Gary Chapman's "Five Love Languages" identified five different ways that we give and receive love. One of the core concepts being that *we tend to show love to our partner in the same way that we want to get love back.* But the problem is that our partners have their own preferences as to how they give and get. We can be trying to show love to our partners, but if it's not their particular "language", then they may not experience love from us as meaningfully as we would intend.

To connect in a more powerful way, we need to show them love in the way that they are most likely to recognize it.

The five "languages" are:

- Words of affirmation (praise, compliments, recognition)
- Quality time
- Receiving gifts (random acts of kindness)
- Acts of service (chores, favors)
- Physical touch

"Acts of service" plays out somewhat differently at the dating level than it does at the marriage level, because, unless you're living together, you're typically not doing each other's chores. However, while dating it's not unusual to see a partner help out around the other's house, take on shared projects, or just persist with doing favors for the other.

While Chapman views these as the central pathways to maintaining intimacy in a relationship, they are actually more of what "opens the door" to going there. If you have a couple who both share the same language of physical touch, they can touch all they want, and feel very loved, but it doesn't assure any relationship of depth if everything remains on the physical level.

Speaking your partner's love language keeps the relationship emotionally afloat, and provides *the motivation* to deepen your relationship, but it isn't a replacement for developing true intimacy.

Of the five languages, "quality time" is the one that is most closely tied in to the relationship's potential growth and deepening intimacy. Learning and applying each other's love language is an example of *initial* growth, but past that, intimacy usually won't develop further unless we're taking consistent intentional time out for "us".

* * *

While the dating ritual is a vital routine, it stops having a meaningful impact at the point that things become *too* routine. Even though a couple will say that they still have date nights, if those times consist of a predictable repetition (dinner and a movie, dinner and a movie…), they start to lose the depth of what this healthy routine is meant to accomplish.

A continuing courtship is attempting to develop a more mature bond, a deeper intimacy, that goes beyond just having lived our lives together. It's going behind the scenes to that inner world where each of us lives, to where we make sense out of life and our experiences, to where we feel and think and wonder about life ahead and behind. For the Christian, it's also the realm of the spiritual world that we have to share and explore together.

Because the Christian couple has a *shared* faith, their spirituality becomes another level to their intimacy. For many, their relationship with God is a very personal thing, and so to open up and share that with your partner can be very powerful. Going to church together, reading the Bible together, praying together, sharing a ministry together, doing a small church group together, can all be creative things that add to the courtship.

Some people aren't good with looking at themselves, their lives, or their motivations (why they are the way they are). They prefer to stay on the surface because going deeper is an unfamiliar place, and maybe even a painful or scary one. You don't know what you're going to find if you haven't been there much in the past. For some, it's perceived as too much work. But our ability to go deeper (aside from being a help to the partner who doesn't know how to go deeper) is what allows us to connect more intimately, and makes us more interesting to each other. It affirms that there are more worlds to be explored together than just the one that's in front of our eyes.

Quality time isn't just about the partner being physically present. That may be a step up from how things usually are, but just being present doesn't mean "interactive". Quality time in a dating routine is doing things that go beyond a passive activity that requires no meaningful dialogue. It's choosing activities that stir our thoughts or emotions, that create new dialogue, and may even bring facets of us to the surface that we don't normally get to see or explore.

Accountability Routines

When it comes to an accountability ritual or routine, this is how the couple monitors necessary change in a very conscious way, as well as provides necessary recognition for positive efforts made. *This is one of the most important keys to maintaining change over time.* The idea is that the more we approach our relationships on a very conscious level in terms of "what's working" and "what needs work" the less likely it is for blind spots to develop or for the relationship to subtly deteriorate.

Many times our tendency is to approach accountability with our partner only when things get to a point of complete discomfort. Or, rather than approaching each other with loving accountability, we allow things to build up until we explode and now the issue's out, but there's a lot of collateral damage to attend to. Having accountability routines in place, where both the positive and not-so-positive are recognized and addressed, creates a necessary platform where it's not about nagging, but keeping the relationship healthy.

There are three rituals you can use to accomplish this:

- The Needs List Utility
- The Sit-down
- The Priority Assessment

The Needs List Utility

An irony in many relationships is that a couple can become very upset by feeling that their needs are going unmet, when, in actuality, both sides may still be putting energy into pleasing each other. However, they often are trying to please each other in the way they *think* their partner wants to be pleased, or how *they themselves* want to be pleased, and are "missing the boat" as a result.

Keep in mind that what is important to you and your partner may change over the course of a relationship. Usually the first major "change" takes place in the first year of marriage, adjusting to the transition from dating to being married. After that, romantic relationships tend to reach critical points about every 5 to 7 years (if life circumstances don't make it sooner), just as your body goes through changes in cycles.

Moves, changes in jobs, or having children can bring about new adjustment periods since they automatically create new demands on the roles of husband and wife. What was important when you first started dating may now be inconsequential or even no longer desired (for example: you don't go out as much socially). And, vice versa, things that were overlooked during the courting period may now have become important as the relationship has become more serious (money becomes an issue). If you're not comparing notes every now and then to make sure you're keeping up with each other's changing surface needs, you may be putting energy into the wrong places and exhausting yourself despite good intentions.

It's important to recognize the difference between knowing what your partner wants from you and how he expects you to accomplish that. You may know that trust is very important to your partner. (Trust is part of the security need.) But do you know specifically what he looks for from you in order to develop that trust? Is it making the occasional phone call from work? Is it never going out to dinner with someone of the opposite sex? Just because you've voiced your needs in general terms does not mean you've gained an understanding of the specifics required to meet that need. It's why the first exercise I do in couples counseling is to have the couple complete a *needs list*.

A needs list serves several purposes.

- It gives a specific direction for meeting each other's needs.
- It helps clarify needs for those that really aren't in touch with their own needs.
- It can help establish a clear priority as to which surface needs are most important to each of you.
- It helps stop the "blame game" of over-focusing on each other's part, and gives you something within your own control to do for the health of the relationship.
- For those couples *considering* marriage, it is a very simple tool to help explore compatibility. If you are identifying

something as a need, something you *have* to have in order to be content in the relationship, and your partner is saying that he is unwilling or unable to provide that, it helps simplify perspective in terms of whether or not the relationship can move forward.

Some people have difficulty with the idea of a needs list because they feel that it is putting the relationship in conditional terms. "I will continue to love you so long as you are doing this, this and this…" But the expectations in a relationship are things you work towards meeting for each other because of your *choice*, because you *love* each other, *not* because they are being demanded. The needs list isn't supposed to be about adding another "to do" list to all of those other lists already in existence. Neither is it supposed to be a complaint list for how each has fallen short. It is simply a direct and accurate guide to what is most important to each of you, and what are the best and most valued ways to show each other you are loved.

The needs list isn't just about what you need that you *aren't* getting, but also the things that you already are. It's a *balanced* exercise. Recognizing that, over time, we tend to focus on the things we need "fixed" and take for granted what is still working, it's just as important to sit back and take stock in those needs that are already being satisfied (giving credit where credit is due).

Recognizing creativity, the needs list isn't about micromanaging our partners' positive behavior towards us. It's helping to lead them to what works best for us, but it's still up to them how exactly they go about it. The idea of identifying several different avenues to meeting each other's needs allows for freedom of choice, in the same way that we might ask our kids, "Give me a top 5 of the things you might like for your birthday".

I'm mentioning the needs list in this chapter on routines because it is something that is directly plugged in to how you choose to go about courting each other, and the sit-downs we are about to discuss. Also, it isn't a one-time exercise. Used wisely, a needs list undergoes refinement from time to time.

Many people's initial needs lists are relatively over-generalized, vague, and unrefined. But, ideally, part of the dialogue that comes out of sharing your needs lists is getting things better defined for each other, more specific. The clearer the request, the easier it will be to accommodate it.

As time goes by, hopefully, the couple is also continuing to intermittently update and revise their lists as the needs shift and as circumstances change.[21]

When needs lists are completed, often what are on the lists are mostly about what's needed from each other in regards to the relationship roles. If this is the case, be sure that you also take some time to add items that address the courtship: what keeps you connected, what ways you still need to have fun together, and what things are reflective of your particular love language.

Predictably, some of the identified needs on a needs list are the relationship issues that have gone unresolved (leading to an unmet need). What makes this additionally complicated is that often partners can be doing things that stand in the way of their own needs being met, such as the person who desires her partner to share with her, but then reacts, rather than listens, when he does. If she wants this need to be met, she *does* need to be careful not to sabotage it. If she truly wants him to share, she has to be willing to hear what he has to say without reacting to or punishing him for it. On *his* side, he needs to continue to risk sharing for the sake of the relationship.

Many of the items on a needs list will require deeper discussions about what can be done to remove the obstacles that *both* sides create to meeting the individual need.

The Sit-down

Most couples who come for counseling typically have stockpiled issues to the point that things are becoming, if not already are, overwhelming. Whatever the reasons for this, one of the most important routines you can introduce into a relationship to deal with this is that of "the sit-down".

---

[21]   To actually do a needs list, refer to the Appendix.

Typically, if there is no accountability routine, the only way change is addressed for the relationship is through one person finally deciding to complain, which, when done routinely, can create a negative, parental feel for the relationship. By over-relying on complaining, we are teaching each other that the only way things get better is if we make each other uncomfortable enough to force change.

The Parent-Child dynamic I mentioned back in Chapter 3 often has the Parent partner routinely directing complaints at the Child partner, because that's the only thing that gets the Child partner to comply. So the Parent has to create continued crises in order to motivate the Child to stay focused on the relationship.

The sit-down routine creates a platform for both positive and negative feedback, so no one has to resort to complaining to bring an issue up. It can be used for:

- couples who have a habit of letting things go too long without discussing them
- couples who seem to never have the time to talk things through
- couples who need a time reserved to discuss issues because otherwise the issues creep into all of the other conversations
- couples who are just learning how to use resolution tools
- couples who are practicing approaching and re-approaching in order to learn how to manage their anger without getting out of control
- couples who are trying to learn how to do regular maintenance on the relationship

The couple initially schedules a time (at the beginning, once a week would be recommended) to sit down and review how the week has gone. If you can't find thirty minutes out of your week to do this, it's a good indicator that your priorities are out of balance. Usually a good day to do the sit-down is on a Sunday afternoon or evening, since it's wrapping up the week behind and getting refocused on the week ahead.

Part of meeting on a regular basis is to give some focused time for recognizing what's been working and what still needs work, to keep track of the progress and to not let the relationship get distracted once again. Because there's time allowed for preparation, to think ahead about what your issues are, how best to express them, and what are some possible solutions, you've got a better chance of success with your conversations. If you don't have time to address something during the week, you know that it can wait until the weekly sit-down to discuss it.

Keeping it to a week at the beginning also has to do with the accuracy of our recall. It's easier to remember what happened just this past week, the details are still in our memory. If you go beyond that, the arguments tend to turn to who is even remembering it accurately.

I am not suggesting that this meeting time be an excuse to delay talking about the things that require immediate attention. The sit-down time is a backup system that acts as a net catching those things that managed to go unresolved during the week.

Another reason for such meetings is that they serve as a way of separating the problems from the rest of the relationship. In other words, couples can get to the point where most of their time spent together focuses on the problems. It even intrudes into date nights. And so the relationship becomes one big problem because whenever you go anywhere you naturally get back into discussing what's wrong. It's important to learn to separate problems from those parts of the relationship that are still working.

For some people, if one little area of the relationship is out of joint, they will not allow themselves to enjoy the rest. This is often when you get into situations where withholding is occurring. One familiar scenario is where one partner withholds sex from the other because he hasn't agreed to her terms in some other area of the relationship. While she may feel that she cannot approach physical intimacy so long as he is ignoring her need elsewhere, it turns the sexual relationship into a control issue, which is a very dangerous thing. **"Do not deprive each other except perhaps by mutual consent and for a time, so that you may devote yourselves to prayer. Then come together again so that Satan will not tempt you because of your lack of self-control."** (I Corinthians 7:5)

I understand that there are factors that interfere with both men and women being able to participate in a physical relationship with their partner whether they want to or not. What I am saying is that *it's important to try to isolate and salvage those areas of the relationship that are still intact because these are what will keep the relationship afloat while the repair work is being done elsewhere.*

Sit-down time needs to be split between giving appropriate recognition for the successes, and refining solutions to the relationship problems as a *team*, not individual accusers of the other. Hopefully, the arrived-at solutions are balanced in that they involve what *both* sides can do to assist with the current issues.

The first time you do a sit-down session at home it may seem very awkward. Some folks don't know where to start, while others have extensive backlogs of things they want to talk about. The typical length of a sit-down is about thirty minutes. It's not a marathon. Keeping it short helps keep the couple focused on what are the most important things to discuss. Each partner should feel that he gets equal time, and gets to address something important to him.

If a conversation is productive, and there's still more to discuss, you might want to go past the normal time frame. And sometimes it might be alright to focus on just one person's issues for that sit-down if the other partner is alright with that and doesn't have something they need to address as well. This isn't about creating an overly rigid structure. It needs to be something that the couple can adapt to their own particular style, so long as that style actually works.

Ideally, the first sit-down should be done after you've completed your needs list. The needs list becomes the initial topic of discussion, where you're making sure each of you understands specifically what the other needs and how they are hoping for those needs to be met. This is an important opportunity to discuss the dilemmas that interfere with meeting those needs.

Some of these conversations might just be replays (identify, resolve) and others may require the whole 4-step process for resolving an issue (identify, validate, explain, resolve) depending on the degree of the issue.

Sit-downs can sometimes be a little overwhelming at first because you are, in a way, attempting to combine the majority of guidelines that are contained in this book into one sitting. You are attempting to:

- stay focused on the issue at hand
- treat each person's side as information rather than something to react to
- remain focused on solutions rather than fault
- validate each other's opinions rather than dominate with your own
- manage your anger
- take turns talking and listening respectfully

You need to have realistic expectations that if you haven't had much success with resolution in the past, it's going to take practice before you see improvement. Which is why it's usually best to start with the smaller issues and gradually address the more complicated ones after you have become more familiar with the routine.

The general structure of a sit-down looks like this:

1. What's working:

    a. What I saw you do for me this past week that I really liked.

    b. What I did for you this past week that you may not have seen.

2. What we're still working on:

    a. The dangling issues (unfinished business) of the week

    b. The ongoing issues (the needs list)

Usually it's better to start with "what's working", because if you just jump into the issues the tendency is for each partner to defend themselves with evidence of when they successfully did meet that need, attempting to balance the partner's efforts at pointing out the times when they didn't. If the couple has already given recognition for the successes, it reduces the need to defend because successes have already been acknowledged.

The "what's working" is the time for each person to give recognition for positive efforts. It's time to give credit where credit is due and to help shape what works best for each other. It helps a couple force themselves to pay attention to the continuing positives.

If you do things in sequence, "what I saw you do" gives the other partner the information they need to be able to list "what I did for you that you may not have seen".

Some people have difficulty at first with the "what I did for you" because they take it as bragging. It's not about bragging, it's about putting the current energy going into the relationship on a conscious level. We often do things for our partner that goes unseen and, as a result, doesn't get credit.

A secondary reason for the "what I did for you" is that it's a nice self-assessment. If we, ourselves, can't think of anything that we did for our partner this past week, it's a nice wakeup call that we need to be investing more energy (and our partner didn't even have to point it out).

The "what we're still working on" is much better phrasing than "how you've failed me once again." I challenge couples to start replacing judgmental words such as "good or bad", "right or wrong", "stupid", etc. with "what's working" and "what's not working" when they discuss issues in the relationship. You can debate all day about whose way is best, or which way is right, but talking in terms of does it or doesn't it work tends to avoid the competitive, judgmental conversations. It's not about does it work for you, or work for me. It's about, does it work for us?

The "dangling issues" are the unresolved issues from the current week, if there are any. These are the short-term projects for the couple.

The "ongoing issues", as indicated, are about the needs list items - the long-term projects.

Usually couples will need to actually write down what solutions they commit to, so it doesn't depend on recall, and then they can follow up in future sit-downs with whether or not it got carried out as agreed on.

Otherwise, it's back to opinions of "I thought we agreed to this", when that's not what was said.

Doing sit-downs isn't about passing blame. It's about sharing ownership for the continued work, giving recognition where recognition is due, and keeping the relationship on a conscious level in order to keep it fit and focused.[22]

Over time, couples will typically reduce the frequency of the sit-downs from weekly to every-other-week to monthly, depending on how much there is to discuss. As the couple gets better at fielding the issues in a timely manner and coming up with applied strategies, the sit-downs become more about just the shared recognition of the positive efforts made.

Priority Assessment

While you're working towards a conscious, more disciplined relationship, it's also important that you're taking time to look at the overall *balance* of the relationship (in terms of how each of you is handling the individual priorities).

There are different priorities in everyone's life: self, partner, children, relatives, friends, work, health and exercise, hobbies/interests, and your spiritual walk. *No one priority should take our constant attention at the cost of everything else.* Rather, the priorities are separate balls in the hands of a juggler. You're continuing to juggle each of these responsibilities and giving them their needed attention. If too much time is spent on any one, the majority of the other balls get dropped. Stress sets in. Chaos looms. Yes, the juggling act in itself can be stressful, but a juggler who has developed that skill, at some point, comes to see the act of juggling as second-nature.

Sometimes work will come first before having lunch with your partner. Sometimes the children will come before a trip to the gym. But overall you're trying to pay attention to where most of your energy goes, and

---

[22] For more specifics on the weekly sit-down, take a look at the Appendix at the end of the book.

what gets the least. The extreme ends are usually where we fall out of balance: over-focused or under-focused.

Of the various priorities, your spiritual walk is slightly different than the rest. Rather than our relationship with God being a separate aspect of our life (as I mentioned in talking about toxic faith in Chapter 2), one's spiritual life, if healthy and active, becomes integrated with all of the other priorities, rather than kept separate.

As people age and available time and energy becomes more precious, most put the majority of their energy into only two or three priorities and tend to start neglecting the rest. But *in times of crises, how well you manage through any particular crisis is often determined by how balanced all of your priorities are.* Men tend to get more of their needs met through their work and hobbies, neglecting social supports. Women tend to get the majority of their needs met through their relationships and their families, often neglecting their health and having any personal interests (though these stereotypes are changing with our two-job family culture).

Some will end up placing an incredible demand on their partner for meeting their needs because they have neglected so many other areas of their lives, especially other social supports. While it is important to be working on meeting each other's needs, no relationship should have the burden of trying to meet *all* of one's needs. A balanced lifestyle, with balanced priorities, provides for this.

Keeping this in mind, another tool for personal accountability that you can use for the weekly sit-down is a priority assessment.[23] While it is designed for the individual, it can just as easily be a couple's activity. So the focus is how much are we, as a couple, in balance.

The outcome of doing a priority assessment is, hopefully, a specific plan for how you're going to implement restoring a more healthy degree of balance in your life. Doing the assessment is also helpful for those folks who think things are already in balance. By actually mapping it out, sometimes they're surprised at what they find. They'd become so caught

---

[23] Again, see the Appendix.

up in the schedules and routines that they'd lost sight of the big picture without even realizing it.

Since we can be too close to our own lives to have perspective on the bigger picture, sometimes it's helpful to invite feedback from our partner on the accuracy of our personal assessment. They may have some good insights (and hopefully not see it as an opportunity to judge).

Aside from being another form of personal accountability, routinely doing this kind of exercise allows you to feel like you are managing the direction (and balance) of your own life, rather than life dictating to you.

Forgiveness Rituals

As children, we are often taught that when you've wronged somebody you're supposed to approach the person you've wronged and apologize ("I'm sorry..."), and then they're supposed to say in return, "I forgive you." But it is a ritual that is a little more complicated in the adult world.

As adults, while it's still important to apologize and forgive, just because someone has expressed that he's sorry, doesn't mean that the person he's offended may be at a place of forgiveness yet. Sometimes true forgiveness takes time. It can't be forced. To say we've forgiven somebody before we're truly able to forgive creates a dilemma, since we've still got our anger or resentment to deal with.

I spent more time discussing forgiveness in Chapter 8 (Rule #23), but it's relevant here that I mention the need for every couple that is experiencing resentment for past mistakes to have a conscious routine where they're making a visible gesture to their partner of "letting go". The ritual we're taught as children starts with ownership ("You were right", or "I was wrong", or, "I shouldn't have done that," or "I'm sorry that hurt you."), before it moves on to forgiveness. As adults, though it doesn't have to be identical to that, ownership of a wrong always makes it easier to move on to forgiving.

Of course, there are details that make this difficult. Maybe the issue in question has yet to be resolved. Maybe the problem's continuing. Maybe the partner is unrepentant. But whatever the case, we are trying to create a mutual standard of forgiving just as we ourselves desire to be forgiven. To refuse to do so is choosing to anchor the relationship to the past rather than freeing ourselves to move forward, which allows resentment and bitterness to take root.

If we are saying, "I'll never be able to forgive you for that," then what we are really saying is there is never any way we will be able to have a restored relationship. Usually in those situations, however, a more accurate statement is, "I will never be able to look at what you did as okay." Which is actually different than whether or not you'll ever be able to forgive. Forgiveness is not about making a wrong okay.

Part of the process of forgiveness sometimes requires a condition in terms of "What I need from you in order to feel like I can move forward again is..." It's important to handle this sincerely and respectfully, rather than a manipulation for compliance. Sometimes a partner's sincere repentance is enough, but sometimes we need specific evidence of necessary change if we're going to be able to trust again.

How a couple chooses to approach a forgiveness routine for past hurts is up to them, but it needs to be something meaningful for the couple. It could be a spoken ritual ("I forgive you."). It could be a certain symbolic gesture (making a list of past wrongs and burning it together) or act of kindness (flowers, gifts, cards, etc.).

Ultimately, if you do a good job with the courtship and accountability routines, the less likely you will ever need to depend on the forgiveness ritual.

The keys behind staying disciplined with these routines are:

- maintaining your motivation (healthy love for each other, respect for yourself)

- honoring that love is more than lip-service, that there should be evidence

- not taking your progress for granted or becoming too comfortable

- attaching a conscious priority to making them happen (scheduling and following through)
- keeping an awareness of the present moment and opportunities to act
- not allowing yourself to become too distracted by other things
- *sharing* the commitment to see them through

Some people need the rigidity of a planned schedule if they are going to follow these routines, while others can be more flexible and creative and still accomplish the core of what I'm trying to get across here. As with everything else in this book, fit it to your own style. You're not going to be perfect in being consistent or getting great results each time in the same way that you can't force time with your partner to always be quality time. But what matters is you're continuing to try, you're continuing to make yourselves available to each other, and, with practice, you *will* get better at it.

The positives gained from staying with the routines (a consistent focus on meeting each other's needs, routinely working through issues without stockpiling them, having a thriving courtship, and keeping your priorities balanced) helps keep your focus over the long run on what's important. They're just helpful ways of maintaining your relationship on a conscious level, keeping your conflicts to a minimum, and staying awake on your journey through life.

Discussion Questions:

1. **How often do you and your partner do things together, just the two of you?** Do you feel it's often enough that you stay connected? Are you able to focus on just having fun when you go out on a date, or do business and problems play a big part in the conversation? Do your dates provide variety, or have they fallen into a predictable routine? What do you look for in dating that helps you feel close and connected?

2. **Are setting dates the responsibility of just one of you, or do you share in initiating and making plans?** Do the two of you

have things to look forward to at the end of the week? Is time alone together something that is still sought after, or has it lost its spark? If everything has become serious, how can you reintroduce fun into your relationship?

3. **Do both of you feel like you specifically know what your partner needs from you?** When was the last time you compared notes on this?

4. **Is there an accountability routine already in place for the two of you?** If not, how do the two of you approach what needs to change? And how do you monitor whether that change persists over time?

5. **How balanced are each of your priorities?** Are there any priorities that are going neglected? How do you measure what is and what is not in balance? Are you and your partner in agreement about the priorities that need work? What's the plan for restoring balance?

6. **Is there a forgiveness routine in the relationship?** How do you go about forgiving each other? Is there anything currently hanging over the relationship that needs to be forgiven? If so, what needs to happen in order for forgiveness to occur?

Part IV

Unique Situations

Chapter 11
Affairs and Conflict

**"You have heard that it was said to those of old 'You
shall not commit adultery.' But I say to you that whoever
looks at a woman to lust for her has already committed
adultery with her in his heart."** (Matthew 5:27-28)

Aside from physical, emotional or substance abuse, there is little that
can happen in a relationship that is as destructive to the foundation as
having an affair. Of the only two criteria in the New Testament that
allow Christians to divorce, affairs are one of them.

In a dating relationship, if the relationship is exclusive and you are
cheated on, it should be the end of the relationship since the primary test
at that relationship stage was finding out whether or not your partner
could be exclusive with you. If they prove this to not be true, it's *not* a
matter of working things out. They failed the test. In a marriage, because
a deeper commitment exists and there are more things to take into
account (such as children), it's often not so simple.

Affairs occur for many different reasons. Let me be very clear in saying
here at the start, however, that *none of the reasons why an affair occurs
actually justifies the act*. But, sometimes, *why* the affair occurred, and
what the couple is willing to do about it, leaves room for the relationship
to be repaired.

Why Does It Happen?

When an affair occurs, the natural reaction of whoever was cheated on is to want to know "Why?" Part of needing to know the "why" is an attempt to gain some sense of control over what's happening. Possibly, the more we know about what happened, the more we'll be able to make sense of things. But part of knowing why also helps us to make a decision about what we need to do next: to stay or go.

Many people who haven't experienced an affair for themselves tend to think that an affair is all about lust and cheap sex. Certainly many movies that depict infidelity promote exactly that. And, sometimes, yes, that's exactly what it is. The offender was immature, self-absorbed and showed little or no emotional discipline and so the affair occurred. But many times affairs occur when the offenders are actually solid family figures. They had morals. They were good mothers or fathers. They loved their partners. Yet, it still happened. Why?

One of the most common statements I hear from clients who've committed an affair is, "I never thought it could happen to me." And that's a very important point. *Often, because people see themselves as being above having an affair, they're not taking the necessary precautions to prevent one from occurring.* Because they think it can't happen to them, they've developed a blind spot. Whereas if they'd realized that they're human, so they're not above temptation, they might have been a little more watchful, a little more aware when they first started to compromise.

Acting on Impulse

Sometimes, affairs occur as momentary acts of passion: a one-night stand, or a business trip where things got out of hand. Usually, these are times where there is a sense of isolation, promoting a disconnection from the rest of our daily lives.

Sometimes, because of that momentary aspect, an impulsive act, it's easier for the partner to forgive because it wasn't anything deeper (it wasn't about love). For others, the opposite is true. The partner could understand it better if it *were* about love. If the feelings were that deep, then it would make more sense that it could overpower the commitment to the relationship. It wouldn't excuse it, but it would make more sense.

Under the Influence

Like it or not, people need to be honest with themselves that when alcohol or other drugs are involved our inhibitions and standards are lowered or disappear. Too many affairs of the moment occur under these kinds of circumstances.

If we know this is the case, that we're more likely to compromise ourselves if alcohol is involved, yet we continue to take that risk, at some point we have to ask ourselves if we're just using the alcohol as an excuse to allow ourselves to make foolish choices.

Times of Crisis

Affairs can occur when we are distracted by other severe stressors in our lives. Death of a family member. Ending of a career. Marital separation. Midlife crisis.

Because our personal identity is already being tested or threatened during such times, our personal lines (standards) often become temporarily vague. We may choose to do things that seem inconsistent and out of character for us because, in the midst of that crisis, we have become somewhat lost.

Small Compromises

For many, what makes an affair possible are the subtle, small compromises that lead us through the process of making much bigger ones. In other words, if things at the start of the outside relationship had been presented so blatantly ("I'm having an affair"), the lines would never have been crossed.

Because we are living in the everyday, it is often difficult to see where the choices we make in the present moment are leading. Often, affairs begin as friendships that develop into flirtations that become something more over time.

At the start, it's exciting. It's fun. Someone likes us. We feel attractive. It's harmless. It's safe. It's not going to go anywhere. And then we take it a step further. Conversations on the phone. Getting together for an occasional lunch. Still "safe". Nothing physical. Just good conversation. Good company. The occasional hug. Maybe a kiss on the cheek in greeting or goodbye. A good friend.

In this process, we're gradually starting to get needs met from someone other than our partners, which, by itself, may still be in the realm of "okay". It's true that in any committed relationship we still need to have outside friendships in order to avoid placing all of our social needs on our partners. Yet, there is such a thing as an "emotional affair" where we're starting to get personal needs met from an opposite sex friend that really no longer has to do with being "social".

What often is so attractive about these relationships is how removed they are from the rest of our lives. We can talk about almost anything with this person, because we don't have to live with them. A sense of intimacy is being created that is somewhat artificial because it's disconnected from the everyday. Since we are able to discuss very personal things without having to be concerned about editing, there is a sense of freedom in this relationship that we may no longer have in our own committed one. In that way, it's hard for even a marriage to compete with the fantasy that an affair takes on (removed from consequences and responsibilities).

It is also because of this unreal aspect to the "friendship" that we can start making potentially distorted attributions about our friend and what they would be like in a romantic relationship.

Whatever the case, at some point, the friendship boundary gets crossed. Maybe not in a big way, but if we were looking at it from a distance, we'd be able to say that that was not something you'd do with a friend. Maybe it's a quick kiss on the mouth instead of the cheek. Maybe it's starting to choose one-on-one activities that are more in the category of dates: going to movies, dinner instead of lunch, etc. Gradually, things are being moved into a romance. And we're creating a current that's starting to gain strength.

Because of the shared nature of these small compromises, there is a sense of "being in it together" that keeps the couple intimately connected yet isolated from the rest of the world.

Compartmentalizing

There is a skill that men, more-so than women, seem to possess called "compartmentalizing". Basically, this is when you set up different "compartments" in your mind that contain the emotion connected with that situation but don't allow it to cross the boundaries of the compartment to affect other areas of your life (all of the other compartments).

Men are often raised in a way that promotes this kind of "skill". They're taught not to cry, to be tough, and not show weakness. And they do that by putting all those emotions in compartments and sealing them off. It's not that the feelings aren't there any longer, they're just being contained.

Women are often given greater permission to be emotional. It's not that they don't have "compartments" like men do, it's just that the compartments' walls are not as high. As a result, one emotional event tends to overflow into the surrounding compartments.

Compartmentalizing is a mixed blessing. It's a good survival skill to learn in that it helps you deal with emotional stress by providing you with a method for separating yourself from it. However, separating yourself from pain isn't always a solution. If it's pain that you cannot do anything to relieve, or is overwhelming to you, then it's sometimes necessary to keep at a distance in order to emotionally function in the present. However, if it's pain that you've caused or play a part in, or pain that's holding you back because you haven't worked through it, then, sooner or later, continuing to compartmentalize it will begin to have an adverse effect on your life.

Compartmentalizing is what often occurs with affairs. It makes it possible for the offender to insist he still feels love for his spouse while the affair is going on. While it's certainly true that he is not *being* loving by having an affair, he can still *feel* love towards both people. He separates the one from the other. That separation of feelings, not allowing the compartments to overlap, prevents him from having to face the impact that his choices actually have on all the other "compartments".

Not allowing the compartments to overlap involves a certain degree of intentional focus. In other words, there is a refusal (conscious or unconscious) to look too closely at the big picture. We are able to allow ourselves to continue to act in a way that we wouldn't normally approve of because we stay firmly rooted in the moment, looking only at the next footstep ahead of us rather than where this path is taking us.

Because we've created this "relationship in a bubble", removed from the rest of reality, we can continue to entertain the notion that everything's going to be okay. What we're doing over here isn't going to impact the relationship over there.

Selfish love versus Healthy Love

Even with those affairs where it is supposedly about love, where the plan may be to ultimately leave the spouses and ride off into the sunset together, it brings into question whether the couple caught in the affair understands the difference between selfish love versus healthy love.

Selfish love is about immediate gratification, what we want now despite how it may hurt us, and others, in the future. While we may be thinking of a future together with this person, we're totally ignoring the impact this is going to have on everybody else we care about by how we're going about it. That's selfish.

Also, if we were truly showing love to this person we were involved with, why would we be willing to risk destroying *her* life, *her* family, *her* reputation, by involving her in an affair? The offender and the lover are, in reality, participating in *mutual neglect, not* healthy love.

Confusing Passion with Love

Many people are confused about mature love versus desire. Because they are able to experience desire for somebody, they automatically assume that it means something deeper. Being "in-love" can be very deceptive because, while the feelings experienced may seem to go very deep, the relationship itself can still be very superficial.

Like it or not, just because you're married does not mean you are going to stop being attracted to other people. Your hormones don't stop functioning. You're still biologically engineered to procreate. So when you come across somebody that is a good biological fit, you're going to notice them. Where things go after that depends on how you choose to deal with it.

If you feed those feelings, through fantasy or actually developing a relationship with that person, they will grow stronger. In the same way that, within your marriage, how much passion stays alive often depends on how much you continue to fuel those feelings for each other.

Just because you're able to feel something for someone other than your partner doesn't mean that the love you have for your partner is false. But *it does make it harder to feel for your spouse while you are nurturing feelings for someone else.* That's one big reason why you can't start working on a marriage again until whoever's having the affair has ended it.

Needs

There is often an assumption that if someone has an affair it must have been because he wasn't getting his needs met in the marriage, which tends to place the blame on the scorned partner.

Before I talk about those situations where this holds true, let me say *that there are many situations where infidelities occur yet the marriage needs were being consistently met* (which is why it's important to never see your own marriage as being completely "above it", no matter how great it may be). I don't say that to give you something to panic over, but just so you'll be cautious and take the proper steps to safeguard against it.

We are all need-driven. I've stated that throughout this book. The core needs can't be denied. They will make themselves known somehow. Those central needs are legitimate and need to be addressed by the committed couple. The problems that arise result from the unhealthy ways we attempt to get those needs met.

Sometimes there *are* relationships where the needs are being starved. Maybe we're not even aware of it on a conscious level, but because we're still "in need", we're vulnerable to other sources that are willing to meet those needs.

Sometimes "the affair" isn't with another person. It's with our job, or a hobby. It has such a strong pull on our time and attention because we were emotionally starving and didn't even know it.

An affair can be so powerful because it provides for all three core needs. It makes us feel *significant* to know that somebody desires us so intensely. It makes us feel *secure* to have somebody we feel we can trust with so much of our personal life. (Though you'd think that knowing if the affair was discovered it would have devastating results would make someone feel anything but secure.) And the companionship and physicality of it satisfies the need for *fun*.

If the affair occurred, at least in part, due to unmet needs, it can sometimes be a relief to the injured partner to know that there is something she can actually work on to improve the quality of the relationship (something within her control). The balance is that, while each person owns responsibility for meeting the needs of the relationship, the offender accepts that unmet needs *never* justify "stepping out" on the relationship. It wouldn't be fair to the partner to make her feel that if she's not always successful at "meeting the needs", she's responsible for the possibility of another affair occurring.

Comparison Shopping

There are some who have affairs because they are chronically second-guessing the decision they made to marry. They become involved in flirtations and more, because they are still looking for a potential partner. They are married, yet exploring options on the side for a better fit.

It's an unending quest because there's always somebody out there who is stronger in one quality or another than the current partner. So even if the offender ends one affair after concluding she's not a good enough fit, it still leaves the question open about the next one that comes along.

The offender has to become willing to step back to respecting the commitment that's already been made. He already chose his partner. If he wasn't content with that decision, he shouldn't have made it to start with. And even if it was a matter of coming to question it down the road, after problems have arisen, the initial commitment is still to honor working on the relationship he's in, not trying to juggle it with others he's tempted to explore.

What it comes down to is, if you're unhappy with your relationship/ marriage, do what you need to do to improve it, or accept responsibility for ending it. Don't complicate it, cheapen it, with an affair.

Many won't approach it in these black-and-white terms simply because they don't want to walk away from what they have unless they know for sure there's something better to go to (which is a needy and using way of approaching relationships).

What the offender fails to recognize is that the person he is risking the marriage over is somebody whose character is already in question. After all, this person is willing, no matter how reluctantly, to have an affair with a married person. What makes him think that her immoral behavior will stop with him? Or what makes her think that his immoral behavior will stop with her? Isn't there going to be somebody else with a particular quality that's better than hers that will start that quest all over again?

Also, while the offender is looking for somebody with superior qualities to his own partner, he isn't considering his *own* qualities by compromising the marriage this way. He is engaged in behaviors that he himself wouldn't tolerate.

Sexual Addiction

Some affairs are due to a sexual addiction. If this is just one of many affairs that have occurred, this needs to seriously be considered. While there are degrees to this, the "entry level" for an addiction is continuing to make a particular unhealthy choice *despite* having experienced consequences for it. If you've committed an affair in the past, paid a price for it, but are now starting into another one, something more deeply problematic is going on than just the affair.

Few relationships can tolerate such issues because it continually undermines any trust that is regained between affairs.

A Way Out

Sometimes having an affair is the way a partner chooses to end his marriage. For whatever reason (fear of confrontation, an avoidant personality, immaturity, etc.), he can't end the marriage directly so he's forcing his partner's hand to make that decision for him. It's his indirect way out. He may not even be doing so on a conscious level, but he knows what will happen if he gets caught, and may not even be trying to cover his tracks.

It can often come as a surprise to the offender, when the affair is finally discovered, that the injured partner is still willing to work things out. The offender assumed that the relationship would just be over, but now, if it *is* going to end, he will still have to be the one to make that decision.

Sometimes the fact that his partner loves him that much that she would stay *despite* his affair makes him reconsider his opinion of her, as well as his feelings towards her. Other times, he starts looking for new ways to sabotage the relationship, so he can still force her to end it.

Boundaries

Some affairs occur due to poor boundaries. Because the relationship lines are thin for the offender, he practices a degree of verbal and physical intimacy with others that should normally be reserved for his partner. The more he discloses intimate information the more he is creating an intimate atmosphere with whoever he is sharing it with. Someone with clear boundaries treats strangers and friends noticeably different than the favor he shows to his partner. Especially in terms of the confidences that he shares, the types of compliments he gives, and the respect he shows for personal space (proximity and touch).

*　*　*

Sometimes it's not that the boundaries were poor, it's that the person of interest for the offender was already "in", such as a best friend, or a long-term colleague. He was "protected" against strangers and friends, because those boundaries were distinct. If he'd been approached by someone outside of his inner circle it would have been easy to pass the opportunity by. But because this person was closer than that, an attachment already in existence, he was vulnerable and likely didn't even realize it.

In these kind of situations, it's predictable for the victim to still be paranoid about *any* outside threat to the relationship, but it's more likely that the only "weak spot" for the offender was for those that were closest. That doesn't have to mean he has to give up all of his other closest opposite-sex friends. It just means he puts more intentional space and boundary lines in place than he did before (though, obviously, it *will* cost him his relationship with the close friend he had the affair with if the marriage is to continue).

Payback

Occasionally, an affair is sought out in order to punish the partner for past behavior. There is little remorse involved because the offender feels justified in what he's doing.

Payback scenarios are inherently complicated because what the "victim" needs most from the offender is some evidence of remorse, yet the offender has little or none to offer.

Having an affair in order to punish a partner for having an affair first is immature thinking (and a lack of character because of the vindictive behavior). If it wasn't okay for him, then it shouldn't be okay for her. By her lowering herself to that level, it doesn't make things even. Since she's doing it intentionally to hurt back, it actually puts her *below* the partner's level and creates a new set of issues for the relationship.

It's hard to imagine a relationship that's spiritually sound and yet an affair occurs. At the same time, it's not all that uncommon to hear of pastors leaving their congregation to run off with the church secretary, or someone that they've been personally counseling. What happened?

Spiritual drift often occurs when accountability is lacking. Because there is an *assumption* that things are spiritually okay, no one bothers to look any deeper, especially the one who is drifting.

Also, because it is right, loving and "Christian" to help others, sometimes individuals don't even recognize when they're starting to cross the lines between being loving versus inappropriate. Brotherly love becomes corrupted into erotic love.

To complicate this, a personal faith can become twisted to accommodate a developing affair because of the over-spiritualizing that sometimes goes along with it. The attraction, and how the two came together, must be "meant to be". Something that is strictly forbidden Biblically becomes rationalized into something God-ordained.

What makes the "why's" difficult to assess is that typically there isn't just one reason for why we do what we do. In any given moment, the choices we make are because of a *combination* of any number of factors. There is rarely one root cause that simplifies and explains everything. While we yearn for such an explanation that would provide us with some degree of security and understanding, it's usually not that simple. And so we have to remain open to exploring its complexity.

Understanding the "why's" as much as we are able *can* provide us with the necessary information we need in order to decide just how big the problem is, and if we're willing to do the repairs.

Likelihood of repair

So, if your partner has an affair, and you're married, what things should you consider in deciding to stay or go? What constitutes ending the relationship?

For some, if an affair occurs even once, the relationship's over. It's a clear line. Others will *say* that that line is a clear one, but, when it's actually crossed by the partner, they find themselves struggling to make a choice.

Things to take into consideration in making such a decision:

- A history of such behavior
- Presence of character
- Sincerity to recommit

A History of Such Behavior

An isolated incident does not mean the same as a recurring pattern. If the offender has never had any prior affairs, there is some room to believe that it was a foolish choice, a serious mistake or lapse of judgment, but something that can still be repaired.

I tend to visualize it in terms of the addictions progression. There are four levels of significance for a potential addiction:

1. Use
2. Misuse
3. Abuse
4. Dependency

Use is using something for what it's intended. Sex is naturally "used' to have children, and to support the emotional/physical connection between husband and wife.

Misuse is using something for other than what it's intended (infidelity), but *without* experiencing consequences for the misuse. If consequences *are* experienced, then the misuse stops.

Abuse is continuing to choose to engage in the behavior, even though it's costing us. We continue to misuse *despite* consequences.

Dependency, too, is continuing to engage in destructive behavior despite consequences, but it also involves some other aspects. There can be a growing *tolerance* (needing to increase the behavior in order to feel the same as when they first started). There can be *withdrawal* (emotional or physical reactions when the behavior is stopped). Engaging in the behavior more than planned. Going out of one's way in order to continue the behavior. The behavior persists despite attempts to stop.

Dependency, in terms of affairs, is sexual addiction.

The person who has had a one-time affair is at the point of *misuse.* If there is enough of a consequence (external or internal) attached to that wrongful act, often the moral line is redrawn and not crossed again.[24]

Attaching a label of "misuse" may seem that I'm putting an affair into a very mild context, but keep in mind that a one-time episode of "misusing" alcohol can get someone killed.

If the affair was an ongoing one and the line was crossed several times but with the same person, yet there were no identifiable consequences for the couple, it could still fall under the category of misuse. Because there were no *external* consequences to snap the couple back to reality, the relationship was able to persist. However, the question remains why were the *internal* consequences (conscience) not sufficient enough to halt the relationship, since there was more than one opportunity to stop.

If the affair *did* experience consequences (such as being discovered), *yet still continued,* most likely an emotional attachment has occurred. The illicit relationship has become a priority to the degree that even real-world consequences aren't going to immediately disrupt it.

What sometimes makes the self-assessment of moral character difficult for the couple caught in the affair, is that, if they're "in-love" (which

---

[24] For people with a developed conscience, their own awareness of what they did is often enough of a consequence to prevent them from re-violating that standard.

is equivalent with being emotionally out-of-control), the couple has often convinced themselves that it's somehow right. ("How can this be wrong if I feel so connected to this person?") There is a tendency to romanticize, idealize or over-spiritualize the experience. They're not coherent enough to recognize that *satisfying a need is going to feel good, even if you're doing it in a destructive way.* On a big picture level, there's no way that what's going on can be justified. But because their world is reduced to the two of them, there is no longer any clear big-picture perspective.

Lack of moral character, emotional immaturity, or dependency (sexual addiction) are the automatic concerns when there have been *multiple* affairs or flirtations. Typically, there have been consequences that have failed to make a sufficient impact, and there is continuing evidence that the problem persists despite attempted interventions.

*   *   *

As far as damage done, just a one-time affair can violate the trust to the degree that the victim may not be able to allow herself to be vulnerable again. For others, because they see the offender's remorse and commitment to correct a horrible mistake, they are gradually able to let go and move on.

How does one know if they can't get past it? Trying to move forward and being unable. That doesn't mean trying once, finding an emotional roadblock, and giving up. That means continued attempts over time (months, sometimes longer) that prove unsuccessful.

Perhaps surprising in this current age of "do what feels good", a large percentage of marriages that experience affairs still try to work through it. The victim is certainly justified in walking away from the unfaithful partner, but many are able to recognize that there is enough still working for the relationship that it is worth trying to salvage.

When a *pattern* of such behavior exists, the problem for the partner becomes, "At what point is continuing to try to work on the relationship showing my partner that he can basically get away with it, because I keep taking him back?" Continuing to take the partner back leads to a loss of the victim's own self-esteem and self-respect, because they are accepting unacceptable behavior, and treating themselves as not worthy of more.

Presence of character

If your history with your partner has been one where he has handled life with discipline (holding down a regular job, managing money wisely, a good parent, an attentive spouse, no substance abuse, good in a crisis), yet an affair has occurred, it isn't likely that all of a sudden he's lost all of that character, or that it was all a lie.

A grievous lack of judgment in one area of a person's life does not erase all of the good in the other areas (though it is certainly going to be difficult for the victim to stay in touch with that fact). If anything, that presence of character is a good indication that that person has the necessary tools to put his life back in order. He may have believed himself to be above making such a mistake, but, hopefully, with having been humbled, he will do whatever's necessary to keep the damage from becoming even greater.

There are some people that go full force at whatever challenge has been placed in front of them. That is how they approach life. They already have the self-discipline to do "what it takes". So when the "challenge" of repairing the relationship is put in front of them, they are usually good at rising to the occasion. So long as they are able to recognize that repairing a relationship is not all about surface behavior (resuming the roles of the marriage) but *depth* of relationship (courting, openness, true intimacy), the likelihood of success can be pretty good.

Sincerity to recommit

A willingness to set things right, as much as that is possible, should be evident from the offender. What most victims are looking for is some sign of true remorse. They need to know that change is taken seriously and will last. Unfortunately, both of those things can only really be proven over time.

For many offenders, their pride gets in the way when their partners start to make demands of them to prove that they are trustworthy. They feel embarrassed enough at what they did, and now feel like they're being asked to jump through hoops to prove themselves. But they need to understand that trust isn't regained overnight and the damage done is for them to own and repair.

This isn't to say that if there were marital problems prior to the affair that these go unaddressed. It's just that, right now, when the wound is still fresh, it's not yet the time.

What many offenders will worry about is, "How long is it going to be like this?" In other words, how long will they have to go through the questioning and the emotional waves? The attitude (and answer) the offender needs to work at accepting is, "As long as it takes".

If the offender loses his patience and attempts to force the victim to "get over it", the message he conveys to his partner is, "I'm not really sincere about this. I just want to get off the hook as quickly as possible."

It's understandable that no one would want to be in a lifelong relationship if equality was never restored. But, over time, there should be a visible progression to the trust being regained. Over time, the wounds should start to heal, though there will always be a scar.

If a year down the road there is just as much need for the victim to have to double-check everything, just as many emotional meltdowns or setbacks, even though there's been no evidence of any continued infidelities, it would indicate that something else is in the way of forgiveness. In such situations, the victim may have become "stuck".

*　*　*

True repentance *is* possible. Sometimes it's not until we're about to lose something, or someone, that we realize just how important they are to us. When boundaries are failing in a relationship and we've become accustomed to taking each other for granted, a crisis of these proportions can restore clarity in a dramatic way. Suddenly we see our partner again as separate, not just an extension of us. We see a real human being, experiencing serious emotional pain that *we've* caused.

The enormity of what we've done is made real, and all of what we are about to lose finally hits us.

Hopefully, while it is a good thing to have perspective restored, it hasn't occurred "too little too late".

Regaining Trust

For most, to regain trust means that the offender's life becomes an open book. Phone records are made readily available. Passwords to internet accounts are freely shared. Time is willingly accounted for. More effort is made to check-in when there are changes in plans. Questions about the unknowns (past and present) are entertained. Obviously, the offender needs to be willing to humble himself to his partner in order to submit to this. It's *not* punishment. It's being accountable in order to regain trust.

Earlier in the book we discussed the difference between accountability versus judgment. Exercising loving accountability towards our partners is calling them on the things that they may be doing that are destructive to the relationship. Sometimes accountability leads to confrontation - drawing a clear line of what is acceptable and unacceptable in the relationship. And sometimes confrontation requires an ultimatum if meaningful change has yet to occur.

Accountability is in terms of what you need from your partner in order to regain trust. If the offender is saying he will do whatever it takes to make the relationship work, this is where the evidence of true change is visible. It's not making unreasonable demands just to control and punish. It's serious time assessing what the victim truly needs in order to initially get past the hurt, and then starting to work on repair.

Sometimes *major* sacrifices need to be made in order to put the relationship first again. If the offender worked closely with the person he had the affair with, a job change may be necessary. If they lived next door, a move may have to happen. There need to be clear, visible boundaries that safeguard the relationship for the victim, even if there is no way the affair could ever begin again. It's unrealistic for the offender to think that a person he's crossed such a personal line with will no longer be a continued temptation with continued regular contact. And it's unrealistic for him to expect that his partner should just take his word for it that it will never happen again. His word, at that point, holds little weight.

The Victim's Role

When we feel betrayed by an affair it's all too easy to "cope" with it by venting. Venting, in itself, is healthy. We *do* need to get those painful feelings out rather than let them fester inside. But we also need to be careful that, when we *do* let them out, we don't do even more damage in the process.

Ultimately, we're hurt because our needs to feel secure and significant in the relationship have both taken a serious blow. Yet by letting reactions get out of hand, by letting our anger run wild so that now *we're* compromising our own standards, we're introducing more problems into the picture and working against our own needs. Yes, it may be because of what *he* did, but that still doesn't remove her from being responsible for what *she* does.

It's expected that emotions will come in waves. Little things she sees on TV, hears on the radio, passes by in the car, will set her feelings off all over again. That's natural. She needs to allow herself time to learn to ride out those waves, rather than letting the waves control her. The more she just represses them and acts like everything's okay, the more likely they'll start to build up. The more she gives herself permission to feel what she needs to feel, she's cooperating with the process, not delaying or putting it off.

Anger is effective to a degree, so long as it isn't about attacking or slinging character judgments. Anger is expected. She *does* need to be able to show her pain, but what makes it more deeply significant for the offender is for her to show it through her hurt and woundedness (the vulnerable side, the injured heart). Ultimately, that's what gives her access to *his* heart again - the quickest way to move him towards true remorse.

Attempts to punish are often out of a desire to make the consequence severe enough that she can feel like he'll take her seriously, so it won't happen again. Which is why many people never stop punishing. Conscious or not, the logic is that if they stop making the partner feel the cost, it'll make it okay to happen again. As long as that discomfort level is maintained, there's an unhealthy security. But if she's ultimately trying to approach forgiveness, letting go and moving forward, sooner than later she will have to give up her efforts at payback.

Because forgiveness is a process, it does take time. It can't be forced, by us or by our partners. In the same way that we need time to grieve the death of a loved one, we need time to grieve the loss of the relationship's trust.

*   *   *

Initially, victims will frequently try to over-control the situation, such as with trying to force the offender to call the former lover to break it off, dictating to him what they want him to say, like a puppet on a string. Or sometimes they want that confrontation to be face-to-face. They want the hateful words that they have to share to come from the offender, rejecting the way they felt rejected, while portraying a united front - the couple back together. They will feel angry if the offender isn't willing to look at this other person exactly the same way they do. Any attempts from the offender to explain the ex-lover's circumstances, or describe her as anything less than evil, is seen as siding with "the enemy" rather than attempts to help the victim better understand this other person's motivations.

If the affair is not already over at the time it is discovered or disclosed, there usually *does* need to be some sort of evidence that it is over other than just taking the offender's word for it. Usually this is best done in a letter or e-mail, which the offender shows to the victim *before* he sends it (evidence that it's happening). This is *not* an opportunity for the victim to dictate to the offender what to write. It's not going to be hate mail, but neither should it be a love letter. Usually in the letter the offender is taking responsibility for his wrongful choice in having the affair, clearly stating that the relationship is over, and that communication from that point on is ended (that his focus will now be on attempting to restore his marriage).

While the victim's attempts to force compliance in the offender *do* give an artificial sense that she has regained some control of the situation, her methods often don't get at the heart of things. Forcing a partner to say what you want them to say, feel what you want them to feel, isn't free will. It's not authentic. So even if the offender is willing to cooperate, his actions are still going to feel hollow to both the victim and the offender if it's not really coming from him.

The uncomfortable truth is that, unless the former lover did something horrific to the offender either while they were together or after they broke up, the offender is naturally going to continue to have positive feelings towards her. Yes, she showed poor judgment by being involved with a married man, but the offender did the same by being involved with her. So, predictably, he's not going to see her as the bad guy, since they were *both* "bad guys."

The *legitimate* underlying need for the victim is to be sure that there is no way this outside relationship can continue, that the "threat" has been removed. But she needs to understand that it's not about the offender hating this other person in order to feel secure again. What's important is that the victim knows that the offender hates *what he did* (cheated). It's not about hating the person, it's about hating the choice.

If it's only about knowing that the offender now despises that particular person, even if he truly does, what about all of the other desirable women still out there? The victim only dealt with a single branch, but there's a lot of other branches that she will now see as potential threats. However, if she's going for the root (the offender hating *the choice* he made), she doesn't have to worry about *any* other women, good or bad, because the only way something would reoccur was if he was willing to make that same choice again.

* * *

When it comes to the questions the victim asks, the extremes are either asking too much, or asking too little.

There *are* questions that are destructive and only serve to create new issues. Getting into the graphic details of what occurred physically

235

with an affair isn't useful information. Asking questions focused on making physical or relational comparisons between the victim and the partner's ex-lover is seldom helpful. The important questions are the ones that help establish 1) what led up to it (origin), 2) how long it went on (duration), 3) how often they met (frequency), and 4) how serious it was (severity). Because the victim is too close to her pain, she usually can't exercise good judgment in discerning the healthy questions from the unhealthy, which is why most couples have to seek out counselors who specialize with affair recovery to help them sort it out.

When you consider the physiology of a trauma, the brain has often become stuck in a loop. It isn't really taking in information anymore because it is in a state of shock. The information we're attempting to take in isn't getting organized in any meaningful way. So we end up gathering the same pieces of information over and over again. At some point the world settles down enough that we can truly start focusing and making sense of things, but how long it takes is different for any one person.

Over time, if the couple finds that the questions never seem to lessen, the victim has to stop and ask herself, "Are these questions really helping me move through this, or are they keeping me anchored to the past?" After a point, questions can become her own personal form of self-torture. If she already had low self-esteem prior to the affair, it can very quickly feed into this destructive ritual. She has to start self-editing by first asking herself, "Is this just me picking at the wound?"

*   *   *

Victims can create their own dilemma because they will ask the offender "why", but *any* explanation will then be seen as an attempt to rationalize the affair. Both sides need to understand the distinction between an *explanation* versus a *justification*. An explanation attempts to give the reasons why something occurred, without excusing it. ("I wasn't thinking it through." "We weren't paying attention to what was happening.") There *are* reasons why the affair occurred that need to be explored if you're going to work at safeguarding the relationship. A justification, however, attempts to justify the act - to *excuse* it, or displace the blame. ("If you hadn't treated me like that, it never would have happened.")

Sometimes victims can't accept a particular explanation because, *for them*, that wouldn't be enough to justify having an affair. But they have to remember that the relationship consists of two separate people. It might not be an "acceptable" reason for her, but that doesn't mean it wasn't for him.

The victim has to realize that her need in asking the questions, past the point she's already asked them, isn't really to get more answers. What she really needs is assurance, security, to feel significant to her partner again, respected, the trust restored. How she's going about it, may actually be standing in the way of that happening.

*   *   *

One big dilemma for the victim is knowing how much she should trust what the offender's telling her, versus continuing to dig for more lies.

There are situations where the offender has owned everything that happened, but the victim is convinced there's more. No matter how much time goes by, even with no further evidence that there's more, the victim refuses to be convinced. The victim's fears are running wild. She may find that, over time, she still can't allow for the benefit of the doubt. This is one of the saddest scenarios because the truth *had* been told, but the trust had been damaged to the degree that it no longer made a difference.

There's an argument to be made for going either direction. Sometimes intuition is correct and because she stubbornly sought out the rest of the story, she found it. And knowing that his confession had been only a partial truth, she feels peace at being able to walk away from the ashes of the relationship. Other times, the confession is complete and further accusations without the information to back it up just serve as attacks that keep things from being able to heal.

So do you choose to err on the side of trusting at the risk of being further deceived, or do you choose to attempt to expose what may still be hidden at the risk of what's left of the relationship? Either path involves a risk. Initially, it's accepting for both the offender and victim that there's going to be an investigation, and that investigation is justified. At some point, though, that investigation needs to be concluded and, if the relationship is to start to grow again, she will have to risk trusting, in degrees. What she is trying to do is to not blindly trust, but base her trust on the visible evidence of the offender's efforts to recommit. The trust needs to be earned.

At some point the victim has to realize that continued questions past the initial investigation is *her* continuing to bring this other person back into the middle of the relationship, not the offender. She wants to know that the other woman's no longer on his mind, but the victim herself keeps putting her back on his mind.

* * *

After the first couple of months of "processing" through the affair, Rule #5 starts to apply ("Bring up the past during an argument only if the problem is still going on.").

If conflict in the relationship inevitably ends up with the "big gun" being brought out (the affair), the victim is keeping the relationship chained to a negative history and giving herself an unfair advantage in any and all discussions. If a long-term relationship is being attempted, at some point, the offender will need to experience being forgiven.

Hanging onto a vindictive spirit will destroy the victim and whatever's left of the relationship. *He* may have had the affair, and, yes, he needs to be responsible for that, but *she's* the one who needs to ultimately be responsible to forgive.

Remember that to forgive does *not* mean to forget. If we forget, then we stop doing the work of safeguarding the relationship. Not forgetting doesn't mean that we keep reminding our partner, and ourselves, what they did. We've forgiven to the degree that we can move on, letting go of our anger, and without having to bring the affair along into the present.

The turning point for healing is often when we start to focus on the things within our control which help to make the relationship work in the present, rather than continuing to obsess about the things in the past that we can't change.

The Offender's Role

Often offenders fail to realize how they can negatively contribute to the victim's need to keep questioning. Slot machines are based on *variable ratio reinforcement*. It is the strongest kind of reinforcement in existence. Because the payoff is intermittent and unpredictable, it keeps us hooked because our experience is that sooner or later there's going to be a payoff. In the same way, often when the victim asks continued questions, even when the routine response has been, "That's everything that happened", if the victim keeps pushing, she'll get a little bit more information than before. So she's learning that she needs to *keep* pushing in order to find out "the whole story".

As much as possible, the offender needs to "put it all out there" at the beginning so it isn't a matter of more and more information coming out. Often what's happening is that everything *was* said but because details keep being asked to be elaborated on by the victim, there's an *appearance* of more things being withheld when it's really just an issue of the detail.

Because of the damaged trust, the information that *does* get withheld, even if it's in order to prevent more pain, usually only conveys the message to the victim, "He's still lying to me."

As I said, it's not healthy to get into graphic detail about the physical relationship, or entertaining comparisons between the victim and the offender's ex-lover, but it's vital that the victim has a sense from the offender that he is remaining open and cooperative with being questioned, not withholding.

Sometimes, though, if the questions are becoming overly habitual or destructive, ruining neutral or positive moments for the couple, it's better for the offender to, on occasion, sidestep the victim's questions and attempt to go deeper to what she really needs *past* all of the questions: validating the victim's pain, taking ownership for his choices, providing sincere assurances, restating his restored commitment, bringing her back to the present moment.

Often, at the point the victim has just found out about the affair, the offender has already made his decision as to whether or not he wants to salvage the marriage. If he's decided to work it out, he's typically already made that emotional transition and urgently wants to start working on repairs in order to start feeling some relief. But the victim hasn't had enough time yet to have made that decision for herself. It's predictable then that the victim will be seen as the one holding things back.

The victim, at the beginning, is trying to put the emotional chaos she's feeling into some kind of order. She may not know yet whether or not she still wants the relationship. She can't even know if she's ever going to be able to trust this person again. She's by no means ready to just start working on the relationship.

So the more pressure the offender prematurely puts on the victim to "get onboard" with things, the more insensitive he's being about where his partner's at. Even though what's being presented is for the good of the relationship, the offender is still making it all about *his* need to move forward (which is another reflection of the affair - something else that was all about him).

What the victim needs to hear is the offender's commitment and willingness to make things work, giving the victim however much time she needs to figure out where she's at and what she needs.

* * *

In trying to show remorse, just because the offender's words have lost their credibility with the victim, doesn't mean he should give up on trying to express his regret. Ideally, this is most impactful if he is someone who can also access his feelings. If the offender is a person who has difficulty bringing his emotions to the surface, this is going to create a particular dilemma. He may certainly be *experiencing* remorse, but it may be very difficult for him to show it in the way his partner is probably looking for. If she is looking for tears, yet the last time he cried was at a funeral 20 years ago, there's probably not going to be tears.

The offender *does* need to work at showing the victim the pain he is experiencing for his foolish choices, but, hopefully, the victim will also be able to accept that how it comes out is not going to be exactly the way it would if the roles were reversed.

If the offender *discredits* the victim's need to see remorse ("Yes, I'm sorry, okay? But I'm not going to break down in front of you."), making her sound overly demanding, while he may have retained his pride, he's probably lost the relationship. She's looking for a true change of heart and all he's showing her is his refusal to bend.

If this is his partner (a person that, no matter how flawed, he's now deeply wronged), it doesn't matter that there were wrongs she may have done to make him feel justified in having an affair. He needs to accept ownership for the pain he's caused. If he wants her to acknowledge his pain at some point, he needs to be willing to acknowledge hers.

If the offender *isn't* experiencing remorse at this point, that's a problem. If his heart has become that hardened towards the relationship to the degree that this serious a wrong leaves him unmoved, then, he's not going to be able to validate his partner's pain, and they're not going to be able to move forward with the relationship because there's been no resolution.

* * *

Consistency is key. In contrast to the victim's emotional instability at this time (mood shifts from day to day), the offender needs to be as much of an "emotional rock" as possible: stable, assuring, hopeful without being dismissive, sensitive, and nurturing. The victim's feelings are like a temperamental volcano that the offender is attempting to soothe and help stabilize. It's not about controlling the victim's reactions. It's about the offender accepting responsibility for how he continues to influence them.

Through the consistency of the offender's loving efforts, over time, he is able to prove his sincerity and rededication to the relationship.

When the Offender's "Stuck"

Sometimes, when an affair has been discovered, the offender isn't able to address the partner's pain because he hasn't yet emotionally recommitted to the relationship. This can be tricky since this time normally *should* be around validating the victim's pain, but, because the offender is still caught up in his own emotion, he's not yet ready to do so. Some might say to the offender, "Get over it!" but there are several reasons that can make it not so simple.

Sometimes the offender already emotionally cut himself off from the relationship. Which is either what made him susceptible for an affair, or a consequence of the affair (emotional attachment). Though the victim wants to work on salvaging the marriage, the emotions the victim is looking for from the offender are often difficult for the offender to "access" because he's distanced himself from them.

Sometimes the offender "stepped out" on the relationship because he was angry at the partner. And he hasn't let go of that anger yet. It's hard to validate the partner's pain because he may still feel *his* pain has gone invalidated for so long. Forgiveness is an issue for *both* of them.

Sometimes the victim will end up smothering the offender (out of fear, neediness, or feeling driven to "win" the partner back). Her efforts fail to draw him closer, and may actually push him further away. It's not that her efforts aren't good ones. They're just premature. The more the offender is "forced" to show intimate, vulnerable behavior, the less able he is to actually feel it. Because the partner's voice is so much louder than his own, it may confuse him as to his own wants. Or, because the emotions desired from the offender are being forced, they don't feel authentic to him.

In these situations, sometimes *both* the offender and the victim need time to decide if they are at a point where they are willing to start working on the relationship again. The victim needs time to get past the hurt and anger. The offender needs time to emotionally recommit to the relationship. If either is forced to move past these points too quickly, it's like flooding an engine, and the relationship can experience a false restart.

It's delicate territory since *the longer the offender is unable to recommit to the relationship, the more emotional pain the victim has to go through while waiting for a decision* (and the more likely the victim will get to a place where she feels the need to force a decision in order to relieve that pain).

By holding back from reentering the relationship, the offender is also perpetuating the theme that, "It's all about him". Choosing to have an affair was selfish, no matter what the circumstances, and continuing to "ignore" the partner's pain in order to sort out his own feelings will likely have a similar appearance.

Yet it's important that both sides feel that each is choosing to stay for the right reasons (not because they *have* to, but because they want to).

When I talk in terms of "reentering the relationship" or "stepping back in", I'm not referring to a physical separation (though that may be happening too). Couples can still be living together, initially testing the relationship by trying to talk their issues out, in order to decide if reinvesting is the right choice for both. So "stepping back in" simply means getting to a place where the offender is willing to try to make it work again.

Usually in order to do this he will need from the victim some of the same things she needs from him. He will need to feel like she's willing to take ownership for her part in the relationship issues, and open to changing what wasn't working. If she's not willing to do this, then what's his motivation to return?

At the same time, as much as possible the couple is trying to start putting conversational boundaries in place between the affair (what the victim needs in order to heal) and the marital issues (what both need to do to work on the relationship), treating them as separate conversations. The more they overlap these conversations the harder it will be. If the offender talks about the marital issues when the victim's trying to address what she needs to heal, the victim will feel like the offender is using the marital issues to justify the affair. And if the victim keeps bringing up the affair when the offender talks about the marital issues, he'll feel like she's still attempting to punish him and manipulating the conversation.

Separations

243

After an affair has been discovered or disclosed, it's not uncommon (and sometimes even advisable) that the couple physically separates for a time. Emotions are too intense, and perspective is chronically threatened by continuing to be around each other day to day. Proximity can keep things stirred up.

Sometimes that separation serves as a natural consequence for the offender's actions. It makes the potential loss of the relationship real for him. But that time apart can just as often be a time for *both* sides to regain some perspective. Ideally, if further down the road they decide to re-approach, it's with *both* of them being at a place of readiness to reinvest.

For black-and-white thinkers, what will sometimes keep *both* the victim and the offender from reinvesting is either needing to *know* that things will work before they reinvest (which isn't realistic), or waiting to feel like their heart's completely "all-in" before they do. But, while the affair certainly needs to be completely over, restoring confidence that the relationship can be fixed only comes in stages, which means the *initial* reinvestment to work on things is often only a partial one. And that's okay.

The couple isn't waiting until *all* of the anger's gone away before they reunite, since much of working through the pain is done together, not apart.

Nor are they waiting to be *certain* it's going to work before they get back together. They are getting back together to decide *if* it can work again, which they will only find out in the actual effort of *trying* to make it work again.

Reinvesting is being willing to respect your initial commitment to the marriage, to make sure you've done everything that you could to make it work before ever deciding that it can't.

Emotional Affairs

Sometimes the situation is not a full-blown affair, but a *potential* affair in the making (an emotional affair, or a growing flirtation). The lines were just starting to be crossed.

The couple is arguing over what constitutes an affair because "the offender" is feeling unjustly accused of having an affair when there wasn't any sexual relationship, and "the victim" is having a hard time dealing with everything that *might* be happening. The victim knows that "something" happened, but the offender keeps insisting it was "nothing".

An undisclosed meeting might have been discovered. There may have been a kiss. There may have been continuing phone calls that indicated more than a surface relationship. But because actual sex hadn't occurred, the offender is taking offense and the victim fears the worst.

Perhaps things wouldn't have gone any further. Maybe they would. It's a gray area because it's based on conjecture of what was already happening, and how far it could have gone if not discovered.

While benefit of the doubt does need to exist, rather than letting our worst fears run with us, accountability for what current evidence is at hand needs to be the focus. Rather than trying to force a particular label on what it was or wasn't, it's better to address the current behavior as an issue of trust for the relationship and what needs to happen to set things right.

Most of the work with flirtations and possible emotional affairs is around redrawing healthier boundaries for the relationship and outside relationships. Much of the time couples in these circumstances have never had direct conversations about what "crossing the line" means for each, it was just assumed.

Emotional affairs and flirtations typically don't require the same extreme solutions as a full-blown affair might require. Redrawing better boundary lines might simply be putting more realistic restrictions on the degree, frequency and type of contact that was considered safe or appropriate for the future, and what level of transparency was required for the relationship going forward in order to restore trust. These restrictions are something that the couple is agreeing to as a *mutual* standard for the relationship, not just directed at one partner. If there *is* something more going on, putting these additional checks-and-balances in place will likely expose it. If the flirtation/emotional affair was something still in the developmental stages, it will serve as a healthy deterrent from it becoming something more.

*   *   *

What constitutes a relationship being called "an emotional affair" is when we are getting emotional needs met from someone else that are normally needs met by our romantic partner. While we do need to depend on some of our relational needs being met by our friends (rather than being completely dependent on our partner), there is a difference between the needs that are met through a friendship versus those met by an emotional affair. However, at the beginning, many emotional affairs start out as just being friends.

Some of the lines that indicate the existence, or beginning stages, of an emotional affair would include:

- sharing intimate details about your relationship with your partner to this other person
- routinely complaining about your partner to them
- saying things to this other person that you would not say if your partner was present
- sharing secrets
- a growing anticipation about seeing/talking to this person
- wanting to share personal news with them first
- making internal comparisons between them and your partner, where they are coming out more favorably
- daydreaming about seeing them, more than you do your other friends
- fantasizing about what they'd be like in a romantic relationship (even without the intent to act on it)
- a progressive emotional payoff with greetings and goodbyes (for example, looking forward to any brief physical contact)

Not all of these have to be true in order to "qualify" you as fostering an emotional affair.

When it comes to having a best friend, the intimacy being greater than just a friendship, the lines can be harder to distinguish at what point it constitutes an emotional affair. By nature of a close friendship, we are typically sharing details about our personal life, looking for support even about our romantic relationships, with this best friend. But by doing so, we are practicing intimacy and need to be careful that we're not nurturing a setting for something more to start.

During the dating years, there is more room for opposite-sex best friends because we are still in the process of finding a marital partner. But at the point we already are in a marriage, we have to be more careful about our personal boundaries with others, even those we trust, because there is more to protect. That's not to say you can't have opposite-sex friends at all, but we need to pay more attention to maintaining clear relational lines, and be respectful of what additional lines our partner may need from us. Especially when our romantic relationships are struggling, we have to recognize that we are more vulnerable to those closest to us.

Obviously, if there's a romantic history with this best friend, there's a greater threat of rekindling something by having intimate conversations, or being in intimate settings with them.

New friendships are greater unknowns because relational lines have had little practice being respected. They have yet to be tested.

Old longstanding friendships where the boundary lines have been practiced for years are less of a potential threat, but this depends on how honest each has been that both just want to be friends.

In a marriage, how these opposite-sex best friend relational lines are respected (in order to not cater to an emotional affair) is usually through the frequency and setting that contact is maintained. The phone calls, texts, or visits happen at a frequency where the marriage is still the obvious priority in comparison. The content of any contact, while personal, is not intimate. The phone calls, or texting, doesn't happen in the middle of the night, or only when the other partner isn't present. There is no sense of secrecy, everything is transparent. The settings of visits are public rather than private, and are always open for the partner to be present.

247

For some couples, the stricter boundary rule for the relationship is no one-on-one time with *anyone* of the opposite-sex (family members being the obvious exception) unless the partner has "signed off" on it. The idea isn't to over-control, or not to trust, it's simply about being respectful and not putting oneself into any overly tempting situation.

For those with poor emotional discipline, or poor personal boundaries, it's unrealistic to even attempt opposite-sex best friend relationships because it's predicting that something's going to happen. Better to not play with fire. For those partners with trust issues, maintaining those best friend relationships from anything other than a distance can be asking too much of them.

Restoring an Emotional Connection

One of the more complicated scenarios for any long-term romantic relationship, whether there has been an affair or not, is when at least one partner feels they have fallen out of love. It's true that, because feelings can't be directly controlled, we can't just force ourselves to feel love again for our partner.

When an affair *has* occurred and the couple has decided to work at reconnecting, often the more a partner tries to *force* himself to feel love again, the further from it he becomes because of the greater awareness that he's *not* feeling it. The refocus point for many couples trying to restore love is that initially the focus is on *being* loving with each other, rather than over-assessing the presence or absence of the feelings.

"Being loving" is reintroducing respectful, considerate behavior towards each other, staying focused on being the godly partner that we need to be, and gradually restoring the courtship. We are relearning how to *guide* our emotions through what we do and what we choose to focus on, rather than letting the initial negative feelings make those choices for us.

Ultimately, recreating love depends on us being able to find something in our partners that we can reconnect with. If we have completely lost respect for them, no longer able to see anything in them that we admire, desire or appreciate, then there is nothing to fuel the connection. Many times, however, there *are* still things that we can rediscover and reconnect with in each other, it's just that our focus has become distorted and all we are currently seeing is the negatives.

* * *

For many couples, to start being physically intimate again, knowing that the offender has been physically intimate with someone else, can be very problematic. It's typically unrealistic to assume that the sexual relationship will just pick up where it left off. And if there were sexual issues prior to the affair, things will often be even more complicated now. In such situations, seeking a couple's therapist, more than recommended, becomes a necessity.

Especially for the person that sees sex as something more than a physical outlet, who needs *emotional intimacy* first before she is able to open herself up to physical intimacy, she needs room to feel that sex is not an immediate demand. Ideally, in such situations, both partners are willing to back off and focus on rebuilding other parts of the relationship, such as the emotional connection, first. Sexual restoration is still viewed as an end-goal, but not an immediate priority.

Many times, just removing sex as a requirement, makes it easier (for whoever's most resistant) to re-approach it at some point, because now it's been put back on the level of a choice versus an expectation.

Affair-Proofing

Part of "affair-proofing" a relationship is done by creating, or restoring, a shared common vision for the couple (more than raising a family, or retirement goals). They need to 1) reattach a priority to the relationship and 2) have a specific plan as to how they're going to continue to take care of it (especially how they maintain the emotional connection over the years ahead). The more that connection becomes a part of their lifestyle, the harder it will be for anything outside of the relationship to distract them from it. For the Christian, this is where the couple refocuses their life on having a godly relationship - God at the center. They have to be careful, though, that this doesn't just translate into shared traditions and rituals, but is actually about *relationship*.

The majority of us are uncomfortable with discomfort. When we *do* experience it, we want to move as quickly out of it as we can, often short-cutting legitimate suffering and failing to learn from what was causing the discomfort in the first place. Choosing to remain disciplined with ourselves, not allowing opportunity for even the seeds of an affair to start growing, means remaining uncomfortable to a small degree with the relationship. Uncomfortable that, if we don't take the threat seriously, it could happen to us (or happen again).

If we understand that many affairs begin simply because the people involved thought they were above it ever going that far, and that's what created the blind spot for them, remaining uncomfortable means never allowing ourselves to get to the point where we think we're "immune".

If you know it *could* happen, then you're going to take better precautions to make sure it *doesn't* happen.

Knowing our Limits and Triggers

As with substance abuse treatment, a good part of "affair-proofing" comes down to knowing *the triggers*, the things that started us in that direction. There are factors inside and outside of us that make it possible (make us vulnerable) to have outside romantic relationships: whether it's when substances become involved, needs go unmet, life stressors become overwhelming, allowing ourselves to get into an overly tempting situation, whatever.

If an affair has occurred, then we already have some firsthand knowledge of where the lines started to get crossed for us, though we may not have wanted to explore them closely. So long as we remain ignorant of them, or unwilling to address them, we continue to remain vulnerable to them.

We need to be honest with ourselves about at what point we started to cross the line, and take serious steps to not even approach that line again. For the individual who hasn't ever crossed that line (never had an affair), that means thinking in terms of what *potential* lines look like for him.

If we know that what made us vulnerable was drinking alone in a public place where there were available partners, then we need to stop drinking alone in public places.

If we know the affair started at the point where we started fantasizing while surfing internet porn, then we need to draw the line at how we spend our computer time, or what security measures we install onto the computer to keep it from being an option.

If problems began when we started spending one-on-one time with someone of the opposite sex, then we need to stay with social groups or doing things as couples.

And that's not to say there is only one line we need to draw. The compromise may have been on several different levels, and require several different lines.

It's also recognizing that the problem isn't just about our behavior, it's also what thoughts allowed us to make those compromises, and perhaps even some beliefs we've chosen to embrace about ourselves and/or our relationship.[25]

Even if the thinking that allowed the affair to start was a *lack* of thought, that's useful information. You know that part of what needs to change in those moments of temptation is to *intentionally* choose to think about those real-life priorities (your partner, your kids, your job, your Christian witness) in order to stay focused.

Needs and Priorities

Because we are all need-driven, it's important that the offender be honest with himself about what needs the affair provided for. Part of forming preventive strategies is clearly defining needs and being diligent about getting those needs met in healthy ways, or he *will* be vulnerable to getting them met through unhealthy means.

---

[25] Maybe a good time to use the 3-Part Solution Model in the Appendix.

Hopefully, at the point both parties in the relationship are trying to heal it, the couple can be honest about what relational needs have gone unmet and make specific plans for how they can, as a team, begin to start better addressing them for both.[26]

The need might be about *fun*. If the home life has become dull and routine, the couple needs to break those rituals in the relationship that get in the way of experiencing passion and fun together again.

But we're also looking beyond the marital needs. Sometimes the marital needs were being met, but the rest of the offender's life was out of balance. He only had a few resources available for meeting his needs. Sometimes affairs begin because of a lack of other social supports, so the legitimate need it initially provided for was one of *support*, not sex.

In attempting to repair the relationship we might try to fix this problem by making our partner our sole support, but that is not a realistic expectation. That places too great a demand on one person. So we still need to find friends, just not friends that would be a threat to the relationship. Ideally, this would be a friend or two who can, at times, be a mentor - someone who's gone a little further in life than we have so they can be a source of wise guidance and a positive influence.

When exploring overall balance in our lives and our relationships (work, play, health, social, family, spiritual), it's a good time to look at where our priorities are and which ones need to shift in order to better meet the overall needs. It's a great time to do the Priority Exercise.[27]

---

[26] Such a time would be a great opportunity to go back and use the Needs List Exercise in the Appendix.

[27] Also the Appendix.

Part of safeguarding is reassessing all of the relationship's routines to see whether they are helping or hindering, keeping it awake or lulling it to sleep.

Stepping back to the *courtship*, do you intentionally approach having intimate, intentional conversations with your partner or do things just stay on a surface level? Do you consciously put effort into letting your partner know he's important to you in the ways that are most meaningful to him? Are there any goals for your shared future that can bring you together as a team with a common purpose? Are those goals something that excite you about the future? Are they something that are just as much your dreams as your partner's? How much does your courtship involve exploring a shared faith and shared passions?

What are the *accountability routines*? Do you actively negotiate conflict or are issues stockpiling? Do you give as much recognition for the positive as you do drawing attention to the things that still need work?[28]

And what are the *forgiveness rituals* - the ways (whether spoken or acted out) that the couple goes through the routine of letting go of past hurts? It often needs to be something visible for whoever is being forgiven, so he can experience the grace that is being applied. But it's also something you're embracing for yourself, in order to move on and be free of inner resentment and bitterness. They need to be meaningful rituals that both sides are willing to adopt.

It's true that healing can't be rushed and reinvesting in the routines is a gradual process. But they do provide a restored direction for relationships that have drifted too far, and a visible path for regaining intimacy.

---

[28] Again, the Appendix, referring to "the Sit-down".

There is no way I can do justice to the process of moving past an affair in a single chapter. And there are more thorough resources out there that I would readily suggest. For those interested in seeking that information, the most popular books counselors recommend for clients (both victim and offender) are "After the Affair" by Spring, "His Needs, Her Needs" by Harley and "Not Just Friends" by Glass.

Chapter 12
Separation and Conflict

Some Pharisees came to him to test him. They asked, "Is it lawful for a man to divorce his wife for any and every reason?"

"Haven't you read,' he replied, 'that at the beginning the Creator 'made them male and female,' and said, 'For this reason a man will leave his father and mother and be united to his wife and the two will become one flesh'? So they are no longer two, but one. Therefore what God has joined together, let man not separate."

"Why then," they asked, "did Moses command that a man give his wife a certificate of divorce and send her away?"

Jesus replied, "Moses permitted you to divorce your wives because your hearts were hard. But it was not this way from the beginning. I tell you that anyone who divorces his wife, except for marital unfaithfulness, and marries another woman commits adultery."

The disciples said to him, "If this is the situation between a husband and wife, it is better not to marry."

Jesus replied, "Not everyone can accept this word, but only those to whom it has been given." (Matthew 19:7-11)

According to Old Testament tradition it was up to the men to request divorces because the women were viewed as property. The men could have any number of reasons for seeking a divorce. This changed with the New Testament, which provided only two grounds for divorce: 1) infidelity and 2) being married to a nonbeliever who chooses to leave (I Corinthians 7: 10-16).

Right from the start you know you're going to experience your own personal spiritual struggle of conscience if you are a Christian and *wanting* to divorce, yet the boundaries of your faith do not condone it. Even if you have Biblical grounds for divorce, so you are morally justified in ending the relationship, it does not necessarily make it the best choice if there is still a reasonable chance for the marriage to be salvaged.

If separating was a hasty reaction, when things finally settle you may find that the emotional logic that drove you was not as connected to reality as you had thought. Staying focused on pursuing divorce is often managed by remaining angry at the partner. After all, if you keep that anger alive, then you never have to think past what drove you to that decision to end it. Still, hanging on to that anger ultimately costs *you* more than anybody else. At some point you will have to consider the whole picture, both the good *and* bad of both your partner and the relationship (*your* part included), in order to better assess what is truly the best course to take.

For the accountable Christian, much of the struggle with moving through a separation is accepting responsibility for our *own* part in the failure of the relationship, which may mean acknowledging that we really haven't gone the extra mile - that there's more we need to try before ending it.

For those who *have* tried everything they could to make things work, including getting outside help, it is sometimes difficult for them to feel like they can be both divorced and still accepted by God. Yet Jesus clearly states, "**I tell you the truth, *all* the sins and blasphemies of men will be forgiven them. But whoever blasphemes against the Holy Spirit will never be forgiven...**" (Mark 3:28-29)

* * *

For the sake of clarity and communication, it's helpful for a couple considering separation to understand the different types. There are basically three:

1. temporary separation

2. trial separation

3. separation with intent to divorce

A *temporary separation* is when a couple is just getting space from each other for a short period of time. There is no need for a separation agreement to be drawn up because both understand it is just a temporary thing. She's going to go stay with her family for a couple weeks. Or he's going to go stay at the cabin at the lake. One or the other, or both, just need some "me" time to regroup and recharge.

A *trial separation* is when the couple separates and, while there may be some doubts as to whether or not they're going to get back together, reconciliation is still considered a possibility, if not the goal. The intent is to initially get some space from each other, work on getting themselves back into balance, and then re-approach the relationship to see if things can be worked out. In these situations, a separation agreement is often completed.

A *separation with intent to divorce* is when at least one partner has made a firm decision that the relationship is over and that there is no option for reconciliation. Sometimes separations with intent to divorce still turn into trial separations partway through the separation once the couple has had some time away from each other. Separation agreements are necessary.

*   *   *

In the state of North Carolina (where I live), you have to be separated a period of a year in order to be able to divorce. In other states, divorce can be immediate. The logic behind the waiting period is due to the unpredictability of people when strong emotions are involved. The span of a year is to insure that there has been time for people to calm down and think things through. Unfortunately, many don't understand that

that is what the separation period is about. As far as they are concerned, being separated is the same as divorce. It's just not gotten its official title yet.

Ideally, couples going through a separation should, at some point, go for couples counseling with a professional counselor who specializes in relationship issues, especially if it has never been attempted before. There are few life-changing decisions that you make in your life: the career you choose, where you live, what faith you choose, who you marry, having kids. Choosing to divorce is such a decision and it's very important that you've really thought things through and exhausted all avenues of assistance.

Typically, the professional that *will* be contacted during a separation is the attorney. But attorneys are there to represent you and only you. They are not there to be fair or to represent both sides. Their job is to get everything possible that could be coming to you, and to get paid in the process. Personally, I have rarely ever seen separations where the involvement of attorneys *improved* the odds of reconciliation, unless part of their policy required the couple to get counseling during the separation. The typical counsel of an attorney during such a time is to *refrain* from any communication with your partner. *They* want to handle any further communication. This may be in part to protect you and not overcomplicate their job, but, it also prevents opportunities for you and your partner to work things out.

Don't get me wrong. I am not suggesting you set yourself up to be taken advantage of by not seeking legal counsel. There is no harm in *consulting* with an attorney to be aware of what your rights are in a situation, but in working out a separation agreement, in my opinion, it's better to go through *mediation*. Mediators represent both sides and try to find a middle ground where both sides are being taken into account and the focus is on workable compromise. The end result is a separation agreement that is just as legally binding.

A separation agreement, while *preparatory* for divorce, does not *obligate* you to divorce. It sets the rules for how things will be handled on each side while the separation is occurring.

* * *

Often, couples who do come for counseling at the point of separating have poor motives for being there. Sometimes they are simply looking for a clear conscience, a "thumbs up" that leaving their dysfunctional partner was the wisest thing they could have done - that even the counselor said they were crazy for staying. In other words, their interest really isn't towards healing the relationship. They have already decided they want out and are trying to use counseling as the seal of approval. Typically, they will sabotage the work required in marital counseling, continuing to bait their partner, not following through on homework, and giving up on new ways of relating instead of actually making a serious attempt at change.

While it is difficult for any success to occur under these circumstances, the initial work of the counselor ends up being to challenge the client's conclusions about the fate of the relationship. Often the client has embraced several myths about the relationship: "It's supposed to work without having to work at it", "My partner's supposed to fulfill all my needs", "I should still feel love even though we're no longer doing the things that create love", etc. If you can uncover the myths, or the misdiagnoses, then, sometimes, you have a starting place to work with and the real work on the marriage can begin. Other times, people don't care if their thinking is faulty. They feel what they feel and so they're going to do what they've already decided to do.

The complaints may be that "We're too different", "We have nothing in common anymore", "We can't talk without fighting", etc. And the experience may be one of feeling abandoned, rejected or abused. But the degree of emotion involved says that feelings are still very much alive, just turned in a negative direction. The couple may not feel loving towards each other, but their feelings are still very much involved in the relationship. Often, it will be evident that the couple is still trying to work things out even though they themselves don't realize it, because they will continue to try to press their point, try yet again to show they're right about something or attempt to be understood, only for things to explode again and both sides scream in frustration. If someone has *really* given up on trying to work things out, he no longer makes the extra effort to be understood, and he no longer engages in the old routine of arguing. He's just done.

If we truly no longer care about somebody, the feelings are typically ones of indifference, not hate. Often, hate is simply reflective of our wounded love. While that love is being masked by our negative emotions, it doesn't mean that love no longer exists.

Sometimes a partner has become "emotionally numb", so the experience for him is that he no longer feels anything towards his partner. Yet, if you think in terms of woundedness, if somebody agitates a wound often enough it overwhelms the pain receptors to the point that the wound now becomes numb. It's not that there's no longer a wound, no longer pain (no longer love), it's just that because the intensity of the emotions have been so overwhelming for so long the brain is defending itself by shutting itself off emotionally. With physical distance, and time away from the things that agitated the wound, feeling (and perspective) sometimes starts to return.

So, too, it can be misleading to be making a decision about ending a relationship when you're taking certain types of medication. For those on antidepressants (and many are these days), they need to remember that these are *mood stabilizers*. They not only prevent lows, but they also prevent highs. The internal experience may be that the thought of divorce leaves them unmoved, so they must no longer care, but it can just as much be a result of the medication they are taking.

Many times couples will come to couple's counseling with negative assumptions (misdiagnoses) about each other's personalities or character, only to find out that with better information regarding communication and conflict resolution they're actually able to start working things out that they never thought they could.

Healthier motives for seeking counseling during a separation are those where the couple is trying to be cautious and make sure that divorce isn't an even bigger mistake. Ideally, the couple is approaching that time apart as an opportunity for each to get themselves back in balance. With that restored balance, it's then reassessing the relationship from a healthier perspective and with better judgment.

Sometimes the outcome of couple's work *is* acknowledging that the relationship is an unhealthy one and that, even with assistance, the most healthy and responsible thing to do is to end it. But at least then the couple can walk away feeling like they went the extra mile and can have some peace that divorcing was the right thing to do.

The separation period is a time to accomplish several things:

1) it's allowing time for emotions to cool in order to regain some perspective

2) time to do some self-assessment on how much your own life is in balance and taking the necessary steps towards getting *you* healthy

3) time seeking counsel to explore if you really have exhausted all resources

4) time exploring the impact that divorce will have on your life

Project #1. Time for emotions to cool in order to regain some perspective.

Some Christian counselors will not abide physical separation for a couple. If you come to them, they will immediately insist that you move back in together in order to work things out. This is primarily due to the danger that the longer you are apart, the less likely you are to come back together. While that *is* a real danger, there are also dilemmas involved in moving back too soon.

For emotionally reactive couples every little thing sets off a larger conflict. Boundaries have deteriorated to the degree that neither side has a balanced perspective, and everything has become reflective, or symbolic, of some greater hurt. The negative feelings easily flare and quickly become explosive. Such couples have not necessarily grown too far apart, but often are *too close* to be able to see things clearly. A little breathing room can help restore some level of boundary, and perspective (with assistance).

To move a couple that is emotionally reactive back together without any preparation time involved is predicting that the war will resume where it

left off. Neither side has been given any new tools to use to help defuse the battle.

Because they are reactive, even if they're getting counseling, the time that they spend with each other outside of sessions can still be so destructive that it undoes anything that the counseling accomplished.

When I see a separated couple that fits the description of being "emotionally reactive", the first rule is that *both sides need to agree not to make any further life-changing decisions for the immediate future*. This means no moving out of state, getting into another relationship, or even moving back in together too quickly.

I use the metaphor of the relationship as a pond, and how one of the primary goals for a couple trying to restore sanity to the relationship is to stop throwing things into the pond, to give the pond time to settle down.

At one point in time that pond might have been a pretty attractive pond. It had a certain sparkle to it. You could see clearly into it. It might have had some pretty impressive fish swimming around in it. It used to be a peaceful place, somewhere you felt at home. And the pond improved over time because of how you tended to it.

But now the pond has gotten all stirred up either because of things that have been thrown into it (attacks on the relationship), something that was buried that's been dug up (the history you bring with you), or even because of nasty weather (life circumstances). You can no longer see into that pond because too much is happening, keeping its waters muddied and churning. You may *think* you know what's in that pond at this point because of your past familiarity with it, but you're having to make some assumptions about it now because the visibility is so poor.

Your primary goal at this point should be to stop your part in keeping the waters stirred. You may be planning on giving up on this pond and go find another one. You may be trying to tend to two ponds at once. But, ultimately, you can't make a good decision about whether or not to give up on this pond until you've given enough time for things to calm down, and for the pond to clear up enough to get an idea whether or not it's become polluted beyond repair.

Some couples, as long as they are living together, day after day, cannot stop themselves from continuing to throw stuff into their pond. Only by getting some physical distance, and emotional space, can they stop complicating things.

It's unfortunate when someone abandons his "pond" only to discover that, when he's stopped throwing stuff at it and it's settled back down, it really was a great little pond, but now it's no longer his. And guess what? That other pond you had your eye on? It may be in a different location, have a different shape, and have different things swimming around in it, but the work of tending it will be the same. And if you don't have very good "tending" skills, your next pond will end up being very similar to the last.

*   *   *

Let me make a quick aside to the person who's trying to tend to two ponds at once (meaning either an affair, or dating while separated). You can't accurately assess two ponds at the same time. By becoming focused on another pond, rather than the one you're still obligated to, you're not going to be able to clearly see what you still have because you're already looking somewhere else.

This violates a few critical relational rules:

1) Don't leave a marriage because of another relationship.

2) Don't jump into a relationship just after ending another.

Each is a prediction for failure if violated. It conveys the picture of 1) a needy person who can't handle being alone, 2) someone who places little value on the importance of relationship transitions, and/or 3) someone lacking in emotional self-discipline.

Relationships can be very fragile things, particularly beginnings and endings. It's incredibly important to deal with your marriage on its own terms. If you're going to make a good, sound decision about the future of your relationship, stay focused on *it*, not on something or somebody else. It becomes an issue of sequence. First things first. If you break that sequence by overlapping relationships, there will be complications that can sabotage *both* the old and the new relationship.

There's no way you can draw a fair comparison between the partner you've been in a relationship with and somebody you haven't been with on a day-to-day basis. It's two different creatures. The draw of a second relationship is the excitement and newness that it brings (without yet having experienced the responsibilities, the obligations, and the problems that that relationship would eventually also have). There's a whole lot of information about that second relationship you don't have yet, and whatever predictions about a future you're making are based on feelings, not facts.

The *feelings* are what makes a person in that situation so torn. You feel excited and alive with this other person. Your feelings for your marriage may be varied: confused, angry, resentful, hurt, numb. But people often fail to realize that feelings aren't these things that happen by themselves. You create those feelings by what you choose to think and how you choose to act (Chapter 9). Your partner's choices may have helped kill or diminish those feelings of love for you, but if your partner's at a place where they're willing to change, it's not a foregone conclusion that those positive feelings can never be brought back. It typically depends on 1) how much damage has been done and for how long, and 2) how ready and how motivated each side is to make the necessary changes.

You need to recognize that attraction and desire is often based on *appetite*. If you're feeding your appetite with feelings and thoughts for somebody else, it *will* starve your desire for your partner. It's unfair to try to gauge your feelings for your partner under such circumstances.

Whether there's a chance to work it out or not, the marriage needs to be considered or rejected on its own merits, not because you've got an escape route planned into another relationship. If you're going to be able to feel at peace in years to come about what choice you made, it needs to be because you respected your *first* commitment, which was to your marriage.

People often fail to understand that, by leaving their partner for another person, they're automatically introducing doubt into that second relationship by how they're choosing to end the first. ("He jumped into this relationship with me before his marriage was even officially over. What if I'm just a rebound?", "He was willing to break his commitment to her. Why wouldn't he be willing to do the same with me?", "He hasn't had time to truly mourn the physical loss of his marriage. What if I'm just a Band-aid for his pain - a quick replacement?", "Is he so needy that he *has* to be in a relationship? That he just can't stand to be alone?") In the passion of the moment, these considerations get overlooked. But as time goes by and feelings die down to where perspective's restored, these are the legitimate concerns that start to surface.

Whether you like it or not, if you want to have minimal fallout from a decision to divorce you have to be respectful of everyone else's legitimate need (your current partner, your kids, the families on both sides) to transition as well. The more you rush change (by getting involved in outside relationships) out of your own need, the harder it's going to be for everybody else to be accepting of the choices you're making. And the more emotional damage you're causing to them in the process.

You might be able to justify that cost because you no longer care about your partner's feelings, but you're forgetting that throughout the separation period you are still going to be needing your partner's cooperation with different things, and now you are making it that much less likely to happen.

And if children *are* present, how do you justify the transitional cost to them? You may oversimplify by saying, "They'll adjust. They're kids." Perhaps, but perhaps not. What is your responsibility as a parent to make sure that adjustment is done as considerately as possible? You may feel that you're showing them "it's okay to not stay in a bad relationship", but you're also unintentionally modeling unhealthy self-love by exiting in a way that is 1) disrespectful to the marriage that was, 2) modeling relationship hopping as being okay, and 3) saying it's okay to make selfish decisions regardless of how many other people it negatively effects.

You may be at a point where you feel like you've suppressed your needs for such a long time, taking care of everyone else, that letting yourself be selfish now feels pretty good, but that doesn't excuse you from handling your own needs in a responsible way. When people change, they will often gravitate to the other extreme, because the extremes are always the easiest to see. So if you were a "giver" to the point of need deprivation, the most visible alternative is to become a "taker". But "healthy and balanced" is this middle world where you still *do* get your own needs met, but in a *healthy* way (one that isn't at everyone else's expense). First things first.

* * *

So many times I'll hear people a few months into their separation say, "I'm over it. I really am." And to look at their lives at that moment you might agree. They have their energy back. They're active again, doing things with friends, maybe involved in some hobbies, caught up at work. But adjustments of that magnitude take time and you need to give yourself permission to take that time because your short-term medicine won't really heal the wound. What you usually have is someone who is very uncomfortable with emotional pain and they so badly want to get through it that they're burying themselves in distractions. If, in truth, they *are* "over it" that quickly then one would question whether or not they were ever actually "in it" to start with.

Yes, sometimes there *are* relationships where the pain has been ongoing for several years, and, by the time the separation has arrived, at least one person has already done most of the emotional work of letting go. But this still doesn't mean you're ready for another relationship. While you may have *emotionally* left the marriage several years ago, you've just left it *physically* in the present, and you need to give yourself time to adjust to being on your own again, or be at risk of practicing relational dependency.

* * *

Sometimes letting things cool and regaining perspective means working towards *forgiveness*. It's recognizing that any bitterness or resentment you're hanging onto may actually be interfering with a clear perspective of what the issues actually are. And, ultimately, hanging onto those intensely negative emotions may be hurting you, and your loved ones *through* you.

Does forgiving mean that you are making what happened when you were together "okay"? Not at all. You're not trying to rationalize or minimize your partner's wrong deeds, though understanding his part in what happened is necessary for a balanced perspective. You *are* trying to accept that there were *two* people involved in the relationship, not just one. And, typically, there were hurtful things done by *both* sides (things *you* may need to be forgiven for as well).

Does forgiving mean that you have to return to the relationship? Not necessarily. It depends on how much work has already been attempted, and failed. It depends on the reasons *why* it failed. Sometimes forgiving is done simply in order to let go of the wounds of the relationship in order to be able to move on with your life.

* * *

Sometimes the things that occur *during* the separation are greater obstacles to reconciliation than anything that occurred in the marriage. This is particularly true when the separation is not a joint decision. The person that is left behind often has the hardest time of it, simply because it wasn't his choice, the choice was made for him. This creates a need to try to restore a sense of control to his life, because a big part of his life has just been removed from his control. This personal crisis can often lead to attempts to *over-control* the situation that can become somewhat destructive or self-destructive.

In addition, the partner that has left will often emotionally shut themselves off from the other, leaving the one left behind feeling like he's now dealing with an inaccessible stranger. Suddenly, he is cut off from being able to know what the other person is doing or feeling, and the "not knowing" can cause significant distress because of everything she *might* be doing or feeling.

That emotional barrier that's now present may be due to several things:

1) It's how the partner who has left is self-protecting. By distancing herself, she is keeping herself from becoming vulnerable again, and, as a result, able to stay resolved with the decision to leave.

2) Depending on the *type* of separation, personal boundaries are sometimes redrawn between what is now each other's "right" to know and not know. Often, the partner who leaves will not explain how they are intending the boundaries to change, she will just change them, creating a mystery for the one who is left of what the new expectations are.

3) Family or friends may have told the partner to do so.

4) Attorneys may have counseled the partner to stop further contact except through them.

Ideally, the couple keeps each other "in the know" as to what changes in how they communicate and changes in their behavior mean and don't mean, just to keep things respectful and informed. They have to understand the more their behavior becomes a mystery, the greater issues it's going to create between the two of them for shutting the other out. For the person who's been left, each change that occurs without discussing it, is one more thing that's being removed from his control, agitating the wound.

The information you get out of a separation can be mixed, simply because of the degree of the emotions that are going on. It's difficult to know how to interpret each other's behavior.

On the one hand, while you may be discovering just how flexible you or your partner's morals have become during this time, it's also keeping in mind that people do really stupid things when emotions are out of control. I do not say that to absolve you or your partner of responsibility in the situation, but often people will hang on to particular acts of stupidity done or said in a foolish moment and deny themselves the opportunity to repair something that still had value.

Yet, on the other hand, how someone handles this chaotic time *is* potentially good information about character. Do they still try to be fair, or is it all about payback? Can you still see efforts to be loving despite the circumstances, or is it all about venting the anger? Are they running off and impulsively spending, bingeing, and partying, or are they trying to handle things in a more mature manner?

Some of this depends on the circumstances of the separation. If you've just had an affair and the relationship has broken up because of it, it's somewhat unrealistic to expect your partner to be trying to draw close at this point.

You do need to be discrete with the information you share with others about the intimate details of the relationship during this time. Often, each side is trying to "convert" others to their side by dumping as much "dirt" as they can about the partner. But, ideally, you should only be talking to a very few personal friends (two or three) about what's going on. These need to be people who can be trusted, who possess good judgment and aren't just there to tell you what you want to hear. Sometimes the damage that is done through gossip and slander is what stands in the way of ever reconciling.

Often, during the separation period, affairs, stalking episodes, harassment and all sorts of other chaotic stuff goes on. People are panicking over their loss and trying everything they can to hang on to their partner, trying to get payback, or trying to move on too quickly. This sudden loss of personal standards is sometimes because when the couple was still together there were rules that were being followed, no matter how loosely, but now "all bets are off". Now that the couple is no longer together, though not yet divorced, the "rules" are no longer clear. But by throwing the "rules" to the wind (out of anger, resentment, spite, newfound freedom, whatever), you are making the road to sorting things out that much more difficult.

Even if you don't plan to reconcile, by abandoning any sense of fair-play, you are setting the stage for a nasty divorce and some serious loss of self-respect. Your emotional maturity is now being put to the test. For those caught up in their own revenge ("I can't help it, they just make me so angry") or neediness ("I can't help it, I just need to be with someone,"), they are now taking an active path in destroying any hope of setting things right.

Now is an opportunity to show your worthiness, not your immaturity, *even if your partner could care less.* Even if there is no hope for the relationship and divorce is inevitable, it is still taking the more mature path and maintaining your own integrity. You need to be able to look back on this time *without* regret over your own behavior. If the relationship does end, it needs to be *despite* how you handled things (responsibly, rather than as a Child).

Project #2. Time to do some self-assessment on how much your own life is in balance and taking the necessary steps towards getting *you* healthy.

A big part of being separated is doing self-assessment and looking at how in balance your *own* life is. It's easy to put the weight of our needs on the marriage when we have nothing else to shoulder our burdens.

How well have you been taking care of your health? What's the status on your friendships, or have you become pretty isolated? How's your spiritual life? Have you allowed it to become nonexistent because of all of the distractions?

This time to yourself is time to get *you* together. If it is possible that you might get back together with your mate, it needs to be as a healthy you, not the "you" that was helping keep things stirred up. A balanced you may have a different perspective on the problems of the relationship. But even if there is no chance of getting back together, you need to be facing the future as a healthy individual or risk repeating some of the same mistakes.

Remember the priority exercise I suggested in Chapter 10? Separation is an ideal time to do this exercise. This becomes your guide in restoring some balance to yourself while living apart. Your plan for restoring the neglected areas needs to be specific enough that you can act on it a little each day. At the beginning or end of each day you may need to do a quick review of where your energy needs to be focused, or how successful you were that day in restoring energy to the neglected areas of your life. Following through on this exercise can also be educational in helping you discover your own resistances to achieving balance.

Why seek balance at all? For some people, putting all their energy into work may seem to be very satisfying to them. (It may have cost them their marriage, but they were happy up until that point.) But when we look to any one source (aside from God) to meet all our needs, we automatically make ourselves vulnerable by becoming overly dependent on that source. If all your worth came from your work and you suddenly lost your job, where would you be? In severe depression, most likely. If you had depended on your partner to meet all of your needs, but now you're separated, how do you think that is going to impact you? Instant crisis. By balancing the priorities in our lives, when one area is under attack or suffering, the other areas help to keep us afloat.

If we can separate our part of the problems (our negativity, reactivity, etc.) and, for the moment, not over-focus on what our partner was doing to set those things off or keep them going, we can reestablish who we need to be in order to regain some self-respect. Granted, this calls for some good judgment which may be beyond you at this point. You may have to turn to someone more removed from the situation to get some help. Sometimes friends and family can serve this role but often friends and family, in wanting to be supportive, can be quite biased.

In searching through what your part of the problems were in the relationship, you can still work on those, to a degree, with the telephone conversations or texts you continue to have with your partner, even though apart. For example, if you had problems with losing your temper while you were together, then the goal in future conversations with your partner is to complete a conversation without "losing it". Your focus during the conversation is solely on controlling *your* reactions to what is said. Your gauge of success is not around how hateful *his* words are, but around how well *you* refrained from feeding into it this time.

This is not to say that there will never come a time when you help educate your partner about his part of the problem, but it is saying that that time is *not* right now (unless he's specifically inviting it). The more you continue to try to criticize at this point, the more you will tend to force each other apart because the inherent message of criticism is rejection, not acceptance. If your partner is honestly asking for criticism, then, fine, go ahead and do so (respectfully and tactfully).

At the point where you are looking at working towards resolution and restoring the relationship it becomes more important to be addressing both ends of the picture. But, initially, the focus is on learning to handle criticism of yourself, particularly since self-assessment *is* self-criticism.

If you find this is very uncomfortable work, owning up to your part in things, what you are probably discovering is your own rigidity or insecurity. And you are finding an area where you will need to do some work. If you can't own up to your own faults then you can't improve. And you can't heal.

*   *   *

Often the separation period is a very lonely, needy time, which is, for many, why it's so easy to get involved in another romantic relationship. What can often be a very positive social alternative is to *get involved in a separated singles support group* (such as DivorceCare). These are often available in the community or sited at local churches. The support group is, as it is named, there for support.

In a support group you will usually find a large diversity of people, separated for various reasons. Some will be coping well, some angry, some in denial, some in anxious crisis, and others in depression but all will be experiencing the common theme of going through emotional pain and trying to figure out how to deal with it best.

Such support groups are *not* pickup scenes. One of the first rules that is identified in group is that the group is not to be used as an opportunity for finding new partners. Isolating yourself with members of the opposite sex from the group is prohibited.

Support groups are a great preventive for depression because they help keep you from withdrawing or isolating yourself too much and they give that important message, "You are not alone". By removing yourself from your marriage, your relationship need (if support is not present) is going unmet. Support groups attempt to partially meet that need in a healthy way. It's a great opportunity for validation of your pain, and, under good leadership, it can also be very helpful in offering you several perspectives that can provide you with a more balanced picture with which to better assess your situation.

For those who are very shy about talking about personal things in front of others, these kinds of groups do not require you to talk in order to attend. You can just go and listen.

For those in financial straits, support groups are usually free of charge.

Project #3. Time seeking counsel to explore whether you really have exhausted all resources.

There is such a great fear in some people of accepting that their marriage has failed, but, in reality, reaching that point can actually be the most healthy thing you could do for the relationship.

Even if you think the relationship was working but your partner doesn't, then it *wasn't* working. A working relationship works for *both* people involved. Very unhealthy relationships are often at the cost of at least one partner's wellbeing. Sure, he may be happy because he comes and goes as he pleases. She takes care of the home and doesn't complain. But, if she's slowly dying inside because she's given up her life to accommodate his selfishness, it's not working!

If the marriage *is* to have a future, it usually requires the old one be put to death. It is a healthy thing to admit your limitations and to recognize when something is no longer working. If you keep pretending, then you'll keep dragging it on and on. Far better to be able to say "Something's wrong here", and do something about it, than continue in a lie.

Think of it in terms of the substance abuse theory where you have to "hit rock bottom" before being willing to truly change. Some folks have to get to a point where things are so uncomfortable that they are finally willing to do *anything* in order to get relief. Hopefully, in this case, that relief will come from being able to admit the need for help in order to start building something new.

The old relationship becomes a template for the new, *not* to recreate the old but to identify those things that *weren't* broken and bring them into the new project. Those things that were deadly to the relationship require strategies, alternative ways of doing things, to prevent them from returning.

The benefit of a separation scenario is that you can approach and retreat. "Let's try this new way of relating to each other, then step back and examine it for bugs." Keep in mind that if the relationship is *not* emotionally chaotic, you don't have to be *physically* separated to do this. If you can get that psychological space within your own home, that is the more ideal path to take.

People tend to have this unbearable picture in their own minds of what the relationship has become, which tends to sabotage things when you try to work on improving it. The message from the counselor who tries to talk a couple back into a bad relationship ends up sounding like "Hey, it's really not so bad. If we spruce things up a little bit it'll be livable again in no time!" Yet, if the building's marked "condemned" (even if you were the one who marked it so), then there's no way "sprucing it up" will make it attractive enough to move back into. But, sometimes, while the construction may be faulty (poor conflict resolution, miscommunication, poor prioritizing), the foundation is still good and, while the house does need to be torn down and rebuilt, it's not a matter of abandoning the property.

For some, the issues go deeper because the foundation itself is poor or has been damaged (poor reasons for being in the relationship, myths and unrealistic expectations about the relationship, trust has been betrayed, unmet needs, poor character, emotional immaturity). While there's much more work to be done in such a situation, if the property's still in a desirable location, and there's been a lot of time invested over the years in fixing up the place, then there are *still* reasons to stay and try to do the necessary rebuilding.

So when do you consider abandoning the site? When the foundation has been so damaged or poisoned that even the surrounding property is no longer a fit place to live. In other words:

- When there have been recurring problems of character that one refuses to address at the cost of the health of the relationship.
- When the impact on an individual has become so destructive that to stay in the relationship becomes an emotional death.
- When the unchanging problems of the marriage are having such a significantly negative impact on the children that remaining in the relationship is harming them as well.

- When things remain so emotionally reactive that no matter how much time is given to allow things to settle down, things don't settle down.

- When all resources have been exhausted and the issues remain unresolved.

If the marriage has become that bad, then it is not truly a marriage any longer. It's very hard to imagine how such a destructive situation can occur if both people in the relationship are committed Christians. When I say "committed", I mean that they are actually *integrating* their Christianity into the relationship, actively *applying* Christ-like behavior and regard toward each other. That's why I think it's important to remember spiritual warfare, where we've allowed ourselves to be manipulated into behaving in very ungodly ways.

The added dimension of difficulty for Christians is that, even in situations where there *are* problems of character, such as recurring patterns of destructive or self-destructive behavior, at what point do we give up on the miraculous? At what point do we have enough information that we can say "enough is enough"? It is true that for some people it's not until they're about to lose their partners that they're finally willing to change, because that's what makes the problems real for them (that's what got them to the point of "hitting rock bottom"). Yet, for others, change only lasts so long as the relationship remains in crisis. When the crisis is over, they go back to their old behavior.

Only you can say what your own limits are, no one else can decide that for you.

Part of the process of measured examination forces each person to look at his own level of commitment to the relationship. When you clearly know what the work is, are you still willing to do it? It's difficult to face your own failings or shortcomings. For some people who are able to see now that they really weren't committed the first time around, it's an opportunity for change and rededication. For others, it's accepting responsibility that the relationship is ending because either they are unwilling to change, or unwilling to continue to try to make it work.

Project #4. Exploring the impact that divorce will have on your life.

Often people are at a point in their marriage where things are so unbearable that divorce represents an escape from all the misery. They know that it's not a "good" thing, but it's relief from pain that otherwise gives no promise of ending. They may be aware that divorce carries with it consequences, but those consequences seem mild in comparison with staying where they are.

Like it or not, though, divorce has an impact on everyone: you, your friends, your relatives, and your kids. The consequences are numerous:

- The reality is that many simply can't afford the expense of separating, or, if they do attempt it, it's having to cope with continuing on a fraction of what the income used to be. To cover the cost of two different homes, duplicate bills, and the legal expenses that are attached, many times it's just not financially feasible. If it was a single-income home, most likely whoever wasn't working will have to now find a job.

- While modern society is much more accepting of divorce, in some career tracks and religious circles there can still be a negative stigma attached.

- On a personal level, it is having to accept that the relationship has failed. For someone who takes marriage very seriously, this is a major hurdle to move past. They have to wrestle through their part and what this says or means about them.

- For many, there are serious emotional scars left behind, often around trust, that prevents them from being able to approach future relationships with anything other than fear when considering a new commitment or willingness to be vulnerable.

- Your friends typically change since most of them were probably married or were friends of both you and your partner. People you felt were "loyal" are suddenly distancing themselves from you, and others you may be distancing yourself from due to your own awkwardness at being in their company.

- Relatives and in-laws can become rejecting, distant, intrusive, or controlling.

Some people are able to make "clean breaks" because they don't have to have further contact with their partners. No children or financial dependency typically means no alimony, no child support - no legal ties. But if it was any of their own "baggage" that created problems in the relationship, they aren't leaving it behind. It's coming with them into the next relationship.

Obviously, the hardest scenario is for those couples who have children because:

- Communication will have to be maintained in order to negotiate financial demands that come up, visitation and other things. You may no longer be married, but you still continue to share parenting responsibilities.

- It means knowing that, at some point, your ex will be romantically involved again and another potential parent will be brought into the picture to whom your children will be exposed.

- It means having to regularly let go of all those things that are beyond your control because your ex-partner is engaged in his own particular lifestyle which your kids will continue to be exposed to.

- It means having to go through the forgiveness (letting go) process on a regular basis, since the continuing contact tends to keep old wounds opened.

Those not considering reconciliation, but who have kids together, may still want to explore the option of doing *co-parenting counseling*, since, even if the relationship ends, their roles as parents don't. The focus of co-parenting counseling is not on rehashing old relationship issues that are no longer relevant, but on being a united front for helping the kids move through their own pain.

* * *

Considering the consequences of divorce is healthy love because it's taking into account the future. You may say "Well, I've already thought of the future. I can't go on like this." But that statement is about how you feel *in this moment* about your *current* degree of pain in your current situation. It doesn't take into account whether you *could* go on in the marriage if things got significantly better.

Many will finally embrace a crisis by ending the relationship without any actual discussion. They just made the decision by assuming that the partner had no interest or was incapable of change. But unless the partner has actually said that, the conclusion can be premature. Better to allow the crisis to give you the courage to openly say "This isn't working the way we're doing it. Either we find a different way, or it needs to end. Are you willing to try?"

For feeling-based people, the majority of their decisions waffle back and forth based on the feeling of the day, the hour, or the moment. But we can't afford to make the decision to separate or divorce based solely on the feelings of an intense moment, or an argument that went too far.

Along those same lines, for those already in the midst of a separation, just because the relationship has a good day doesn't mean things are going to work out. And just because the relationship has a bad day, it shouldn't mean it's over.

We want to simplify these big decisions by narrowing things down to black-and-white terms. "He's evil." "She's good." But the fact-of-the-matter is it's more complicated than that. We each have both good and bad aspects. Realistically, we can't focus on just one without taking the other into account. But you'll see partners waffling back and forth depending on which they're focused on, the good or the bad. We have to take *both* into account.

Even then, it's not if there's *more* good than bad (more pros than cons), because just one bad quality or behavior can be so significantly destructive to a relationship that none of the other good ultimately matters. We need to know how to attach an appropriate weight to the issues that exist in order to have a clear perspective - something we're usually too close to see at the start of a separation.

Trial Separations and Reconciliation

For many couples considering a separation, or separated couples considering a reconciliation, both separation and reconciliation are approached fearfully because the couple has no idea what either entails. Obviously, there are real risks with each.

For those considering a separation, they may know things aren't working now and feel distance is necessary, but they're afraid of the potential consequences and all the "what if's" that they might not have considered if they do.

As I mentioned last chapter, for those considering reconciliation, many think that in order to re-approach the relationship they have to be at a point where they're "all in", ready to sign back up for the rest of their lives, but usually that's not what it's about. A couple is re-approaching the relationship to see *if* things can be worked out, not making uncertain promises that it will.

The overall progression of a trial separation between a couple that is open to considering reconciliation sometimes looks like this:

1. A separation agreement is drawn up between the couple, or with a mediator or attorneys involved, that establishes how the finances are going to be handled while apart, as well as child visitation. (If a separation agreement *doesn't* exist prior to a partner leaving the home, in some states the partner risks the legal label of "abandonment" being attached.)

2. The couple physically separates. The first one-to-three-months the focus is on each partner having space to work on themselves (often through individual counseling), getting their individual lives back in balance, and deciding on whether or not they're willing to attempt to reconcile.

This time period is a true separation where each is essentially living his own life (though not dating others), and getting a sense of what the partner's physical absence truly feels like. They have to be careful because, if the couple attempts to soothe each other too much during this time by continuing to fill the role of partner, though apart (having sex, having dates, doing chores for each other, etc.), it can interfere with a necessary sense of loss and can make the separation experience inappropriately "doable".

Some people fear this period, afraid that if they're not meeting the partner's physical needs that the partner will seek out others who will. But this is a testing time of each other's character: how fairly they handle things with each other (versus vindictively) and how disciplined they are with handling their own needs. If the message is, "I can't go that long without sex or a relationship. If you're not going to provide it for me, I'm going to have to find someone who will," aside from being a manipulation, that's a pretty clear statement about his level of commitment to the relationship. Remember, *being separated isn't being divorced.* You may be separated, but you're still legally married. You may not be currently filling the roles of husband and wife, but you *are* still husband and wife.

3. At the three-to-six-month point, a decision as to whether or not to *attempt* reconciliation is made. *But the couple does not immediately move back in together.* (This is typically the point where couple's counseling begins. Prior to this, individual counseling is usually occurring.) Initially the couple re-approaches each other by stepping back to a simpler level of relationship, such as when they were dating. They relearn how to just be with each other without all the baggage brought into every conversation.

Often there are three pieces going on at the same time: 1) the dating piece, whose only focus is on restoring a degree of connection, 2) the couple's counseling piece, that is attempting to help the couple work through the bigger issues and introduce better communication methods, and 3) the accountability piece, where the couple is continuing to handle the business of the day while starting to practice fielding the smaller issues together.

The dating relationship gradually progresses in terms of how much time the couple spends together, going from dating once or twice a week, to spending weekends together, to several days a week together.

The cushion is that, if at any time the situation blows up, the couple can retreat to their own places and regroup and re-approach once things have calmed down.

4. Somewhere between six to 12 months, depending on how successfully things have progressed, the couple makes a decision with the information at hand to either 1) move back in together, feeling like there's a sufficient amount of information that says things have changed for the better, 2) extend the separation period because not enough improvements have yet been made to make the leap back to living together, but there's been sufficient improvement to justify continuing to work on things, or 3) agree to proceed towards divorce due to lack of progress.

This is just one approach to a separation, with some general timelines attached. Because otherwise it can be such a chaotic time, it helps to have some degree of structure, an overall plan, to help grant some sense of direction.

The idea is to not rush, to make sure there's been sufficient time given to be apart and sufficient time in coming back together. To move too quickly creates doubts for later on ("I really wish I'd had more time to get myself together." "We had a vacation from each other, but nothing's really changed with how we relate." "I don't feel like I'm back for the right reasons."), and can put a couple back in place without the necessary tools to make things meaningfully different.

Obviously, there are other factors, such as finances, that may not allow for "the luxury" of how much time you spend apart, but if rushing a decision results in a premature divorce, it's not going to be saving you any money in the long run.

Some couples don't need a year. Some can do the majority of the above in the span of three to six months. It really depends on how much damage has been done and how much needs to be worked through.

As I said earlier, you're trying to step away from letting momentary feelings make all the choices - whether it's an impulse to run, or an impulse to reunite. You're trying to work through to reason, taking into account the big picture and how moving forward or ending the relationship impacts everyone.

If you've spent years creating this relationship, it needs to be given the respect it deserves in considering its possible end.

Afterword: Balance

There is a word that most teens learn in science class called "homeostasis". *Homeostasis* refers to your body's built-in tendency to always be seeking a state of balance within its various systems. The interesting thing about it is that the body is *never* in perfect balance. One system serves to excite, another serves to calm. One relays pleasure while another relays pain. There are all these natural checks and balance systems that are at different levels of operation, each responsive to another. While describing our internal workings, homeostasis is also reflective of our outer world as well. We are in a constant state of seeking balance in our lives, finding a workable medium that allows us to move forward in the world, not hold us back.

When our lives are out of balance, when bad things happen, when we've been emotionally hurt by someone or have hurt someone we love, we experience emotional pain. How we attempt to deal with this emotional pain can decide whether we move forward in life, because we've restored balance, or become "stuck".

There is an important parallel between physical pain and emotional pain.

Physical pain is a warning signal to the rest of the body that something is injured and needs tended to. While we may fear the actual experience of pain, *the fact that we are experiencing physical pain when we are injured is a healthy thing. It's our body's warning system functioning as it should.*

If you were experiencing physical pain, yet there was *no* injury, your body would be *malfunctioning*, giving false warnings, as with the situations where a limb has been removed yet the patient continues to feel ghost pains as if the limb were still attached. It would also be a malfunction if you *weren't* experiencing physical pain when you *should*, such as with conditions like leprosy where the nerves have died. The smallest of wounds can go untended, even becoming gangrenous, because there is no signal of pain drawing our attention to it.

So, too, *emotional pain usually exists as a healthy flag to call our attention to the fact that something isn't right.* In those instances, it is our mind operating as it should, directing us to the problem. If we are in the midst of a painful situation, it makes perfect sense that we would experience discomfort during that time. If we understand that experiencing emotional pain can be a *healthy* process that exists to help us identify what needs fixed, then it isn't something to be feared or run from.

Are there miscues regarding emotional pain, as there can be with physical pain? Sure. A chemical imbalance, such as can occur with clinical depression, can result in experiencing emotional pain even when there is no reason to be depressed. And with character issues, you'd *expect* a person to be experiencing emotional pain as a result of a destructive lifestyle, yet there is an absence of emotional discomfort.

If we are not in the habit of self-assessing, sometimes it is difficult to isolate the cause of our emotional pain and know what needs healed. And if we are unversed in handling emotional pain, or had no models of how to deal with it, we may feel a complete lack of direction in how to actually go about working through it. But the first step, as with physical pain, is to *attend* to the pain (not ignore it or push it away), and attempt to identify what's causing it.

*　*　*

Seeking balance in a relationship, handling the emotional *discomfort* that comes from having allowed it to have fallen out of balance, means:

- working at resolving conflicts as they occur rather than letting them build up
- working at keeping things in perspective by balancing the maintenance needs with the intimacy needs (the work with the play, the roles with the connection)
- working at not letting the relationship become too needy or too neglected
- working at keeping the communication healthy, where there is active listening and validation

- working at being consistently supportive, loving, caring for and respecting each other
- working at rewarding the positive, rather than over-focusing on the negative
- working at balancing grace with loving accountability
- working at being solution-focused rather than problem-obsessed

Basically, maintaining balance in a relationship requires *effort*. Which can be viewed as either another burdensome obligation or as the positive work that is necessary to keep the relationship alive and thriving. Ultimately, *if the relationship is tended to on a regular basis, the less effort it requires (and less emotional pain is experienced), because it doesn't stray that far off course.*

Because we've learned how to pay attention to emotional discomfort, and not to fear it or ignore it, we can use its information to honestly address necessary change in the relationship and within ourselves.

Since needs continue to change as time goes by, and there are always other responsibilities demanding our attention, adjustments are a continual part of life. At the point of best balance you should feel the least stressed and the most effective because you are using your energy in the most productive ways.

* * *

I have attempted to write these chapters with a balanced perspective: presenting the extremes in the different scenarios, while, hopefully, capturing the desirable middle. No doubt there are exceptions to the guidelines laid out here, but, hopefully, you've approached the reading in terms of how it applies rather than how it doesn't.

For some, the idea that our happiness and the success of our relationships is partly our own responsibility creates anxiety. But it should also be a relief to know that there *are* things we can do to improve the quality of our existence, and to have the kind of quality relationships we desire with our partners.

As Christians, we have God's blessing on our efforts to create a godly relationship according to His guidelines. We can rely on His promise to be faithful to live up to His Word. But it's just as vital that we assume responsibility for ours.

"If it is possible, as far as it depends on you, live at peace with everyone." (Romans 12:18)

Appendix

Tools & Exercises

The Conflict Model

Reaction
Instinct
Fight or Flight - Offensive/Defensive - Attack/Withdraw
Superficial/Staying on the Surface
Punish/Judge/Control (Parent) or Tantrum/
Manipulate/Mudsling (Child)
Extremes
Talking from the Anger
Closed Statements
Assumptions & Judgments

Healthy exits

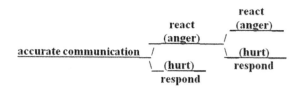

Response
Controlled reaction - Staying vulnerable
Working through it
Going Deeper
Reason/Explore (Adult)
Finding a Middle Ground
Talking from the Hurt
Staying with Questions – Exploration - Educate
Benefit of the doubt

The Resolution Process

Identify Issue > **Validate** > Explain/Process > Resolve
       listen   **2-part Solutions**
       acknowledge
       apologize
       ownership

The ABC's of a Fair Fight

Identifying the Issue:

1. **Choose your battles, and battlefield, wisely.** Pay attention to the time and place you choose to discuss an issue. And be sure that the issue is important enough that it requires discussion.

2. **Identify the intent of approaching a conversation to your partner. Don't assume that he knows it.** Do you simply want a listening ear, to share your feelings, to get feedback, or are you wanting to resolve an issue? It helps to identify what you are looking for before you get into a conversation. That way you avoid guesswork on the other's part and you are more likely to get your need met.

3. **Confrontation is based on facts. Don't confront based on fears and doubts.** Fears and doubts are based on *possible* or *suspected* occurrences, not *known* occurrences. Confrontation only works if it is done in a loving manner, not a judgmental one. If you are tempted to confront based on your fears and doubts, then, what you probably need to do is seek information *first* in order to get your facts straight. What we often *truly* need is assurance - about love, trust, fidelity, etc.

4. **If necessary, attach a priority to the issue, so there is some sense of how important or unimportant it is.** When a lot of issues are being identified, it's important that there is some sense of scale to it all or the list will feel overwhelming. If needs are going to be met, each partner needs to have some sense of which issues require a focused priority.

5. **Bring up the past during an argument only if the problem is still going on.** Occasionally, there will be a past issue that has gone unresolved and felt to be a major contributor to the present mood of the relationship whether or not that situation

has reoccurred. In situations like that, a re-approach is justified. However, in general, it is unfair to bring up the distant past since it distracts the focus from current issues, and is often used as a way to punish the partner.

Validating the Issue:

6. **Balance the negative with the positive.** Just as it's easier to walk through a house and notice what needs to be done rather than what's already been done, it's important to stop and force ourselves to pay attention to what's still working. How can you positively motivate your partner to change only by complaining? When approaching your partner about an issue, try to think of a few positives to share first so he can see that you recognize there are good things happening too. If you are the first to identify the positive in your partner, it keeps him from feeling the need to defend himself.

7. **Own up to your contribution to the problem first, and it will open the door for the other to examine his part.** This isn't suggesting that you assign percentages to how much was you and how much was him. And it isn't suggesting you admit your part and then push him to admit his. If I can focus on my end of any dilemma and approach a solution, I am inviting the other to help me without ever "pointing the finger". We typically try to force our partners to admit to their part in a problem, but this often pushes them into a defensive stance.

8. **Take turns talking and listening.** While this seems elementary, it is incredibly common that the longer you have known somebody the easier it is to take shortcuts with your communication. And the most common experience in miscommunication is, "They're not listening to what I said".

9. **Be respectful of your partner's perception of an issue. Don't define reality for the other.** If your partner feels a certain way, you can't tell him that he doesn't feel that way. No matter how old the relationship, you need to operate from a position of giving the other the "benefit of the doubt". Each of us has our

own perceptions of an experience but reality is somewhere in the middle. If you want the other to help you with a solution, you need to give credibility to what he says, even if you don't agree with it.

10. **Be willing to be wrong.** The wise partner is able to recognize that admission of wrong can be a faster path to resolution than many others. It's not just remaining vulnerable. It's about accepting ownership for your part in a problem. If you are staying focused on maintaining an honest relationship, and are trying to create a safe place for both you and your partner, admitting wrong is an act of trust.

11. **It's okay to disagree.** Some conflicts do not require resolution. It is unrealistic to expect that your partner must have the same opinions or agree with everything that you do. Don't make an issue out of every little thing that comes along.

Processing the Issue:

12. **Keep in mind the goal of the conversation.** Is what you're about to say relevant to the current issue? Will it help clear or muddy the water? Is it to the benefit of the relationship or harmful? Discuss one issue at a time. Avoid counter-issues or becoming sidetracked.

13. **Exercise loving accountability while avoiding value judgments.** Try to separate the act from the individual, avoiding words that are a judgment of someone's character (lazy, jerk, slob, tightwad, etc.).

14. **Approach the conversation with options, not ultimatums.** Ultimatums are often inappropriately used as a form of control or manipulation. If you haven't already discussed options for *possible* solutions, go there first. Don't issue ultimatums unless you are prepared to act on them.

15. **Try to treat emotionally-weighted words as information rather than attacks.** In a conversation that contains sensitive

personal content, try to focus on how this information can be used to gain better understanding. If the words are ones spoken in anger, try to move past your partner's surface communication and get at the underlying needs that have been threatened.

16. **Remain vulnerable**. It is more important to talk from our vulnerable pain than from our anger. Vulnerability is less likely to draw an attack since it is an act of kindness, not vengeance. If you are open to admitting your **own** shortcomings, it can encourage your partner to examine his, without becoming defensive.

17. **Don't negatively compare your partner to others**. Be careful of drawing comparisons too frequently, either positive or negative, between your partner and others. It indicates that you are using others as a gauge of your approval for your partner.

18. **"Never" and "always" need to be stricken from the couple's vocabulary**. There is no such thing as a behavior happening never or always. Using these words in an argument comes off as a blatant exaggeration and doesn't allow for those times when the negative behavior wasn't occurring, or when the positive was. It also puts the partner in a position of feeling like, "Why should I try?" if they are not getting any recognition for the times when they *have* tried.

19. **Make requests, not demands**. This is your partner, and you need to show respect if you want respect. Since you're not in charge of the relationship, it's not a good idea to assume that role with your partner by telling him what he "has" to do. If you want to keep things on the level of choice, be sure to term things as requests.

Resolving the Issue:

20. **Some of the best solutions are the old ones. In seeking solutions don't try to reinvent the wheel.** We often discover that old strategies worked for the relationship in the past but we just stopped using them. Since they're not completely new ways

of doing things, it will be easier to adapt them because there's already a certain familiarity.

21. **If you have already given some thought to possible solutions before you "come to the table" with the issue, it will move the process more quickly to a solution.** It's easy to bring up an issue in order to focus on how unfair or inappropriate an event or behavior was - a means of punishing. However, it's more helpful to approach an issue focusing on options. Don't go into the discussion with *the* solution, but, rather, *possible* solutions.

22. **Solutions should be tolerable to both sides, not a recurring imbalance of one side "giving in". Try to avoid black-and-white solutions.** A true compromise is the result of trying to find the middle ground where the needs of *both* are being addressed. Try to avoid two-dimensional thinking in attempting resolution since it operates in extremes (his way/her way, right/wrong, never/always) and usually implies a judgment.

23. **To forgive does not mean to forget.** To forgive someone for a wrong act means to accept (not agree or condone) what has occurred and move on, letting go of the emotional baggage that is attached. However, it is not advisable to forget an event since, "He who forgets the past is doomed to repeat it". Once an act has been forgiven, it is not appropriate to bring it up to assist an attack or recreate an issue. Forgiveness does not mean an absence of consequences.

24. **Try to resolve issues as they occur. However, each person should retain the right to put off an argument until he feels he can handle his part responsibly.** The longer anger or resentment festers, the greater the damage to the relationship. If it is not possible to resolve an issue before going to bed, then, at least, call a truce with a commitment to re-approach later. In order not to say something hurtful out of anger, it is better to give yourself time to calm down and think things through. Issues, however, should *not* be put off indefinitely.

25. **Decisions made from strong emotion are not going to be good decisions.** When you are having strong emotions your thinking is no longer clear. You may *feel* like you are still thinking, but it is your emotions that are guiding your thoughts, not your intellect. Feelings change from day to day. Reason is more stable and a better foundation from which to make clear decisions.

26. **Be sure "the solution" is clear to both sides and specific enough that it can be immediately applied.** People have a tendency to speak in general terms when reaching a solution. They don't define the specifics and so the exact expectations for each person are not often laid out. If a specific plan is made, it is much more likely that both sides will comply because the expectations have been clarified.

EXERCISE 1: The Listening Exercise

While the following exercise probably feels somewhat overly simple, and maybe even awkward to do, if you can reintroduce the overall concept into your conversations you should find that both sides feel more "heard" and, as a result, more willing to work things out. It's often immediately rewarding in that if you have had little success in the past with feeling heard, or your partner feeling heard, that it *is* within your ability to meet this need for each other. The education involved in this exercise is part of the process of relearning each other's language. By breaking a conversation down into pieces, you learn to separate the emotion and avoid the tendency to react to what the other person says. You are learning to treat what each person says as information, removing some of the emotional baggage from your past history that you may ordinarily attach.

1) Pick a current issue or discussion topic for the relationship (hopefully something that is not overwhelming or has too much baggage attached). The conversation needs to stay focused on just one topic, without other issues being brought into it.

2) Whoever's issue it is starts out. If there are two sides to the issue, somebody needs to be picked to be the initiator. The initiator starts by voicing his perspective of the problem. He is not attempting to insult or judge his partner. He is simply focused on expressing his viewpoint of the situation, so his voice should remain calm and explanatory. Both sides need to have an attitude of patience in hearing each other out. The initiator is going to give his entire side, but he's only going to do it two or three sentences at a time.

3) The listener controls the amount of information that the initiator is giving. About every couple sentences she needs to stop the initiator to tell him what she hears him saying, before allowing him to go further. Rather than the listener *responding* to what she heard, or defending against what is being said, she simply *paraphrases* back to the initiator what she heard the initiator say. This *isn't* a word-for-word repeating, simply an attempt to summarize the content.

4) If the listener "got it right" by capturing the gist of what the initiator said, the initiator continues a step at a time until he's managed to express

all that he wanted to say about that topic. (The reason for keeping it to two or three sentences is that if you say much more than that the listener won't be able to restate it all because too much information is being given.)

If the listener got it "wrong", the process is repeated until she can accurately express to the initiator what the initiator is trying to say.

5) Once the initiator has finished stating his side, and the listener has finished paraphrasing, the listener should take a moment to find something that she can *validate* about what the initiator has said. (This does *not* mean that the listener has to agree with the initiator's opinion. It simply means that the listener tries to show simple respect for the initiator's viewpoint. It can be as simple as saying "I can understand, if that's how you were looking at it, why you would feel that way." Or maybe asking, "What could I do that would be validating for you with this topic?" finding something that the initiator can give the "thumbs up" on, that he feels both understood and validated for.)

6) It now becomes the *initiator's* turn to be the listener, restating what is being said to him without reacting or responding with his own opinion. Again, the goal is to accurately reflect what is being said in the correct tone it is being said, and then, once the viewpoint has been stated completely, taking time to validate it, *before* going on to correcting any misunderstandings, or working towards solutions.

At this point, the new initiator can either go into her side of the issue (if there is one), or simply respond to her partner's concerns - though still taking it a piece at a time. When she is done, and she gets validated, the sides flip again, back and forth, until the whole issue has been discussed.

That is the primary focus of this exercise: *attending, restating/clarifying,* and *validating*.

If a resolution is being sought, then the process can continue, moving on to discussing the suggested solutions, but taking turns doing so. If this is a 2-sided issue, then the couple will talk it through to a solution for each partner.

Note: If taking it this slow you still have problems with taking turns, give whoever's turn it is an object such as a small pillow or ball. So long as they hang on to the object, it's their turn. Once it's the other person's turn, the pillow or ball gets passed on to them.

EXERCISE 2: The Three-Part Solution Model

1) Take two separate pieces of paper. Divide each sheet into three sections: behavior, thinking and beliefs/feelings. Choose a problem you're having either in your own life or with your relationship (your part of it). The first sheet represents you in the present. The second sheet represents the ideal, what you're working towards.

2) What are the *behaviors* that occur that either are the problem or resulting from the problem? For example, if the identified problem is getting angry, the behaviors that go along with that might be "I say cruel things to him", "I lecture him", or "I'll be mean to the kids" and "I withdraw". List them on the first sheet under the behavior section. Try to be as specific as possible.

What are the specific *thoughts* you have that are either creating the issue or contributing to the issue? Usually, the first thought in the chain is more of an observation. For instance, "He didn't take out the garbage again" is just an observation. There is no interpretation or assumption involved. But it may then lead to, "Once again he didn't do what he said", which might lead to, "It really bothers me that I can't count on him", which might lead to "If he cared about me, he wouldn't be doing this." Write the whole train of thought that goes along with the problem on the first page under the thinking section. Feel free to track as many trains as are connected to the particular problem.

What *beliefs or feelings* continue to occur that are complicating things? Continuing with the example just given, the feelings might be: anxious, depressed, sad, lonely, unloved, disrespected, betrayed, angry, disappointed, neglected, etc. The beliefs may be, "He doesn't care about me," "I can't count on him". Our beliefs can be conclusions based on how we feel, or our feelings can be based on what we're choosing to believe. It can go either way. Write down whatever your feelings or beliefs are that are related to, or driving, the problem.

3) The second page represents the ideal - the positive replacements for the negative aspects. Under the behavior category, write down the positive *behaviors* that you need to be doing to replace the current negative ones you're engaged in. In this instance, it might be, "Try to

educate him in a non-lecture way that this isn't about the trash. It's about him keeping his word.", "Letting him know I feel like I'm unimportant to him, rather than attacking him (talking from the hurt and not the anger)", "Let the minor things go", "Controlling my temper". Try to think of as many positive alternative behaviors as you can. The more options you have the better.

Go on to the thought section, second page. What *thoughts* would effectively counter the problem thinking? For instance, "The garbage being taken out when I want it to is my preference, not a need - not worth getting that upset about," "He does show me in other ways that he cares". The counter positive thoughts you're coming up with need to be thoughts you can embrace because they are credible and have weight. Don't list thoughts that you really can't buy into. They need to be ideas that, when you consider them, effectively deescalate where your feelings would take you.

Lastly, list the feelings and beliefs that would be desired. In this instance, "I want to feel valued", "I want to feel like I have some control over what gets done", "I want to feel like everything doesn't depend on me."

The beliefs: "He *does* care about me, he just doesn't always show it the way that I want him to." "He does care about me, I just sometimes fail to see it when he does." "I can count on him, but I need to be realistic about what he can do." "I *can* count on him with many things, but I need to be respectful in bringing those things to his attention, and can't expect him to do everything perfectly." Initially, those beliefs you are trying to create may seem far from where you are, but the more you actively work on the behaviors and thoughts that created the negative beliefs, the more power you'll be putting into creating the desired positive beliefs. Obviously, her husband has some degree of responsibility in helping support the desired beliefs, especially those concerning him, but the important part is that the wife's focusing on what she can do in order to manage her reactions.

4) Having completed the pages, I usually suggest getting rid of the first one. It served as the template for establishing what you're working towards, but your focus now needs to be on the ideal you're trying to create. The second chart becomes your gauge at the end of each day as

to how well you've progressed towards making that picture a reality. And it serves as a reminder of the things you can do and think about when you're being tempted to backslide or are feeling distant from remembering your alternatives.

––––––––––

The model can be used with individual problems or problems of the relationship. If you do the exercise as a couple, you'd need a set for each person's part of the problem. Such a chart also works well when you're exploring a "wound" with your partner and trying to think of strategies for healing it.

Often, the easiest sections to fill out are the ones that that person is the most "in touch" with about themselves. Stereotypically, women tend to be able to fill in the "feeling" sections the easiest, while men have the easiest time with the "behavior" section. The thoughts behind the feelings and behaviors are often the harder things to identify.

EXERCISE 3: The Needs List

The Needs List is a list of both his/her needs, NOT desires. These are the things that you feel are *vital* to maintaining a long-term relationship.

1. Each fills out his own list without sharing them just yet. The list should consist of *both* the needs that are currently not being met as well as those that are. If you can't come up with some specific needs on your own, think in terms of the three core needs: security (trust and control), significance (valued and respected) and fun (quality and freedom). List specifically how you look for your partner to meet each one. Try to be detailed rather than vague. "I need to feel loved" is way too vague. How *specifically* do you look to feel loved by your partner? The more specific you can be, the easier it's going to be for your partner to have a clear idea of what you're looking for.

2. Prioritize the list. Assign a value to the top three or four items that are the most important to you but also need the most work. (This gives the partner an indication of the best places to start, and where their energy and attention will have the most immediate impact.)

3. *Prior* to showing each other your lists, take the time to *guess* each other's lists. This is NOT an opportunity to punish each other for getting it wrong. This is about seeing how closely you understand what's important to each other or how far things have drifted.

4. Go ahead and actually share the lists with each other. This is an opportunity to look at the lists and have your partner define anything that seems vague to you. Each person needs to have a clear understanding of what is being requested in order to effectively address that need.

5. Turn your lists over to each other. At this point, the "list" is out of each other's control. Your responsibility is to work on the list your partner has given you, NOT on keeping track of how well your partner is doing in managing YOUR list. The focus is

back on what is in your own control to do for the relationship to prosper. *Both* of you are making a commitment to respect and work on each other's needs.

If needs are listed that either feels they can't meet for the other, now is the time to discuss them. If you are saying you have to have something and hearing a "No", you have come to a roadblock. If it is a, "No, I can't *yet*," or, "I'm working toward that but I'm not there yet," then there's room to work. If it's a "No. Not now. Not ever," then the relationship has reached a potential "deal-breaker".

The needs list isn't written in stone. If you think of better ways to meet those needs as time goes by, feel free to revise your list.

EXERCISE 4: The Sit-down

What it comes down to:

1) What's working?

- What I saw you do (this past week) that I liked.
- What I did for you (this past week) that you may not have seen.

2) What are we still working on?

- Dangling issues from the past week (unfinished business)
- Ongoing projects (needs list)

When you're first practicing it, the Sit-down should occur, ideally, on a weekly basis. Aside from being a time to address lingering issues, it's an opportunity to give needed recognition for the work that's being done, positive feedback for the successes, and fine-tuning the works-in-progress. It also:

a) gives you continuing practice with your resolution skills

b) helps act as an ongoing barometer for the relationship (with feedback being provided in a neutral but supportive way)

c) helps you prioritize issues

d) helps you think things through in terms of what the issue actually is, how to best present it, and what are some possible solutions

e) shows your partner your willingness to work on things by participating in the process

Suggestions:

1. Keep a list during the week of any issues, concerns or other items that you want to bring to the sit-down. They can be small or large, the goal is to capture the things that you might otherwise be forgetting or avoiding.

2. You can start either by addressing what's already working, or going to the list. It depends on what works best for the two of you. Just be sure to cover both.

3. For the first couple of sit-downs it's recommended that you initially pick some of the "milder" issues for better chances of initial success. Once you "get the hang of it" you can start approaching the bigger ones.

4. When you review the list both sides should attach a priority to the ones that are most important to be discussed. If you can't agree on a proper priority, just be sure to review at least one item important to each of you.

5. The atmosphere and focus should be one of sharing, providing information and seeking solutions, not an opportunity to attack.

6. Don't expect to cover everything on the list in one sitting. Don't turn it into a marathon. Allow for about 15-30 minutes to discuss things. If you have more time, fine, but don't force it. What you don't get to this week can be postponed until next week (or sooner, depending on the immediacy).

7. Don't expect to get everything "right" the first time. The idea is to practice hearing each other out, validating each other as you go, taking the time to really listen, and then to move on to solutions (if a solution is being requested). Success isn't measured by how many items on the list you resolve, but more-so that you've successfully taken the time to stay with the routine of the sit-down and made the effort at discussing issues.

8. Keep in mind that people tend to stop short or go too far. If you're giving up after the first ten minutes, you aren't being patient enough and definitely aren't treating things as information. If you've reached a workable solution, don't over-discuss it.

9. Remember to keep things balanced by discussing BOTH parts of each issue: what BOTH of you are contributing to the issue at hand, as well as what BOTH of you can contribute to the solution.

10. If you find yourself getting sidetracked, stop every minute or so and check to see if you're still discussing the agreed on topic from the list. If you're bringing up other topics that aren't on the list, decide if they warrant discussion time of their own and add them to the list if necessary, but stay with the issue at hand.

11. Stick with the resolution tools (the ABC's): stay focused, don't bring up the past unless it's still playing a part in the present, identify what it is you need, avoid making judgments, be willing to be vulnerable and willing to be wrong, try to find solutions that are win/win for both that may also require just a bit of stretching too.

12. Find your points of agreement, remembering to validate, moving towards solutions, rather than being problem-obsessed.

Just remember, practice develops competency. And competency develops confidence at being able to make the relationship work.

EXERCISE 5: The Priority Assessment

1. Take a sheet of paper and write down the different types of priorities in your life: friends and family (social), health (exercise and diet), kids, spouse/partner (courting), job, interests/hobbies/fun (you), and spiritual.

2. Now take a few minutes and think of where the majority of your time and attention is going. For the priorities that are getting the most attention, draw a larger circle around them. For the areas that are the most neglected, draw a smaller circle. This is an easy visual to show where your energy needs to be going. You may need to be subtracting time and effort from the larger circles and diverting them to the smaller ones.

3. Take some time to itemize the things you do for each particular category. By itemizing, you may find that it wasn't as much as you thought, or maybe it was more than you thought. If you want to get serious about it, you can even itemize the frequency of those activities or the amount of time that goes into each on a normal week. (If you're open to it, invite your partner's opinions as to the accuracy of your assessment.)

4. Now take a second sheet of paper, which will represent "your life in balance". Write down the same categories, but now itemize the things you could realistically start doing in the neglected areas that would restore some balance to the picture.

5. Now that you've identified what you could be doing, you need to make a specific plan for how you're actually going to *start* doing those things in order for it to become a reality. That plan needs to start with the first simple steps that would lead into accomplishing the greater task. For instance, if one of the things you'd listed was to take an evening class, the first few steps might be to order a class listing, decide what evenings you have to work with, and decide from that listing what class you were interested in that fit with your available evening. The steps need to be small enough, and immediate enough, that you can start acting on them within that week. Depending on how

easily distracted you are, you might want to continue to review the priority list on a weekly or monthly basis to measure your progress and keep yourself on track.

If you *don't* have a specific plan, it probably will not happen. You'll just know that it *should* happen. The priority assessment serves as your own personal accountability system.

In addition to doing this as individuals, you can also do a priority assessment for the relationship, looking jointly at how the time is being spent, and where changes need to occur. This can be delicate territory since it requires a good deal of respect shown for each person. It's very easy to slip into the miscommunications of, "My time is more important than your time", or "How you spend your time is a waste of time".

CPSIA information can be obtained at www.ICGtesting.com
Printed in the USA
BVOW08s2044170316

440784BV00001B/49/P

9 781425 966317